Lobscouse
&
Spotted Dog

Lobscouse
&
Spotted Dog

Which It's a Gastronomic
Companion to the
Aubrey/Maturin Novels

Anne Chotzinoff Grossman
Lisa Grossman Thomas

W. W. NORTON & COMPANY
New York   London

Excerpts from Patrick O'Brian's Aubrey/Maturin series reprinted by permission of W. W. Norton & Company, Inc. All page numbers refer to the W. W. Norton editions.

Patrick O'Brian interview with Charlton Heston sponsored by Friends of English and the Department of English at UCLA. Copyright © 1995 by Patrick O'Brian. Reprinted by permission of Georges Borchardt, Inc., for the author.

Patrick O'Brian interview with Robert Hass sponsored by City Arts of San Francisco and Pacific Vista Productions. Copyright © 1995 by Patrick O'Brian. Reprinted by permission of Georges Borchardt, Inc., for the author.

Recipe for Custard Sauce based on Vanilla Custard Sauce, from *Sweet and Savory Sauces*, by Lorraine Bodger (Simon & Schuster, 1995).

Drawings from *Ashley Book of Knots* by Clifford Ashley. Copyright © 1944 by Clifford W. Ashley. Used by permission of Doubleday, a division of Bantam Doubleday Dell Publishing Group, Inc.

The text of this book is composed in Adobe Caslon with the display set in Adobe Caslon Italic and Semibold. Composition by ComCom Typesetting Services, Inc. Manufacturing by the Haddon Craftsmen, Inc. Book design by Charlotte Staub

Library of Congress Cataloging-in-Publication Data

Grossman, Anne Chotzinoff.
    Lobscouse & spotted dog : which it's a gastronomic companion to
the Aubrey/Maturin novels / Anne Chotzinoff Grossman, Lisa Grossman
Thomas ; foreword by Patrick O'Brian.
        p.   cm.
    Includes bibliographical references and index.
    ISBN 0-393-04559-5
    1. Cookery.   2. Gastronomy—History.   3. Food in literature.
4. Literary cookbooks.   I. Thomas, Lisa Grossman.   II. Title.
TX714.G77   1997
641.5—dc21   97-17676
                                                   CIP

ISBN 0-393-32094-4 pbk.

W. W. Norton & Company, Inc., 500 Fifth Avenue, New York, N.Y. 10110
www.wwnorton.com

W. W. Norton & Company Ltd., 10 Coptic Street, London WC1A 1PU

2 3 4 5 6 7 8 9 0

To Patrick O'Brian,
the Onlie Begetter

Contents

List of Recipes by Category

Pig's Trotters
Roast Pork
Soused Hog's Face
Sucking Pig

POULTRY
Côôôôq au Vin
Lacquered Duck Bathed in
    Rich Sauce
Poule au Pot
Roast Pollo

GAME
Civet de Lapin
Jugged Hare
Millers in Onion Sauce
Roast Buffalo
Rrâââble de Lièvre
Squirrels in Madeira
Stewed Boar
Venison Pasty

SAVORY PIES
Boned Larks in a Pie
Goose and Truffle Pie
Mrs. Pullings's Pie
Pigeon Pie
Sea-Pie
Strasburg Pie
Veal and Ham Pie

MADE-DISHES
Lobscouse
Pilaff
Solomongundy
Vine-Leaves

LEGUMES & GRAINS
Dried Peas Beaten . . .
Dried Peas with Lumps of
    Pork

Indian Khichri
Polenta
Spoon-Bread
A Whole Leaf of Pondoo

FRUITS & VEGETABLES
Bashed Neeps
Breadfruit Biscuit
Breadfruit Toast
Pickled Gherkins
Sour Breadfruit Pap

SAVORY SAUCES
Brown Onion Sauce
Caper Sauce
Mayonnaise
White Sauce Beautified with
    Cochineal
Wine Sauce

BREADS
Bidpai Chhatta
The Last of the True French
    Short Bastards
Ship's Biscuit (Hard Tack)
Ship's Biscuit for a Single
    Mess

CHEESE
Toasted Cheese

SAVORY PUDDINGS
Black Pudding
Dog's Body/
    Pease-Pudding
Haggis
Steak and Kidney
    Pudding
White Pudding

Foreword

All flesh is grass: and it has been said that the man who finds out how to make two blades grow where one grew before serves the republic admirably well.

It may also be said that a woman who causes two dishes to stand upon an American table is more valuable to her country than the hero of any election. This is particularly true when the second dish is that noble pudding a Spotted Dog, gleaming on its plate and accompanied by true egg custard.

I have travelled the length and breadth of the United States, a country to which I am profoundly attached and in which I have met with great kindness: yet only once in all those thousands of miles did I meet with a pudding (an Indian pudding in fact, produced by the most amiable of admirals in a Boston tavern). Otherwise even the most splendid of dinners ended with a curious blank; and that is one of the many, many reasons why I urge people to read this admirable book, the fruit of prolonged research combined with even longer periods of first-hand practice, the whole designed to improve the quality of life, bringing back much that was lost with the advent of the industrial revolution and restoring a dinner-table worthy of an even heartier Thanksgiving.

PATRICK O'BRIAN
France, 1997

Preface

When the Patrick O'Brian fever broke out among our friends, we took the infection early, we succumbed immediately and completely. We started to devour the novels with indecent haste, little suspecting where they would lead us. Truth to tell, it was probably the music that first captivated us, right from the opening lines of *Master and Commander*. The last movement of the Locatelli was still playing—we were already hooked.

And then. And then we began to notice the food. Almost from the beginning, we were struck by its pervasiveness, its importance. We were so powerfully fascinated by the descriptions of meals, eaten not only aboard ship but in ports of call in every corner of the world, that we felt compelled to explore further. We were entranced by the names. What is lobscouse? What is burgoo? What on earth is a thumping great spotted dog? We had to know.

What began in frivolity continued in earnest, and it has been an extraordinary education for us. Our cookery book is perforce a work of historical fiction—but we have tried to emulate Mr. O'Brian in point of accuracy and meticulous research. Along the way we have gained some unexpected insights into not only what people ate and how they prepared it, but what it tasted like—and why.

The late eighteenth century produced a spate of cookery books and a certain amount of refinement in the art of writing recipes. Our excitement at having discovered a trove of these works was slightly tempered, after a while, by the realization that a great proportion of the recipes published between 1750 and 1810 were lifted verbatim from Hannah Glasse's 1747 classic, *The Art of Cookery Made Plain and Easy* (and she in turn had stolen shamelessly from her predecessors). Nevertheless, we did have a wealth of sources from which to draw material.

In writing and testing our recipes, we have retraced the footsteps of the notable cooks of the period. While we have done our best to compensate for their lack of precise directions, we have adopted their improvisational and sometimes slapdash approach to cookery, so closely allied to our own; adjusting and combining their recipes, as they would have done, to suit our materials and our palates. These are not so much modernized transcriptions of old recipes as they are re-creations, fashioned after the spirit and the manner of another time.

The problems of reconstructing eighteenth-century cookery are not unlike those of reproducing the sounds of eighteenth-century music in a modern world. In studying the sources of the period, it has become obvious that the modern palate has changed every bit as much as the modern ear. This must be partly attributable to environmental changes, as well as to different farming practices, new methods of food preservation, and so on. The result of these and whatever other factors obtain is that we now have startlingly different notions of what food should taste like.

On the one hand, we wanted to introduce some of these astonishing new/old tastes; on the other, some of them are shockingly unexpected; and in any case we know that it isn't really possible to recreate the original, because too much *in us* has changed irretrievably. So, as with the music, we believe the intelligent solution is to seek a compromise: to try to work with an understanding of the way things were done two hundred years ago, but to take into account the fact that any performance always consists at least in part of its audience. In either case one must adapt to present-day conditions, at least to some degree, or lose a great deal of the message to be conveyed.

We have conceded as little as possible to the amenities of the modern kitchen. We have roasted haunches of meat on a spit in front of an open fire. We have raised coffins and made Sea-Pies. We have Inspissated the Juices of Lemon, Lime, and Lettuce. We have made Portable Soup.

We have combined sweet with savory according to the tastes and exigencies of the time—for preservative reasons as much as for flavor. We have studied the social and economic *raisons d'être* for the raised pie and the two wholly different traditional approaches to its construction. We have made a dozen different kinds of suet puddings, and in the process traced the etymology of most of their names to a single root. We have followed the evolution of pudding itself back to its Roman sources and established its common ancestry with sausage.

These are the foods that Jack and Stephen ate. We do not recommend them to the unimaginative or faint of heart: some of them call for exotic, revolting, or fearfully expensive ingredients; many take upwards of a week to make; most of them cheerfully violate all the nutritional tenets of our health-conscious age. They are all, however, practical and authentic recipes, tested to our satisfaction (and to the detriment of our waistlines) in our own kitchens.

Go thou and do likewise.

Authors' Note

O ur criteria for selecting these dishes were somewhat informal: we have chosen those whose names and descriptions appealed to us—being careful not to omit any of Jack Aubrey's particular favorites—and we have tried to give a sense of the scope, richness, and variety of the fare.

Wherever possible, we have organized the recipes according to where and when they were served in the novels—who cooked them, who ate them, who loved them, and why—but our attempts to impose a logical order have met with limited success. In some cases the sequences were clear-cut and unequivocal, in others far less so; the result being that elegant made-dishes, seamen's rations, and Killick's Toasted Cheese are sometimes presented cheek by jowl.

Since we were privileged to be able to use epigraphs from the novels for each recipe, one of the most serious problems we faced was the embarrassment of riches. Occasionally, when dealing with a dish that appears repeatedly in different situations, we have chosen to place it in one context while borrowing a favorite quotation from another. If the juxtapositions seem a little arbitrary or incongruous, we can only plead that there were some passages we simply couldn't bear to leave out.

Acknowledgments

I must frankly own, that if I had known, beforehand, that this book would have cost me the labour which it has, I should never have been courageous enough to commence it.

So says Mrs. Beeton, in the preface to her *Book of Household Management*. So say not we. We knew when we embarked on this project that it would be an enormous amount of work, and we knew it would be an unprecedented adventure—but in our wildest speculations we could not have foreseen the sheer fun of it. And we could never have anticipated the astonishing generosity we encountered on all sides: wherever we turned we found people willing—nay, eager—to help in any way possible, providing materials, advice, ideas, information, and access to unimagined resources.

We cannot possibly hope to list everyone to whom we are indebted, though we can certainly try.

Our thanks to the following libraries and institutions for their kind assistance, especially in some of our more arcane research: the Janus Museum (Allan Janus, curator); the New York Academy of Medicine Rare Book Collection (Michael North, librarian); the New York Public Library; the New York Yacht Club (Joseph Jackson, librarian); the Schlesinger Library at Harvard University; and the Suffolk County Library System, especially the Babylon Public Library.

We are grateful to these particularly fruitful sources of both exotic ingredients and specialized knowledge: Aux Delices des Bois; Dan, Len, and Rich of the Babylon Village Meat Market; Bayou Crawfish Company; Blood Farm; Rich Bogath of D'Artagnan, Inc.; Nach

Waxman and Matt Sartwell of Kitchen Arts & Letters; Cate Olson and Nash Robbins of Much Ado Books; Myer's of Keswick; Ocean Dynasty; James McKenna, Martin Jancheson, Lynette (the cow) and Norman (her calf), of Old Bethpage Village Restoration (Nassau County Department of Recreation and Parks); A. F. Rustice Liquors; Sherry's; and Sonny Mattera of Village Prime Meat Shoppe.

During the two years it took to write this book, our efforts have been fueled to a great extent by the members of the on-line community dedicated to Patrick O'Brian, known variously and collectively as the Norton list, the Gunroom, and Searoom-l. Among the literally hundreds of "listswains," all of whom have been kind and receptive, the following have been conspicuous for their devotion to the cause: Jean Anderson, John Berg, Hank Burchard, Gibbons Burke, Louis Cohen, Joseph "Joe Row" Ditler, John Drouot, Alison "Aphids" Fitts, Nick Flowers, Allan "Ponto" Janus, Michael Krugman, Paul Murphy, Ada Santiago Phelps, Steve Phelps, Hope Robbins, David and Susie Smith-Petersen, Lynn Steele, Gerry Strey, David and Toni Strother, Tay Tahk, David Wallingford, and Ellen Zimmerman.

We relied heavily on the *Lobscouse & Spotted Dog* Irregulars, an army of friends, relatives, neighbors, clients, and acquaintances, all of whom have gone above and beyond in various ways: David Anderson, Christine Ammer, Joan and Jerry Apt, Jane Asche, Ann and Ian Barribal, Catherine Barribal, Phyllis Brady, Catherine Brown, Kiki Cassidy and Alice Steinmetz, Rosanne and Tom Cassidy, Blair Chotzinoff, Robin Chotzinoff, Saikrupta Das, Barbara Davis, Sarah Dobbis, Martha Driver, Ellen Lovell Evans, Cara Flanagan and Rob Jones, John Flanagan and Susan Roberts, Gregory Garnant, Bill and Ditty Gentry, Peter Hackett, Susanne Hendricks, R. Carter Holliday, Martha Jacobsen, Madhur Jaffrey, Judith Jones, Tim Jurgielewicz, Dean King, Ronald Kluesener, Giuliana Lopes, Dan Lufkin, Denis and Melinda Malich, Gordon Messing, Vincent O'Shea, Ludwig von Pap, Arlene Feltman Sailhac, Jean Scopinich, Ruth and David Seidman, Brad Stone, Deborah Tulchin, and Joseph Wisnovsky.

Brave New World: we have actually met comparatively few of the following people at W. W. Norton, yet thanks to the quirks and wonders of modern technology we have worked more or less intimately with all of them. Among them they have managed to make sense of an uncommonly convoluted manuscript on an extremely demanding schedule—and without them this book would not exist and certainly would not be what it is: Starling Lawrence, Patricia Chui, and Traci Nagle, our editors; Nancy Palmquist, managing editor; Debra Morton Hoyt, art director; Charlotte Staub, designer; Patricia Anthonyson, production manager; Justine Trubey, head of electronic publishing; and Dan Saffer, Kirsten Miller, and Stephen King, who are jointly responsible for the *Lobscouse & Spotted Dog* Web page.

Finally, our gratitude to the following, who shall measure?

Dennis Flanagan, dear man, who introduced us to the works of Patrick O'Brian, and who has consistently encouraged, praised and humored us; he has a great deal to answer for;

Barbara Williams, our dear friend and agent, who first lit the fire under us and then kept it burning; who worked tirelessly with, for, and around us; who aided and abetted, endured and participated, fostered and promoted, throughout;

Lorraine Bodger, a cheerful mentor, a patient and unerring guide through the labyrinthine mysteries of cookbookery; whose experience, good sense, and unfailing enthusiasm supported us through many a dubious experiment;

Mr. and Mrs. O'Brian, for their gracious assistance and invaluable advice, and for their wisdom in the ways of Pudding;

Paul Monette, teacher, adviser, friend—for the semicolons . . . and for so many other things;

Herbert Grossman and Donald Edmund Thomas, whose contributions and whose sacrifices to the greater good are incalculable: for two years they ate the food, washed the dishes, put up with us, and almost never complained.

Lobscouse
&
Spotted Dog

The Roast Beef of Old England

Words and Music by Richard Leveridge

When might-y roast beef was the Eng-lish-man's food it en- nob- led our hearts and en- rich- ed our blood: Our sol- diers were brave, and our court- iers were good. Oh, the roast beef of old Eng- land! And oh, for old Eng- land's roast beef!

But since we have learned from effeminate France
To eat their ragouts, as well as to dance,
We are fed up with nothing but vain complaisance.
 Oh, the roast beef, &c.

Our fathers of old were robust, stout, and strong,
And kept open house, with good cheer all day long,
Which made their plump tenants rejoice in this song.
 Oh, the roast beef, &c.

When good Queen Elizabeth sat on the throne,
Ere coffee and tea, and such slip-slops were known,
The world was in terror if e' en she did frown.
 Oh, the roast beef, &c.

In those days, if fleets did presume on the main,
They seldom or never return'd back again;
As witness the vaunting Armada of Spain.
 Oh, the roast beef, &c.

Oh, then we had stomachs to eat and to fight,
And when wrongs were cooking, to set ourselves right:
But now we're a–hm!–I could, but good night.
 Oh, the roast beef, &c.

CHAPTER ONE

The

Captain's

Table

There was a very old naval tradition that required a captain to give his guests a meal unlike that which they would eat in the gunroom, thus making his entertainment something of a holiday, at least in respect of food. Even in very long voyages, when private stores were no more than memories and all hands were down to ship's provisions, the captain's cook would make a great effort to prepare the salt horse, dog's-body and hard tack rather differently from the gunroom cook; and Jack Aubrey, a Tory, a man who liked old ways and old wine, one of the comparatively few officers of his seniority who still wore his hair long, clubbed at the back of his neck, and his cocked hat athwartships in the Nelson manner rather than fore and aft, was the last to fly in the face of tradition.   —The Far Side of the World, *79*

Aubrey sat in the solitary splendour usual in some captains but rare in him—he liked seeing his officers and midshipmen at his table and particularly his surgeon. Not that Stephen could in any way be called a guest, since they had shared the cabin these many years. . . .
          —The Truelove, *32*

Jack Aubrey is passionate about a great many things: ships, music, women; life in general—and food in particular. He has strong feelings about coffee, he is exuberantly devoted to his dinner, and he is never happier than when confronted with suet pudding in one form or another. His friendship with Stephen Maturin, born of their mutual love of music, is cemented by their mutual love of food during their memorable first dinner together.

Everything in this chapter is served in the captain's dining cabin, either by or to Jack Aubrey or his brother officers, friends, and guests. Depending on the captain's (or admiral's) private means, his personal stores occasionally allowed for very elegant dining indeed, since if he could afford it he usually had his own livestock aboard, and could therefore command eggs, milk, and fresh meat—at least in the first few months of a voyage. Then again, a captain in reduced circumstances, or in the early stages of his career, might very well have to make do with the standard-issue salt pork and dried peas.

Jack is open-handed and hospitable no matter what the state of his finances; no one is better adapted to making hard tack and rancid cheese seem like a celebratory banquet. But when he does have the resources, he delights in planning elaborate meals: resplendent plate, the best wines, and as many courses and removes as possible; and while his lavish style of entertainment is sincerely intended as a mark of esteem for his guests, no one enjoys it more than he.

Breakfast

Skillygalee   Pig's Fry

The Last of the True French Short Bastards

Pickled Salmon   Pickled Tunny

Stirabout   White Pudding

Kedgeree   Coffee

Veal and Ham Pie

Skillygalee

Skillygalee was their only resource. Brigid therefore faced a bowl of very thin oatmeal gruel, sweetened with sugar and tempered with butter. She thought it the finest dish she had ever eaten, a more-than-birthday indulgence: she ate it up with naked greed and begged for more, and when at last she was told that she might get down skipped about the deck singing 'Skillygalee, skillygaloo, skillygalee ooh hoo hoo hoo' with a persistence that only very good-natured men could have borne. —The Commodore, *140*

Skillygalee may be derived from "skilly," which *The Sailor's Word Book* defines as "poor broth, served to prisoners in hulks," composed of "oatmeal and water in which meat has been boiled." John Masefield remarks that the " 'skillagolee,' or oatmeal gruel, issued to the men for breakfast, was invariably bad. The greatest proportion of it went to the pigstys, as uneatable by mortal man. . . . The oatmeal was of a pretty bad quality to begin with, but by the time the cook had wreaked his wicked will upon it by boiling it in his coppers with the unspeakable ship's water, the mess had become disgusting beyond words. Few of the sailors could eat it in its penetrating, undisguised nastiness."

Actually, when properly made, with good oatmeal, it can be as delicious as Brigid found it.

2 tablespoons oatmeal	¼ teaspoon salt
4 tablespoons cold water	2 tablespoons butter
Boiling water	2 teaspoons sugar

Grind the oatmeal into a very fine powder. Mix thoroughly with the cold water and let the mixture settle about 30 minutes. Gradually stir in 1 cup boiling water. Bring to a boil, stirring constantly, and continue to cook over medium heat, still stirring, for 10 minutes. Remove from heat, add the salt, butter and sugar, and stir until the butter and sugar are melted. If the gruel is too thick, thin it with another tablespoon or so of boiling water.

Serves 1

Pig's Fry

Jack's steward cautiously sidled near, muttering something about 'the gunroom's pot', and Stephen said, 'I believe he means that coffee's up.'

It was: and as they drank it benignity returned, helped by fresh cream, bacon, eggs, pig's fry, the last of the true French short bastards, toasted, and Sophie's orange marmalade. —The Mauritius Command, *97–8*

The essential ingredient for Pig's Fry is a pig's harslet (or haslet): its heart, liver, lungs, and sometimes pancreas. Pig offal, being unsanctioned by the powers that be, is rather difficult to obtain, at least in our part of the world; split-second timing and a cloak-and-dagger approach may be necessary.

Living as we do in the highly sanitized late-twentieth-century United States, we were a little taken aback at first by the intimacy of the experience. We met our pig, even knew him by name. Charlie was still alive when we put in our request for offal; minutes later, we had his harslet. Then it began to dawn on us that what seemed a little gruesome to us would have been perfectly commonplace to the people of Jack's time; they lived closer to the land and to the realities of husbandry, often raising and butchering their own livestock as a matter of course. (We were even more forcibly reminded of this on certain other occasions, most notably when we killed and butchered rats and when we made black pudding. It gave us a better understanding of what we were doing, an odd sense of kinship with the cooks whose work we were trying to recreate.)

The size of the harslet will vary with the size of the pig—we had a particularly generous supply of offal, and we found about 1½ pounds of liver to be sufficient.

1 pig's harslet (heart, liver, lungs, and pancreas)	2 tablespoons chopped fresh parsley
1 large onion, peeled and thinly sliced	Salt and pepper
Large handful of fresh sage, coarsely chopped	1 egg beaten with 1 table-spoon water
Oil for frying	Juice of ½ lemon
2 cups bread crumbs (or more as needed)	1 lemon, cut in wedges

Cut a piece of the lung approximately the same size as the heart. Put these (and the pancreas if you have it) in a pot with water to cover. Bring to a boil, reduce heat, and simmer, covered, about 20 minutes. Remove from water and chop coarsely.

In a large frying pan, heat 2–3 tablespoons oil. Sauté the onion and sage until the onion is limp. Add the chopped heart and lung (and another 2 tablespoons or so of oil if necessary) and cook until heated through. Remove from pan and keep warm.

Combine the bread crumbs with the parsley, and salt and pepper to taste. Slice the liver in ½-inch-thick pieces. Rinse the slices and pat them dry. Dip each slice first in the egg and then in the bread crumbs, turning to coat on all sides.

Using the same frying pan, heat 3–4 tablespoons of oil and fry the liver in batches over medium heat until it is browned on all sides.

Spread the heart and onion mixture on a warmed serving dish. Arrange the slices of fried liver on top, sprinkle with lemon juice, and garnish with lemon wedges.

Serves 8

The Last of the True French Short Bastards

The bastard in question is a literal translation of *pain bâtard*—i.e., a loaf of French bread, shorter and thicker than today's typical baguette, about 16 inches long by 3 inches wide. According to Felix Urbain Dubois and Elizabeth David, the name derives from the fact that the dough is something of a hybrid between the very soft and the very firm.

This breakfast is eaten aboard *Boadicea* shortly after her landfall in Simon's Bay. Some weeks previously, off the Dry Salvages, she has captured the French frigate *Hébé,* appropriating not only her captain's private stores but also his cook. The last of the true French short bastards is presumably all that remains of these stores (except perhaps for some dried sausages, some truffles and foie gras in goose grease, and some dozens of noble wines . . .). One very good reason for toasting them, perhaps, is that by then the bread must have been barely edible.

We do not give a recipe for the bastard because period sources for such breads are virtually impossible to find: then (as now) even the thriftiest of housewives bought them from a *boulangerie.* Some women made their own dough, but even they usually took it to a professional oven to be baked.

Pickled Salmon/Pickled Tunny

The breakfast was indeed magnificent. The steward, aware of Captain Aubrey's appetite and willing to do his ship honour, had broken out almost all his remaining stores: the third part of a Brunswick ham, kippered herrings, pickled salmon, seventeen mutton chops coming hot and hot, besides eggs, a kind of toasted scone, and two pots of orange marmalade, small beer, tea, and coffee as the Doctor had recommended it to be made.
—The Fortune of War, *305–6*

'We are sure to be able to pick up some pickled tunny at Barka, let alone other stores.'
—The Ionian Mission, *163*

It is traditional, with pickles, to give some idea of their keeping qualities. But no matter how much pickled salmon we make, somehow it is always eaten before we have a chance to find out. Jack eats this for breakfast—but we find it very good as an hors d'oeuvre or a first course.

1 salmon, about 4½ pounds	3 tablespoons salt
1 gallon water	1 teaspoon peppercorns
Small handful of fresh rosemary	1½ cups dry white wine
Small handful of fresh borage	1½ cups white vinegar
Small handful of fresh parsley	2 small bay leaves
Small handful of fresh marjoram	4 whole cloves
	½ teaspoon whole allspice
	Pinch of mace

Clean and scale the salmon, if necessary.

Put the water, herbs, salt, and ½ teaspoon of the peppercorns in a fish poacher. Bring to a boil. Add the salmon, bring to a gentle boil, reduce heat, cover (not too tightly; there should be a little room for steam to escape) and simmer 5 minutes.

Remove the salmon and let it cool. Remove and discard the skin and bones. Cut into fillets that will lie cleverly in a deep glass or crockery dish. Let both fish and poaching stock cool to room temperature.

Cover salmon fillets with 3 cups of strained stock (a little more if necessary to cover the fish); discard unused liquid. Cover tightly and refrigerate overnight.

Let the fish and broth (which will have set to a jelly) warm to room temperature.

Put the wine, vinegar, bay leaves, cloves, allspice, mace, and the remaining ½ teaspoon of peppercorns into a saucepan. Bring to a boil, reduce heat, and simmer, covered, 15 minutes. Remove from heat, cool to room temperature, and add to the fish. Refrigerate 3 days or longer.

Serves 10–12

Variation: Pickled Tunny: Substitute fillets of fresh tuna for the salmon. The broth will not form a jelly, but otherwise the process is the same.

Stirabout

> *'Stephen, have you forgot breakfast?'*
> *'I have not. My mind has been toying with thoughts of coffee, stirabout, white pudding, bacon, toast, marmalade and more coffee, for some considerable time.'*
> —The Letter of Marque, *162*

"Stirabout" is originally a generic Irish term for any porridge made by this method, whether from oats, flour, or some other kind of meal. The *Oxford English Dictionary* suggests that it is synonymous with hasty pudding, and can even be used to refer to polenta. Made this way, as Jack and Stephen would have eaten it, there is little practical difference between Stirabout and oatmeal—the proportions are not quite the same, but there is not much to choose between them.

1 quart water	1½ cups steel-cut oats, flour, or
1 teaspoon salt	meal

Bring the water to a boil. Add the salt. Gradually stir in the oats. Continue to cook, stirring constantly, until the oats soften and the mixture thickens, about 15 minutes.

Serve with butter, sugar, and/or cream.

Serves 4

White Pudding

The cooks of the period are tantalizingly reticent about their sausage-stuffing procedures. "Fill your Guts," they say, leaving method and equipment to the imagination. Apparently it was one of those things that one was just expected to know.

In the dim, dank recesses of our cellar we discovered a simple, slightly tapered cylindrical implement (about six inches long, and three-quarters of an inch in diameter at its narrow end) that may or may not have been intended for the purpose, soaked our casings, forced them over the tapered end of the instrument, and went to work. Our technique left something to be desired, and we frequently found ourselves having to reverse direction to eliminate air bubbles that had mysteriously appeared. The final results were a bit uneven and the process messy in the extreme, but when it was all over we had several strings of undeniable sausages—and a considerable feeling of accomplishment.

25	feet of large (hog) sausage casings	1	large onion, peeled and finely chopped
	Cold water for soaking	1	cup milk
2	cups steel-cut oats		Large handful of fresh sage, chopped
4	cups water		Pinch of ground cloves
½	pound leaf lard, minced or cut in small dice		Pinch of mace
		2	teaspoons salt

Soak the casings in cold water for at least 2 hours.

In a saucepan, gradually stir the oats into the 4 cups of water. Bring to a boil over medium heat. Reduce heat and simmer 15 minutes, stirring constantly. Remove from heat.

When the oats have cooled, combine them with the remaining ingredients. Stuff the oat mixture into the casings until they are fairly full, tying off individual sausages either with a twist in the casing or with a small piece of string.

Bring a large pot of water to a boil. Remove from heat, add ½ cup of cold water to stop the boiling, and put in the sausages. After 5 minutes, prick the sausages with a needle and return the pot to the heat. Bring to a boil and simmer 30 minutes, pricking the sausages again as they rise to the surface.

Remove the sausages from the pot and hang them in a cool, dry place for a day or two.

To serve, soak the sausages in hot water for 15 minutes, then fry them over medium heat until they are browned on all sides.

Makes about 2 dozen 4-inch sausages

KEDGEREE

Kedgeree appears three times in the Aubrey/Maturin novels: at Fox's breakfast table in Pulo Prabang, in Jack's cabin aboard *Diane* off the False Natunas (both in *The Thirteen-Gun Salute,* 216 and 283), and at Ashgrove (*The Commodore,* 79), where Jack listens "with half an ear to Stephen's minute and circumstantial account of the Madras fashion of making kedgeree."

The dish originated in 1340 (or possibly even earlier) as an Indian rice-and-bean or rice-and-lentil porridge. In the early nineteenth century, Anglo-Indian cooks replaced the lentils and spices with fish, eggs, and cream to make the English version known today. Which form it was that Jack and Stephen ate would have depended in large part on the nationality of the cook; since that was unspecified, we decided to do both.

Indian Khichri

This is fairly close to Stephen's Madras Kedgeree, which could also include nuts such as roasted cashews, and might use mung beans instead of lentils (both of which qualify as *dhal,* a generic term for legumes that also covers yellow split peas, red lentils, soy beans, chickpeas, etc.).

1 cup green lentils (or other *dhal*)	¼ teaspoon cumin seed
	¼ teaspoon ground coriander
3 tablespoons oil or ghee	6 whole cloves
1 onion, peeled and coarsely chopped	½ stick cinnamon
	½ teaspoon ground turmeric
1 clove garlic, peeled and finely chopped	1 bay leaf
	1 cup long-grain rice, washed in several waters
1 inch-long knob fresh ginger, peeled and coarsely chopped	2 cups water
	Salt and pepper

Soak the lentils for 30 minutes in boiling water. Drain and put in a pot with cold water to cover. Bring to a boil, covered, and simmer 10 minutes. Drain.

In a large stewpot, heat the oil and sauté the onion and garlic until they are soft. Stir in the ginger, spices and bay leaf. Add the rice and stir to coat evenly with oil. Add the lentils, the water, and salt and pepper to taste (be especially generous with the pepper). Bring to a boil, reduce heat, cover, and simmer 20 minutes or until the rice is tender but not gummy. Remove the bay leaf and the cinnamon stick before serving.

Serves 4

English Kedgeree

There are creamier versions of this dish, in which raw eggs are beaten lightly and stirred into the sauce as it cooks—but the use of hard-boiled eggs is more typical of the period.

1 pound cold, cooked white fish (such as haddock or cod)	3 tablespoons heavy cream
	½ teaspoon dry mustard mixed with ½ teaspoon water
2 cups cold, cooked rice	Salt, pepper, and cayenne
3 tablespoons butter	
2 eggs, hard-boiled and coarsely chopped	

Remove any skin and bones from the fish. Flake it finely.

Melt the butter in a saucepan, add the fish and the rice, and cook over medium heat, stirring occasionally, about 5 minutes. Reduce heat, stir in the eggs, cream, mustard, and other seasonings to taste, and cook until heated through.

Serves 6

Coffee

Captain Fellowes greeted his guests with the utmost cordiality, with apolo-
gies, explanations, and a breakfast-table covered with all the luxuries that
a ship only a few days outward-bound could offer: beef-steaks; mutton-
chops; bacon; eggs in all their charming variety; soft-tack, crusty or toasted;
mushrooms; pork sausages; a veal and ham pie; fresh butter; fresh milk; fresh
cream, even; tea and cocoa: everything except the coffee that Jack's and
Stephen's souls longed for.

   'You are very good, sir,' said Stephen, '... Would there never be a drop
of coffee, at all?'...

   'Oh no, sir. Oh no. This is a cocoa-ship, sir; though tea is countenanced.'

   'Coffee relaxes the fibres,' called out the Thunderer's *surgeon in an au-*
thoritative voice. 'I always recommend cocoa.'

   'Coffee?' cried Captain Fellowes. 'Would the gentleman like coffee?
Featherstonehaugh, run along and see whether the wardroom or the gun-
room has any.'

   'Coffee relaxes the fibres,' said the surgeon again, rather louder. 'That is
a scientific fact.'

   'Perhaps the Doctor might like to have his fibres relaxed,' said Captain
Dundas. 'I am sure I should, having stood to all night.'

   'Mr McAber,' called Captain Fellowes down the table to his first lieu-
tenant, 'pray be so good as to encourage Featherstonehaugh in his search.'

   But no amount of zeal could find what did not exist.

                                                           —The Commodore, *15–16*

This passage from *The Commodore* is an extraordinarily painful one to
anyone who cares about Jack and Stephen. Coffee is nearly as important to them as pudding, perhaps even more so. In the eighteen
novels, even excluding mentions of coffee-houses and coffee-rooms,
the word appears some 486 times. Killick's increasing skill at making
it is a running thread, from the withering "Killick's version of coffee"
in *Master and Commander*; through various stages of outrage, such as
the "familiar tang" of rat excrement in *The Mauritius Command* and
the "purplish brew," the "vile boiled coffee" in *Desolation Island;* to the

triumph of *The Commodore:* "Of all the many virtues, Preserved Killick possessed only two, polishing silver and making coffee; but these
he possessed to such a high degree that for those who liked their
plate brilliant and their coffee prompt, freely roasted, freshly ground
and piping hot it was worth putting up with his countless vices."

Even when it was boiled ("a crime not far short of hanging") or
adulterated, the coffee that Jack and Stephen drank was several cuts
above the "Scotch coffee" sometimes brewed for the men: an evil
concoction of burnt ship's biscuit boiled in water and sweetened with
a small amount of brown sugar. As for the real thing, the brewing of
coffee was and is such a subjective matter that we felt it would be un-
wise to try to improve upon the actual recipes of the period.

To Make Coffee

The right way to make coffee, is to heat the berries in a fire-shovel,
till they sweat a little; and then grind them, and put the coffee-pot
over the fire with water; when hot, throw the water away, and dry
the pot by the fire, then put the powder into it, and boiling water
immediately over the same; let stand three or four minutes, and
pour off the clear. By this means the hot water meets the spirit of
the coffee; whereas if you boil coffee, as the common way is, the
spirit goes away, so that it will not be so strong nor quick to the
taste.   —William Ellis, *The Country Housewife's Family Companion* (1750)

To Make Coffee

To a quart of boiling water add an ounce of coffee well-ground. Set
it over the fire and let it just have a boil up; try that the spout of
your coffee pot be clear, that it may pour out. After this let it stand
a few minutes that the grounds may settle, and it will be fit to
drink. Some sweeten coffee with Lisbon, and others with Loaf
sugar, but sugar candy is better. And it is now very common for
those who like mustard, to put a teaspoonful of the fine Durham
flour among the coffee as soon as it is ground: this helps the flavour,
and is very wholesome.

—Mrs. Martha Bradley, *The British Housewife* (1757)

Then there is always Miss Annabella Plumptre, who would be perfectly at home aboard the *Thunderer:* "Coffee," she says in her *Domestic Management; or, the Healthful Cookery Book,*

affords very little nourishment, and is apt to occasion heat, dryness, stimulation and tremours of the nerves, and for these reasons is thought to occasion palsies, watchfulness, and leanness. Hence it is very plain that it must be pernicious, to hot, dry, and bilious constitutions. If moderately used, it may be beneficial to phlegmatic persons, but, if drank very strong, or in great quantities it will prove injurious even to them.

Veal and Ham Pie

Our first raised pie. The utterly implausible idea of building a pie without benefit of dish, mold, or buttressing of any kind. Uncharted territory. Ultimately, a revelation.

Both the method of construction and the combination of flavorings seemed like such a gamble at the time that it is no wonder we embarked on the venture with profound misgivings. Looking back on it now, from our present lofty pinnacle of raised-pie experience, we are amazed by our temerity, and even more so by our success.

(For information about preparing raised pies, see "About Raised Pies," p. 279.)

1 recipe (4½ pounds) Hot Water Paste (p. 269)
1 recipe (1¾ pounds) Forcemeat (p. 266)
¼ pound mushrooms, quartered
1 large onion, peeled and cut into ½-inch pieces
2 teaspoons butter or oil
2 pounds veal, cut in ½-inch to ¾-inch dice
1 pound ham, cut in ½-inch to ¾-inch dice
Flour for dredging
2 teaspoons grated lemon zest
1 tablespoon coarsely chopped fresh sage
1 tablespoon finely chopped fresh parsley
Salt and pepper
1 egg, beaten with 1 teaspoon water
1 cup rich stock (see note)

Put a quarter of the Hot Water Paste in a bowl, cover with a damp cloth, and set aside in a warm place.

Form the remaining Hot Water Paste into a ball and place on a well-greased pan. Working quickly while the dough is warm, begin to raise your coffin, continuing in stages until it is about 8 inches across and 3½ inches high. Chill the coffin for at least an hour, or until it is firmly set.

Preheat oven to 450°.

Sauté the mushrooms and onions in the butter until they soften. Remove from heat. Dredge the veal and ham in flour. Combine the mushrooms and onions with the meats; add the lemon zest, sage, parsley, and salt and pepper to taste, and mix well.

Spread a thin layer of Forcemeat on the bottom and inside walls of the coffin. Spoon the meat mixture into the coffin. Spread a thin layer of Forcemeat over the filling.

On a floured board, roll out the remaining Hot Water Paste until it is about ³⁄₁₆ inch thick. Cut a circle slightly larger than the diameter of the coffin. Cut a ½-inch hole in the center of the circle. Place this top crust over the pie. Moisten the edges of the two crusts with the egg wash and seal them tightly together by crimping with your fingers.

Cut decorative shapes (leaves, anchors, knots) from the pastry scraps and arrange them on the top crust, cementing them in place with the egg wash. Brush a thin layer of the remaining egg wash over the top of the pie.

Heat the stock almost to boiling. Using a small funnel, carefully pour as much as you can through the hole in the crust. Place the pie in the oven *immediately* (if you wait, the hot stock will begin to melt the coffin).

Bake 15 minutes at 450°, turn the oven down to 350°, and bake 1 hour 15 minutes.

Note: We make the stock out of the bones and trimmings from the veal and the ham, boiled up with an onion, a carrot, a rib of celery, salt and pepper, and a few pieces of Portable Soup (p. 240)—but any good brown stock will serve the purpose.

Serves 6–8

cA Dinner for the Officers

Lobscouse	Sea-Pie	Strasburg Pie
Frumenty	Syllabub	Spotted Dog

from *The Far Side of the World,* 78ff.

Lobscouse

'It is one of the oldest of the forecastle dishes, and eats very savoury when it is well made.' . . . This was a rich man's lobscouse . . . the potatoes and pounded biscuit that ordinarily made up the bulk of the dish could scarcely be detected at all, being quite overpowered by the fat meat, fried onions and powerful spices. —The Far Side of the World, *82*

[The cook] had no sense of taste or smell . . . yet he was much loved aboard, being . . . uncommonly generous with his slush, the fat that rose to the surface of his coppers from the seething meat. Apart from what was needed to grease masts and yards, the slush was the cook's perquisite. . . . —The Far Side of the World, *80*

Most English dictionaries, while they do define Lobscouse as a sailor's stew or hash, don't seem to have any clear idea as to the word's derivation. "Of obscure origin," they say, or "origin unknown"—and then proceed to offer vague etymological connections to loblolly and Liverpool. We prefer to believe, as one source suggests, that Lobscouse began as a Nordic dish, as in the Norwegian *lapskaus* ("hodgepodge"), the Danish *labskovs,* or the Dutch/German *labskaus.* (Actually, the Norwegian dictionary says *lapskaus* comes from the English "lobscouse," while the Danish dictionary says *labskovs* comes from the Low German *labskaus,* which the German dictionary says comes from the English "lobscouse." It seems none of them is willing to take the credit.)

We have no proof of age for the dish, beyond the fact that the earliest known English reference to it dates from 1706; clearly, though, it is an old and well-established nautical tradition in several countries. As of 1970, *lapskaus* was on the official menu for the seamen's mess of the Norwegian-American Line—and to this day *labskaus* is so popular in the German port of Hamburg that some restaurants there serve nothing else. (Many of them garnish it with a fried egg, which in our minds only serves to underscore the resemblance between Lobscouse and modern corned beef hash.)

We challenge anyone to disprove our pet theory: that Lobscouse originated with the Vikings.

2 pounds corned beef	6 juniper berries, crushed
2 pounds corned pork or	1 teaspoon ground allspice
smoked ham	1 teaspoon ground nutmeg
1 bay leaf	1 teaspoon mace
4 large onions	½ teaspoon ground cloves
6 large potatoes	½ teaspoon ground cardamom
4 large leeks	Dash cayenne
8 ounces Ship's Biscuit (p. 102),	Salt
or enough to produce	Fresh-ground pepper
3 ½ cups crumbs	

Place the corned meat in a pot with bay leaf and cold water to cover. Bring to a boil and cook, covered, over medium-low heat until tender (2½–3 hours). Remove the meat from the pot and discard the bay leaf. Skim and reserve the slush (fat). Reserve 3 cups of the cooking liquid.

(If you are using smoked ham instead of corned pork, you may want to pre-cook it as well, though this is not strictly necessary. We feel it improves the texture, so we usually cook it with the beef for about an hour.)

Trim the meat and cut it into ¼-inch dice. Peel the onions and potatoes and cut them into ¼-inch dice. Put the potatoes in cold water to cover.

Remove the root tips and the tough green ends of the leeks. Cut the remaining portion in quarters, lengthwise, and wash thoroughly under running water, separating the layers to remove any grit. Cut into ¼-inch slices.

Place the Ship's Biscuit in a plastic bag and pound it into coarse crumbs with a marline-spike—or a belaying pin, a mallet, or any other large blunt instrument.

Heat 6 tablespoons of slush in a large frying pan over high heat. Add the meat and cook, stirring occasionally, until it begins to brown (10–15 minutes). Remove the meat from the pan and set aside, draining as much fat as possible back into the pan.

Sauté the onions over medium heat in the same pan (adding a little more slush if needed) until they start to soften. Add the leeks and cook until the onions start to brown. Drain the potatoes, add to the onion mixture, and cook, stirring often, about 5 minutes. Add the browned meat. Cover and cook over medium-low heat until the potatoes are almost tender (5–10 minutes).

Stir in the pounded biscuit and 1½ cups of the reserved cooking liquid (less if you like your Lobscouse very dry, more if you prefer it soupier). Add the spices, and salt and pepper to taste (be very generous with the pepper). Mix well. Cover and cook another 5 minutes.

Serves 8

Sea-Pie

'Pies at sea,' he said, 'are made on nautical lines, of course. They are quite unlike pies by land. First you lay down a stratum of pastry, then a layer of meat, then a layer of pastry, then another layer of meat, and so on, according to the number of decks required. This is a three-decker, as you can see: spar-deck, main-deck, middle-deck, lower deck.'

'But that makes four decks, my dear sir,' said Martin.

'Oh, yes,' said Jack. 'All first-rate ships of the line, all three-deckers have four. And by counting the orlop you could make it five; or even six, with the poop. We only call them three-deckers, you understand. Though now I come to think of it, perhaps when we say deck we really mean the space between two of them. . . .' —The Far Side of the World, *83–4*

As Jack implies, the Sea-Pie is defined not by its contents but by its construction. You can put almost anything in a Sea-Pie—in fact you can, if you choose, make a different filling for each deck. The quantities in this recipe are based on a literal three-decker; we have not yet succeeded in building a higher one. If your ambition runs to more decks, you will need to adjust the amounts of pastry accordingly.

The Sea-Pie described above is actually Jemmy Ducks's infamous, "vulturine" goose-pie. Since we have another recipe for goose-pie (Pullings's truffle-studded surprise for the Doctor, p. 65), we have given a slightly more generic version here. This pie, of course, can also be made with goose—but in that case we recommend cooking it rather longer than Jemmy did his.

(For information about preparing raised pies, see "About Raised Pies," p. 279.)

1½ recipes (about 6¾ pounds)
    Hot Water Paste (p. 269)
1½ recipes (about 2⅔ pounds)
    Forcemeat (p. 266)

For *each* deck:
  6 mushrooms, quartered
  1 small onion, peeled and cut
    in ½-inch pieces
  2 teaspoons butter or oil
1¼ pounds meat (ham, pork,
    veal, chicken, goose, etc.),
    cut in ½-inch to ¾-inch
    dice

Flour for dredging
½ cup peas or diced carrots
    (optional)
2 teaspoons grated lemon
    zest
1 tablespoon coarsely chopped
    fresh sage leaves
1 tablespoon finely chopped
    fresh parsley
Salt and pepper

1 egg, beaten with 1 teaspoon
    water
1 cup rich stock (see note)

Put half the Hot Water Paste in a bowl, cover with a damp cloth, and set aside in a warm place.

Form the remaining dough into a ball and place on a well-greased pan. Working quickly while the dough is warm, begin to raise your coffin, continuing in stages until it is about 9 inches across and 4 inches high. Chill the coffin for at least an hour, or until firmly set.

Preheat oven to 450°.

Sauté the mushrooms and onions in the butter until they soften.

For each deck filling, dredge the meat in flour and combine with whichever of the seasonings and other ingredients you choose.

Spread a thin layer of Forcemeat on the bottom of the coffin. Spoon one of the fillings into the coffin. Spread another thin layer of Forcemeat over the filling.

On a floured board, roll out one-third of the reserved Hot Water Paste (leaving the rest in a warm place) until it is about ³/₁₆ inch thick. Cut a circle slightly larger than the diameter of the coffin. Cut a companionway—a ½-inch hole—in the center of the circle. Place the circle on top of the filling, pressing the edges gently into the coffin walls.

Continue in this manner, adding layers of Forcemeat, filling, Forcemeat, and pastry, until you have the desired number of decks.

Cut the circle of pastry for the final deck slightly larger than the others. Cut the companionway as before, and place the crust over the pie. Moisten the edges of the top crust and of the coffin walls with the egg wash and seal them tightly together by crimping with your fingers.

Cut decorative shapes (leaves, anchors, knots) from the pastry scraps and arrange them on the top crust, cementing them in place with the egg wash. Brush a thin layer of the remaining egg wash over the top of the pie.

Heat the stock almost to boiling. Using a small funnel, carefully pour as much as you can down the companionway. Gradually lift the funnel as you pour to make sure that some stock goes to each deck. Place the pie in the oven *immediately* (if you wait, the hot stock will begin to melt the coffin).

Bake 15 minutes at 450°, turn the oven down to 350°, and bake 1 hour 15 minutes.

Note: We make the stock out of the bones and trimmings from the meat, boiled up with an onion, a carrot, a rib of celery, salt and pepper, and a few pieces of Portable Soup (p. 240)—but any good brown stock will serve the purpose.

Serves 10–12

Strasburg Pie

'By God, Stephen, this is the most famous Strasburg pie. Have you had any?'

'I have not.'

'Let me give you a piece.'

Ordinarily opium so cut Stephen's appetite that after a considerable dose he took little pleasure in meals, but this time he said 'It is uncommonly good,' and passed his plate for more.   —The Letter of Marque, *189*

It is certainly true that this pie is uncommonly good. It is also without question the richest thing we have ever eaten. We are in awe of Stephen's request for a second helping.

1 whole fresh foie gras, about 1¼ pounds	1 pound bacon
1 pound Puff Paste (p. 270)	1 egg beaten with 1 teaspoon water

Preheat oven to 450°.

Trim the foie gras, removing any dark spots.

On a lightly floured board, roll out three-quarters of the Puff Paste until it is about ¼ inch thick.

Trace the shape of a hinged metal pâté mold on a piece of paper. Cut it out to make a pattern for the top crust.

Line the pâté mold with the sheet of Puff Paste, crimping and trimming as necessary. Leave a ¾-inch overhang. Line the pastry with bacon, draping it so that it covers the bottom and hangs over the sides.

Put the foie gras into the mold, cutting and packing as needed to make it fit. Fold the bacon over the foie gras, and lay additional bacon strips on the top, so that it is completely covered.

Roll out the remaining Puff Paste until it is large enough to cover the pâté mold. Cut it to size using the paper pattern. Cut a small hole in the center of the top crust.

Place the top crust over the mold. Bring up the overhanging edges of the bottom crust, brush them with the egg wash, and cement them over the rim of the top crust, pressing gently to seal.

Cut decorative shapes from the pastry scraps and arrange them on the crust, covering the seam, and secure them in place with the egg wash. Brush a thin layer of the remaining egg wash over the entire top crust.

Place the mold on a rimmed cookie sheet and bake at 450° for 10 minutes. Reduce heat to 350° and bake for another 20 minutes.

Cool thoroughly on a rack and unmold carefully onto a serving dish.

Serves 20

Frumenty

'What about pudding? Did you ask Mrs Lamb about pudding? About her frumenty?'

'Which she is belching so and throwing up you can hardly hear yourself speak,' said Killick, laughing merrily. 'And has been ever since we left Gib. Shall I ask the gunner's wife?'

'No, no,' said Jack. No one the shape of the gunner's wife could make frumenty, or spotted dog, or syllabub, and he did not wish to have anything to do with her.   —The Far Side of the World, *78–9*

Frumenty (also furmity, firmety, formete) probably originated somewhere in Touraine, France, around 1300 or perhaps earlier. The name is from the French *froment,* meaning "wheat." In medieval times Frumenty was sometimes made with broth rather than milk (very elegant households used almond milk—"swete mylk of almandys"); it was occasionally savory rather than sweet, and was generally served as an accompaniment to meat. By the late eighteenth century it was invariably sweet and was considered a breakfast or dessert dish.

The ingredients for Frumenty do not vary much from one source to another, but the proportions are wildly inconsistent; so the development of this recipe was based, more than most, on educated trial and error. Our first Frumenty was a fairly insipid affair, our second simply dreadful. The third attempt was quite acceptable, and once we had spiked it heavily with rum and floated a great deal of thick cream on it, we found ourselves liking it very much indeed. (Almost any-thing will taste good if you add enough rum and cream to it.) Of course, this sort of indulgence is not without its perils—it was spiked Frumenty, after all, that caused Henchard to sell his wife and child at the village fair in *The Mayor of Casterbridge.* Perhaps the seller of Kil-lick's "wife" in *Desolation Island* was similarly inspired.

1 cup cracked wheat	½ teaspoon mace
1 quart water	Generous pinch of saffron
2 cups milk	2 egg yolks
¼ pound dried currants (about ⅞ cup)	1 tablespoon heavy cream
	3 tablespoons sugar
1 teaspoon salt	Rum and/or heavy cream for serving (optional)
½ teaspoon ground nutmeg	

Put the cracked wheat and water in a large saucepan over fairly high heat. Bring to a boil, remove from heat, and let stand, uncovered, overnight. The wheat will quadruple in volume.

Pour off any liquid that has not been absorbed by the wheat. Add the milk, currants, salt, and spices, and bring gradually to a boil. Simmer 10 minutes, stirring occasionally. Remove from heat.

Beat the egg yolks with the heavy cream and stir into the wheat mix-ture. Return to heat and simmer 10 minutes, stirring often. Add the sugar and stir to combine.

Spoon into bowls. For those who like their Frumenty spiked with rum, stir in about a teaspoon per portion. Or float a tablespoon or so of heavy cream on top of each portion. We strongly recommend that you do both.

Serves 6–8

SYLLABUB

Syllabubs fall into three categories: Everlasting, Whipt, and From the Cow. The first is essentially a flavored whipped cream; the second, much the same thing, but floated in a glass of sweetened wine. The last, and most exciting, is the result of the "clabbering" effect of squirting milk directly from a cow into a bowl of sweetened wine (or, in regional variations, sherry, cider, brandy, etc.).

We were fortunate enough to have usufruct of a real cow, but we have also simulated one with some success. There is historic precedent for this: Hannah Glasse says, "You may make this Syllabub at Home, only have new Milk; make it as hot as Milk from the Cow, and out of a Tea-pot or any such Thing, pour it in, holding your Hand very high."

In either case the result is a surprisingly delicate and delicious concoction, reminiscent of Miss Patience Muffet and her curds and whey.

Whipt Syllabub

4 cups red wine	2 cups heavy cream
¾ cup sugar	8 sprigs fresh rosemary (op-
Juice and grated zest of 2	tional)
large lemons	
1 cup medium-dry sherry (or	
½ cup sherry and ½ cup	
Madeira)	

Sweeten the wine with ¼ cup of the sugar. Stir well to dissolve. Divide evenly among 8 goblets.

Reserve 1 tablespoon of the lemon zest. In a large bowl, combine the lemon juice with the remaining zest and the sherry. Add the remaining sugar and stir to dissolve. Pour in the cream and whip with a wire whisk. As the froth rises, take it off with a spoon and lay it gently on the surface of the wine in the goblets.

Sprinkle with the reserved lemon zest and garnish each with a sprig of rosemary. Chill at least an hour before serving.

Serves 8

Variation: Everlasting Syllabub: Omit the sweetened red wine, whip the cream until it is quite stiff, and spoon directly into the goblets.

Syllabub from the Cow (Windsor Syllabub)

2 cups port	whole nutmeg
2 cups medium-dry sherry	
8 teaspoons sugar	
1 milch cow; *or* 2 quarts un-homogenized milk; *or* 1½ quarts homogenized milk plus 2 cups heavy cream	

In a very large bowl, combine the port, sherry, and sugar, and stir to dissolve.

Milk the cow directly into the bowl until you have approximately 2 quarts of milk. (Be prepared to start all over again if the cow knocks over the bowl—or steps in it—both of which happened to us.)

If you do not have access to a milch cow, use unhomogenized milk or, as an absolute last resort, a combination of homogenized milk and heavy cream. Heat to cow temperature (approximately 103°) and pour into the bowl from cow height, preferably using a soft, squeezable bottle with a nipple and violently expressing the milk therefrom, to approximate the force and angle of the real thing.

Pour the Syllabub into goblets and grate a light dusting of nutmeg over it. Refrigerate 1 hour before serving.

Serves 8

Variation: Staffordshire Syllabub: Instead of port and sherry, use 4 cups cider and 1 cup brandy, and increase the sugar to 5 tablespoons.

Spotted Dog

The pudding was Jack's favourite, a spotted dog, and a spotted dog fit for
a line-of-battle ship, carried in by two strong men.

'Bless me,' cried Jack, with a loving look at its glistening, faintly translu-
cent sides, 'a spotted dog!'

'We thought as how you might like one, sir,' said Pullings. 'Allow me to
carve you a slice.'   —The Ionian Mission, *83*

It was a cheerful meal. Jack was a good host, and . . . he was fond of the lit-
tle brutes from the midshipmen's berth . . . and he amused himself and the
young gentlemen extremely by dwelling at length on the fact that the coun-
try they had just quitted was practically the same as Dalmatia . . . so fa-
mous for its spotted dogs. He himself had seen quantities of spotted
dogs—had even hunted behind a couple of braces—spotted dogs in a pack
of hounds, oh Lord!—while the town of Kutali was positively infested
with spotted youths and maidens, and now the Doctor swore he had seen
spotted eagles. . . . Jack laughed until the tears came into his eyes. In a Dal-
matian inn, he said, by way of pudding you could call for spotted dick,
give pieces of it to a spotted dog, and throw the remains to the spotted ea-
gles.   —The Ionian Mission, *351–2*

Spotted Dog, Roly-Poly and Boiled Baby are all referred to at various times as Jack's favorite pudding, with perfect truth in every case.
When Jack's not near the pudding he loves, he loves the pudding he's
near. Nevertheless we must put in a special word for Spotted Dog. It
is a handsome object, brown and appetizing; it has a moist, dense,
cake-like texture; it is sweet but not too sweet, spicy but not too spicy,
and altogether satisfying.

(For information on preparing and cooking puddings, see "About
Puddings," p. 273.)

4 cups flour	¼ teaspoon ground nutmeg
¼ cup sugar	1¾ cups dried currants
½ teaspoon salt	½ pound suet, finely grated
1½ teaspoons ground cinna-	1 cup milk
mon	2 eggs, lightly beaten

In a large bowl, mix the flour, sugar, salt, cinnamon, and nutmeg. Stir in the currants, breaking them apart (the flour will coat them and keep them from clumping together). Mix in the suet. Add the milk and eggs, and work the mixture thoroughly with your hands.

Scrape the batter into a greased 6-cup pudding-basin. Tie a well-floured cloth over the pudding. Place the pudding in a pot of boiling water, cover, and steam for 2 hours.

Unmold and serve hot, accompanied by Custard Sauce (p. 264).

Serves 12

Christmas at Sea

Sucking Pig   Roast Pork   Mince Pies
Christmas Pudding

There are not many Christmas feasts in the Aubrey/Maturin novels, nor is there much variety in the fare. Christmas at sea can be a fairly depressing business, and as often as not it is signalized by little more than a double ration of salt pork and Plum-Duff.

Despite our best efforts, we were unable to reproduce some of the more exotic Christmas dinners. We could not obtain the salted penguins and "the wrong kind of turtle" eaten to such dramatic effect in *The Mauritius Command;* not to mention the porpoises, "rather strangely jointed by the ship's butcher," which "were served out for Christmas dinner and declared better, far better, than roast pork" in *The Yellow Admiral.*

Nevertheless, we firmly believe that our pork was better, far better, than roast porpoise.

Sucking Pig

The catering-officer at once ordered a massacre of geese, ducks, sucking-pigs.
Yet in spite of the season and the rich smell of festivity there was no Christmas spirit in the ship at all. Stephen's first impression was that she was the gloomiest vessel he had ever known.   —The Fortune of War, *95*

The *Java* may have been a gloomy vessel, but it seems unlikely that the sucking pigs had anything to do with the dismal atmosphere. We cannot imagine a more cheerful Christmas dinner than one based on roast pork. This is a fairly simple recipe for the period; Hannah Glasse, for instance, has a much more elaborate one that runs ". . . make a hard [force]Meat, with a Pint of Cream, the Yolks of six Eggs, grated Bread and Beef Sewet, seasoned with Salt, Pepper, Mace, Nutmeg, Thyme, and Lemon-Peel; make of this a pretty stiff

Pudding . . ." and that also calls for basting with butter and cream. We chose this one, adapted from Meg Dods, because it worked so well when we used it for a smaller pork roast (given in the next recipe).

We have not been able to determine the origins of the custom of putting an apple in a sucking pig's mouth; but we do know that it probably was not typical of Jack's time, when most cooks split the head and stirred the brains into the sauce. But splitting a pig's head—as we knew from our experience with Soused Hog's Face—is a nasty, difficult task. We decided to use the possibly anachronistic apple; it seemed the better part of valor.

(For information on spit-roasting, see "About Roasting," p. 282.)

1 sucking pig, about 20 pounds	Salt
Large handful of fresh sage	Sage and Onion Stuffing (see p. 32)

Wash the pig and wipe it dry, inside and out.

Rub the pig, inside and out, with sage and salt. Spoon the stuffing into the cavity. Sew up the opening with stout cotton string.

Center and secure the pig on the spit. Set it to roast before a clear fire. A pig of this size should take about 4 hours—it is done when it reaches an inside temperature of 160°.

Serves 20

Roast Pork

'And so, sir—a trifle of crackling?'
'If you please,' said Jack, holding out his plate. 'How I love roast pork.'
—The Truelove, *141*

The classic accompaniment for a pork roast like this is Brown Onion Sauce, p. 263.

(For information on spit-roasting, see "About Roasting," p. 282.)

1 half leg of pork with skin,   Flour for dredging
   about 8 pounds, at room   1 tablespoon fresh sage
   temperature
   Sage and Onion Stuffing
   (recipe follows)

Bone the pork. Sew it together at one end, making a pocket for the stuffing.

Spoon the stuffing into the cavity of the roast, and sew up the opening. (This is a dreadfully messy job, as the stuffing will try to ooze out—and will probably succeed.) Using butcher's twine or stout string, tie the meat tightly into a firm oblong package. Center it on the spit, dredge it with flour, and set it to roast in front of a clear fire.

After the pork has been cooking about 1 hour, remove it from the fire. With a very sharp knife or a small scissors, carefully score the skin in 1-inch squares. Tear the sage in little pieces and stuff them into the cuts in the skin.

Return the meat to the fire and roast it for about 2 more hours, or until it reaches an inside temperature of 160°. Put it on a platter, remove the spit, cover the meat loosely, and let it rest at least 15 minutes before carving.

Serves 10

Sage and Onion Stuffing

1 large Spanish onion, peeled   1 teaspoon dry mustard
   Small handful of fresh sage   1 egg
¼ pound stale French bread,   Salt and pepper
   coarsely crumbled (about
   1 cup)

Blanch the onion in boiling water for 5 minutes. Add the sage and cook 30 seconds more. Strain and chop coarsely. Add the bread, mustard, egg, and salt and pepper to taste. Mix well.

Makes enough for an 8-pound pork roast; we quadrupled the amount for the Sucking Pig.

Mince Pies

'I will just see my people aboard,' said Jack. . . . When he reached the cabin, Captain Lambert was calling for 'a glass of brandy, there, and mince pies; but only small ones, d'ye hear me, only small ones.' . . . 'What did he mean by mince pies? . . . Mince pies. Why, of course: it must be Christmas in a day or two.'
—The Fortune of War, *94*

Mince Pies are indelibly associated with Christmas. Indeed, until the mid-seventeenth century, they were known exclusively as "Christmas Pies"—they were usually rectangular, to represent the cradle of Jesus, and the dried fruits and spices were supposed to symbolize the gifts of the Magi. The Christmas Pie of Little Jack Horner was a Mince Pie, though in his case it contained something more than meat and fruit. Sir John Horner was responsible for the delivery of a Christmas Pie to Henry VIII; and the plum he pulled out was the deed to a piece of confiscated church property—one of several hidden beneath the crust.

Under Puritan rule, Christmas Pies were briefly outlawed as emblems of Popery, but they resurfaced shortly afterward in less controversial guise, as Mince or "Shrid" (shred) Pies. Under any name, they represent a very old tradition—the practice of preserving meat by combining it with dried fruits, spices, sugars, and alcohol dates back at least to medieval times, and may even have originated in ancient Rome.

Today, alas, mincemeat has lost something in translation—too often it is neither minced nor meat—but in Aubrey's time it was still faithful to its roots.

2 recipes (1 pound) Short Pastry (p. 271)
½ recipe (½ pound) Puff Paste (p. 270)

1 quart Mincemeat (recipe follows)

Preheat oven to 450°.

On a lightly floured board, with a lightly floured rolling pin, roll out the Short Pastry until it is about ⅛ inch thick. Cut the sheet of pastry into 4 circles big enough to line 4 small pie dishes (the ones we use are 4½ inches in diameter). Line the dishes with the crusts. Fill the pies with Mincemeat.

Reflour the board and rolling pin, and roll out the Puff Paste until it is ⅛ inch thick. Cut 4 circles slightly larger than the pie dishes. Cut a small hole in the center of each, and place them on the pies. Crimp the edges together.

Bake 10 minutes, then turn the oven down to 350° and bake for about 20 minutes.

Makes 4 small pies

Mincemeat

- 3 pounds shin of beef
- 1 pound suet, finely grated
- 1¾ cups dried currants
- ¾ cup raisins
- ¾ cup sultanas
- ½ cup candied orange peel, coarsely chopped
- ½ cup candied citron, coarsely chopped
- 1 pound tart apples, peeled, cored and coarsely chopped (about 3 cups)
- Juice and coarsely chopped zest of 1 lemon
- Juice and coarsely chopped zest of 1 Seville orange
- 2 tablespoons grated ginger
- 2 cups sugar
- 1 teaspoon mace
- 1 teaspoon ground cloves
- 2 teaspoons ground nutmeg
- 1 tablespoon ground cinnamon
- 1 teaspoon salt
- ½ cup cider
- ½ cup brandy
- ½ cup red wine

Put the beef in a pot with water to cover. Bring to a boil, reduce heat, and simmer, covered, 2 hours, or until the meat is tender enough to fall off the bone.

Take the meat out of the pot (you may want to season and save the stock, as we do, for future use). When it is cool enough to handle, remove and discard the bones, fat and gristle. You should have about 1 pound of meat.

Shred or coarsely chop the meat, and mix it thoroughly with all the other ingredients. Put the Mincemeat in a sealed container and set it to ripen in a cool, dark place. It will be ready for use after about 2 weeks, or it can be refrigerated for several months (ours has been aging for about a year now, and it gets a little more interesting every day).

Makes about 3 quarts

Christmas Pudding

'Killick, pray tell my cook to make a special effort today: we shall have three Company's captains to dinner. And you may rouse out a case of champagne in case we meet early. Sling in half a dozen in a wet blanket from the crossjack yard. . . .'

Early they came and late they left, pink and jolly, after a dinner that ended with the Christmas pudding for which Jack's new cook was so justly famous, and measureless wine. A cheerful dinner. . . .

—The Far Side of the World, *121–2*

Christmas Pudding evolved from Plumb Porridge, another medieval concoction in which dried fruit and alcohol originally played a supporting and preservative role, while meat (generally beef shin) took center stage. Between the mid-seventeenth and the late eighteenth centuries, the meat gradually faded out, leaving only a vestigial quantity of suet. But the tradition of long cooking and long storage persisted. Some old recipes recommend up to four days for the first cooking time, though we have never had the patience to try this. No one really knows how long this sort of pudding can be kept, but a plum pudding that has not ripened at least a month or two is hardly worth eating. We make ours a year in advance, as the cooks of Jack's time would have done. And in all our research we have not found a single recorded instance of a well-brandied plum pudding going bad.

(For information on preparing and cooking puddings, see "About Puddings," p. 273.)

1 cup flour
2 cups soft, fresh bread crumbs
½ cup dark brown sugar, firmly
    packed
½ teaspoon salt
1 teaspoon ground cinnamon
½ teaspoon mace
½ teaspoon ground nutmeg
½ teaspoon ground ginger
¼ teaspoon ground cloves
1 cup dried currants
1 cup raisins

1 cup sultanas
  Zest of ½ lemon, coarsely
    chopped
⅓ cup candied orange peel,
    coarsely chopped
⅓ cup candied citron, coarsely
    chopped
¾ cup slivered almonds
¼ pound suet, finely grated
3 eggs, lightly beaten
¾ cup brandy, plus ¼ cup for
    flaming (optional)

In a large bowl, combine the flour, bread crumbs, sugar, salt, and spices. Stir in the fruits and nuts (the flour and bread crumbs will coat the fruits and prevent them from sticking together). Mix in the suet, then add the eggs and ½ cup of the brandy. Work the mixture thoroughly with your hands.

Scrape the batter into a greased 6-cup pudding-basin. Tie a well-floured cloth over the pudding, allowing a little room for expansion. Place the pudding in a pot of boiling water, cover, and steam for 5 hours or longer. You will almost certainly need to add more boiling water as it cooks.

Take the pudding out of the water and let it cool. Remove the cloth and pour in the remaining ¼ cup of brandy. Cover tightly and store in a cool place for 3 weeks or longer.

To prepare for serving, uncover the pudding, tie it up again in a floured cloth, and steam it for at least 2 hours. Remove it from the pot, untie the cloth, and unmold onto a serving dish.

Decorate with sprigs of holly, and serve flaming, as follows: Warm ¼ cup of brandy in a small saucepan, pour it over the pudding, set it alight, and serve it forth accompanied by Hard Sauce (which see, p. 265).

Serves 6 to 12

Kickshaws

Toasted Cheese   Comfits

Breadfruit Biscuit   Breadfruit Toast   Maids of Honour

Shrewsbury Cakes   Ratafia Biscuits

Kickshaws can be almost anything at all, as witness their derivation from the French *quelque chose*, literally "some thing." The word is often used to denote little foreign messes (Jack's contemporary, Horatio Hornblower, once referred to the *Zakouski* at the czar's table as "foreign kickshaws"), but it can refer to any kind of small miscellaneous edible oddments. There are some historic recipes for Kickshaws in old English cookery books, and they are chiefly remarkable for bearing no resemblance whatsoever to each other. We have reprinted a couple of them in Chapter VI; meanwhile we are using the name as a catch-all for our own handful of "some things."

Toasted Cheese

'. . . *Killick, belay there; are you now about the cheese?*'
'*Which it's just coming up, ain't it?*' *said Killick angrily. He . . . muttered something about 'those that worshipped their bellies . . . blowing out their gaffs by day and by night . . . never satisfied.*'   —Desolation Island, *204*

Various wounds . . . had so slowed down their fingers that in places they were obliged to indicate the notes by hooting; and as they felt their way through the difficult sonata time after time they made the night so hideous that Killick's indignation broke out at last and he said to the Captain's cook, 'There they go again, tweedly-deedly, tweedly-deedly, belly-aching the whole bleeding night, and the toasted cheese seizing on to their plates like goddam glue, which I dursen't go in to fetch them; and never an honest tune from beginning to end.'   —The Ionian Mission, *48–9*

*They might have pleased Corelli's ghost, as showing what power his music
still possessed for a later generation: they certainly did not please Preserved
Killick. . . . 'Yowl, yowl, yowl,' he said to his mate on hearing the familiar
sounds. 'They are at it again. I have a mind to put ratsbane in their toasted
cheese.'*   —The Wine-Dark Sea, *19*

*They would have brought it to an unusually handsome close if Killick had
not blundered in, tripping over a little stool, unseen because of his tray, and
saving their supper only by a miracle of juggling.*

*At one time this supper had consisted of toasted cheese held in a remark-
ably elegant piece of Irish silver, a covered outer dish that held six within
it, the whole kept warm over a spirit-stove: the dish was still present,
gleaming with a noble brilliance, but it held only a pap made of pounded
biscuit, a little goat's milk, and even less of rock-hard cheese-rind rasped
over the top and browned with a loggerhead, so that some faint odour of
cheddar could still just be made out.*   —The Wine-Dark Sea, *61*

Two of Preserved Killick's three areas of expertise are represented
here: toasting cheese and polishing silver (for the third, see "Coffee,"
p. 14). In Aubrey's day, Toasted Cheese was synonymous with Welsh
Rarebit (or Rabbit, as the case may be . . . but that's another discus-
sion)—but the Welsh Rarebit of the time was a much simpler affair
than it is now. Under either name it consisted of bread (soft tommy,
if possible, otherwise hard tack or whatever was available), toasted
and placed in a dish, covered with grated or thinly sliced cheese, and
browned under a salamander. Occasionally there might be intima-
tions of today's Welsh Rarebit: soaking the toast in porter; sprinkling
the cheese with mustard.

What kind of cheese? " 'Killick shall toast you the Parmesan
cheese.' " " 'Which that Bristol cove gave some to Purser's steward.
Cheddar. And I got it off of him.' " "A piece of the almost imperish-
able manchego or parmesan. . . ."

The actual toasting can be accomplished by passing a red-hot implement over the cheese (or conversely, today, by passing the cheese
under a red-hot broiler). Almost any red-hot implement will do—and
almost any red-hot implement fits the broad definition of a salamander. Historically, Killick could certainly have had a salamander of
the culinary kind; but if he did, there is no mention of his using one.
Perhaps, cross-grained perverse old bugger that he was, he actually
preferred his loggerhead (which also qualifies as a salamander of sorts;

in fact, there is a passage in *Treason's Harbour* where the gunner "came hurrying aft with his salamander"—which was probably actually a loggerhead).

As the voyages dragged on, both the bread and the cheese became less and less appetizing, until at last the only attractive feature of the preparation was Jack's famous silver cheese-dish. Meg Dods refers to this popular item as a cheese-toaster, and it was an elegant and imposing affair, not unlike today's chafing-dish, composed of a series of small dishes set into a hot-water reservoir, which in turn was kept warm by a spirit lamp.

Bread (soft tommy, hard tack, or whatever you can find)	Cheese (cheddar, manchego, Parmesan, rind raspings, or whatever you can find)

Slice (if applicable) and toast the bread and place it in a heated cheese-toaster. Grate or thinly slice the cheese over the toast.

Heat a salamander (or poker, loggerhead, or whatever you can find) until red-hot. Hold it as close as possible to the cheese, which will eventually melt and become brown (you may have to reheat the salamander once or twice).

Serves 2 amateur musicians

Variation: Soak the toast in porter, or sprinkle dry mustard over the cheese before melting—or both.

Comfits

The bottles came and went: the tension wore away and away—talk flowed free in Spanish, English and a sort of French. There was even laughter and interruption, and when at last the noble pudding gave way to comfits, nuts and port, Jack sent the decanter round, desiring them to fill up to the brim; and raising his glass he said, 'Gentlemen, I give you a toast. I beg you will drink Sophia.'

'Sophia!' cried the Spanish captains, holding up their glasses.

'Sophie,' said Stephen. 'God bless her.' —Post Captain, *496*

Comfits were dried candied fruits or seeds. Caraway comfits were by far the most popular, and they were usually made commercially. It was a laborious and exceedingly time-consuming task: each tiny seed had to be dipped individually into sugar syrup, twelve times or more. We did not have the patience to duplicate this process, but it is possible to approximate the flavor with a little less effort.

2 tablespoons caraway seeds   ⅓ cup sugar

Put the seeds and the sugar in a heavy saucepan and cook over medium heat until the sugar starts to take on a golden color. Remove from heat. Working as quickly as possible, dip a fork into the mixture and shake it by drops onto a greased cookie sheet. Allow to cool and harden completely, then store in a cool, dry place.

Makes approximately 2 ounces

Variation: Substitute 3 tablespoons sliced almonds for the caraway seeds.

Breadfruit Biscuit

'You remember Breadfruit Bligh?'
'I do not.'
'Of course you do, Stephen. Bligh, that was sent to Tahiti in the Bounty before the war, to collect breadfruit-trees for the West Indies.'
                                                                    —Desolation Island, *22*

'Could you do with a cup of coffee and a breadfruit biscuit?'
'I could, too.'
'Killick! Killick, there.'
'Sir?' said Killick, still unnaturally meek, though a shade of the familiar shrewishness could now be detected. Indeed, he had recovered enough assurance to bring them only a meagre plate of the dried breadfruit slices, he being devoted to them himself.   —The Truelove, *209*

It is the oddest thing: so far as we can determine, breadfruit is supposed to be generally available in the continental United States, but when we needed some it was nowhere to be found. We finally found ourselves in the peculiar position of arranging to have this perfectly legal fruit smuggled in.

We had better confess that we do not share Killick's devotion to breadfruit biscuit . . .

1 "fit" (ripe) breadfruit

Peel the breadfruit and cut it in half. Discard the spongy core and cut the fruit into ¼-inch slices. Set the slices on racks in a warm, dry, well-ventilated place for about a week, or until all the moisture has evaporated.

Makes about 2 dozen

Breadfruit Toast

'Try one of these toasted slices of breadfruit: they eat well with coffee. The chief's sister sent me a net-full, dried.'   —The Truelove, *179*

. . . although the breadfruit toast was not unpleasant.

1 "fit" (ripe) breadfruit

Peel the breadfruit and cut it in half. Discard the spongy core and cut the fruit into ¼-inch slices. Toast the slices on both sides until brown. Butter (if possible) and serve with coffee.

Makes about 2 dozen

Maids of Honour

Jack was in tearing high spirits, but his great respect for music kept him in order throughout the quartet. It was during the collation that followed— a pair of fowls, a glazed tongue, sillabub, flummery and maids of honour— that he began to break out.   —Master and Commander, *185*

The captain's cook, Adi . . . understood the whole range of naval cookery from Constantinople to Gibraltar; and although his maids of honour brought Rosia Bay to mind rather than Richmond Hill, they went down wonderfully well.   —The Letter of Marque, *154*

In Jack's day Maids of Honour were also commonly known as cheesecakes; which is curious because they haven't a vestige of cheese about them, nor are they cakes so much as tartlets. But in any case they do go down wonderfully well.

1 recipe (½ pound) Short Pastry (p. 271) (or ½ pound Puff Paste, p. 270)

Filling:
⅔ cup almonds, coarsely ground
2 tablespoons grated lemon zest

2 tablespoons lemon juice
4 drops rose water
1 egg
¼ cup sugar
1 tablespoon flour
2 tablespoons heavy cream
2 tablespoons butter, softened
Pinch of ground nutmeg
Pinch of salt

Preheat oven to 350°.

While the pastry dough chills, put the filling ingredients in a bowl and stir until thoroughly blended.

Lightly grease a medium-sized 12-cup muffin tin. Roll the pastry out on a floured board, with a floured rolling pin, until it is about ⅛ inch thick. With a fluted cookie cutter (or the rim of a glass) cut rounds slightly larger than the tops of the muffin cups. Put one round into each cup, pressing it gently into the bottom. Each shell should be ½–¾ inch deep.

Spoon the filling into the cups—it should come almost to the top of the pastry shell.

Bake 25 minutes.

Makes about 2 dozen

Variations: Before filling each pastry shell, spread about ½ teaspoon of raspberry jam in the bottom. You may also cut narrow strips of pastry and cross two of them over the top of each tart just before baking.

Shrewsbury Cakes

All three were now lashing into the baked rice pudding, he observed, the treacle tart, . . . the Shrewsbury cakes, with every appearance of cheerful appetite. —The Nutmeg of Consolation, *107*

Shrewsbury Cakes come in many different forms. They were quite often made with caraway seeds, and we have occasionally seen a larger, thicker version that included currants. Ours is not the most typical combination of flavorings—but it has been wildly successful.

½ pound (2 sticks) butter
¾ cup sugar
1 egg
2 tablespoons brandy
4 teaspoons freshly ground
   coriander

½ teaspoon mace
3 cups flour
½ teaspoon salt (if you are
   using unsalted butter)

Cream the butter and sugar together until fluffy. Add the egg, brandy, coriander and mace. Mix well. Sift the flour (and the salt, if appropriate) into the butter mixture, and work in thoroughly. Shape the dough into a ball, wrap it in wax paper, and chill until firm (about 1 hour).

Preheat the oven to 350°.

Work with half the dough at a time, keeping the other half cold. Roll it out on a floured board, with a floured rolling pin, until it is ³⁄₁₆–¼ inch thick. Cut into squares or diamonds with a sharp knife, or into shapes with any cookie cutters you fancy. (This dough does not suffer from repeated handling; you may combine the scraps and roll them out again as often as necessary. You will need to work fast and use quite a lot of flour, as the dough is very short and quickly becomes sticky.)

Place the cakes fairly close together (they will not spread) on lightly greased cookie sheets. Bake 9–10 minutes. Let cool slightly on the sheets before transferring them to racks.

Note: Beware of rolling these cakes too thin or baking them too long—they will be crisper but will lose some of their distinctive flavor. Do not let them brown. They should be barely golden around the edges, if that.

Makes 6–8 dozen large or 10–12 dozen small cakes

Ratafia Biscuits

At last, when the cloth had been drawn and the King's health drunk in a glass of port suited to a very young head, they took their coffee and ratafia biscuits . . . in the great cabin.   —The Yellow Admiral, *126*

In the eighteenth century Ratafia Biscuits were closely related to macaroons. Today the subtle distinction between them has become blurred: what was then known as a Ratafia would now be considered a macaroon; whereas what was then called a macaroon does not have a modern parallel. Both were light, fragile biscuits made of almonds, egg whites, and sugar—but Ratafias were flavored with bitter almonds; macaroons were not.

The word itself is apparently Creole, but its roots are probably Latin. According to legend it began as a toast, *rata fiat* ("consider it done"), and in the late seventeenth century it came to mean the liqueur in which the toast was drunk, which by then was generally an apricot- or almond-flavored brandy. Subsequently it was applied to several different confections and liqueurs made from members of the rose family: cherries, peaches, apricots, and especially almonds.

The proportion of bitter almonds to sweet varied greatly from one biscuit recipe to another, and does not appear to have been influenced by the early-nineteenth-century discovery that the former are a source of prussic acid. Today they are available only by prescription, unless you choose to crack open apricot pits and use the kernels thereof (a legitimate and historically accurate, though equally poisonous, substitute). If you are really concerned about cyanide poisoning you can accomplish much the same thing and save yourself a great deal of trouble by using pure almond extract, which is made from bitter almonds with the cyanogens miraculously removed by modern technology. We have done both and survived to tell the tale.

The traditional use of paper for baking Ratafias seems to have evolved from edible "wafers" in the early seventeenth century, through "wafer paper" in the eighteenth, to "cartridge paper" in the nineteenth, to brown paper in the twentieth. (Some cooks in the early nineteenth century, notably Jane Austen's friend Martha Lloyd, dispensed with paper and baked their biscuits on "tin plates flour'd." We tried this, and it produced a terrible mess and a nasty taste of burnt flour.) Ordinary grocery bags, cut to fit a cookie sheet, are an excellent substitute.

3 ounces sweet almonds, blanched and peeled, and 1 ounce bitter almonds or apricot kernels, peeled; *or* 4 ounces sweet almonds, blanched and peeled, and ¾ teaspoon pure almond extract	1½ cups sugar 2 egg whites 8 drops rose water Ice water

Preheat oven to 325°.

Line a cookie sheet with brown paper.

Pound or grind the almonds as fine as possible. Gradually add the sugar, egg whites and rose water (and the almond extract, if you are using it), beating the mixture all the while until it becomes a thick paste.

Using a teaspoon dipped in ice water, drop little mounds of the mixture on the brown paper. They will spread while baking, so place them about 2 inches apart.

Bake 20–22 minutes, or until puffy and delicately browned.

Remove the paper, biscuits and all, from the cookie sheet. Let it cool for a few seconds while you wring out a cloth in cold water. Lay the cloth out flat, and place the sheet of biscuits on top of it. After a few minutes the paper will release its hold, and you can lift the biscuits off to cool on a rack.

Repeat the process (with fresh pieces of brown paper) until you have used all the batter.

Makes 2½ dozen

Made-Dishes and Puddings

Curry   Pilaff

Lacquered Duck Bathed in Rich Sauce   Plum-Cake

Jam Roly-Poly   Boiled Sago Pudding

Cabinet Pudding

> What is technically called a *made-dish* presupposes either a more elaborate mode of cookery than plain *frying, broiling,* or *roasting;* or else some combination of those elementary processes,—as, for example, half-roasting and finishing in the stew-pan, which is a very common way of dressing a *ragoo.* All dishes commonly called French dishes are of the class *made-dishes,* such as *fricassees* and *ragoos, meat braised, larded &c.* and so are *hashes, curries,* and generally all viands that are *re-dressed* or *re-made.*
>
> —Mistress Margaret Dods, *Cook and Housewife's Manual* (1826)

Made-dishes—the more outlandish and convoluted the better—were an opportunity for the cook to display special skills. They almost always included elegant sauces and exotic flavorings, and generally involved reducing the main ingredient to an unrecognizable pulp, or "disguising" or "transmogrifying" it to resemble something else. They also quite often contained such fanciful additions as cocks' combs, ox palates, pigeons' eggs, forcemeat balls, truffles, morels, artichoke bottoms, fried oysters, toasted sippets, and brain-balls—preferably all tossed in together. Made-dishes were often "foreign"—English adulterations of Indian dishes, such as Curries and Pilaffs, or French "fricaceys" and ragouts of small game (Hannah Glasse gives a recipe for a French method of dressing partridges, and disapprovingly calls it "an odd Jumble of Trash").

Curry

Dinner in the Wasp's *low triangular cabin was a very different matter. Since this coming night's activity called for a mind as clear as it could be Stephen had begged for thin cold coffee: Mr Fortescue drank no wine at any time, so the bottle he had provided for his guest stood untouched between the lime-juice and the tall brass pot while the two of them devoured a great mound of curry so Vesuvian that it paled the tropic sun.*

—The Mauritius Command, *128*

Since the *Wasp* belonged to the East India Company, we have mixed our metaphors a bit here—the Curry Powder is based on traditional Indian blends (though it does owe something to Dr. William Kitchiner's influence), but the dish itself is a hybrid, a bastardization, an English variation on an Indian theme.

1 clove garlic, peeled	2 pounds cold cooked lamb or
2 small onions, peeled	mutton, sliced
1 tablespoon Curry Powder	2 cups rich brown stock (or re-
(recipe follows)	constituted Portable Soup,
1 teaspoon salt	p. 240)
1 tablespoon butter (or a little	½ cup heavy cream
more as needed)	Juice of 1 lime
¼ cup plain yogurt	

In a mortar, pound together the garlic, one of the onions, the Curry Powder and the salt.

Slice the second onion. In a large pan, melt the butter and brown the sliced onion. Add the curry mixture and cook over low heat, stirring constantly with a wooden spoon, until well blended and aromatic.

Stir in the yogurt. Add the meat and the stock. Bring slowly to a boil, reduce heat, and simmer gently 15 minutes. Add the cream and continue to cook until heated through. Stir in the lime juice. Serve with rice.

Serves 6

Curry Powder

The Vesuvian quality of any curry blend is a subjective issue, and can vary greatly according to the type of chilies used. Depending on how volcanic you like your curry, you may want to double—or halve—the quantity of chilies given here.

2 tablespoons coriander seed	2 tablespoons ground turmeric
2 tablespoons cumin seed	¾ teaspoon ground cinnamon
1½ teaspoons mustard seed	¾ teaspoon cayenne
1½ teaspoons fenugreek	1½ teaspoons ground ginger
¾ teaspoon ground allspice	¾ teaspoon crumbled dried
1½ teaspoons peppercorns	chilies

In a large frying-pan, dry-roast the coriander, cumin, mustard, fenu-greek, allspice, and black pepper, stirring frequently, until they darken. Allow to cool. Combine with remaining ingredients and grind to a powder.

Makes 9 tablespoons

Pilaff

Martin said '. . . the assault terrified your new cook, sir. We were talking to him about a pilaff for your supper when the howl broke out: he uttered a cry in what may have been Armenian and ran from the room, crouched inhumanly low.'

'A pilaff? What an admirable notion. I dearly love a good pilaff. You will give us the pleasure of your company, Mr Martin?'

—The Letter of Marque, *152–3*

Like Curry, Pilaff (Pilloe, Pellow, Poloe, Pollou, Pilau . . .) had wan-dered far from its origins by the time it became popular in Europe. Jack's Dasni cook, Adi, would not even have recognized Charles Carter's recipe (which called for two pounds of butter and a pound of bacon) as a pilaff. Since it was Adi who made this particular pilaff, we have tried to give it a predominantly Azerbaijani flavor—except perhaps in one respect. We puzzled for quite some time over the question of what kind of rice he might have used. Since the *Surprise* was in the Channel off Shelmerston, it stands to reason that the rice came from England; and the rice of choice in both England and France at the turn of the nineteenth century was—Carolina Gold. Poor Adi.

3 pounds boneless lamb or mutton (neck, shoulder, breast, etc.), cut in 2-inch pieces

3 tablespoons butter

2 quarts stock (see note)

1 large onion, peeled and cut in ¾-inch pieces

2 cloves garlic, peeled

2½ cups long-grain rice

½ teaspoon mace

½ teaspoon ground cloves

Large handful of fresh rosemary

Large handful of fresh savory

Large handful of fresh thyme

2 tablespoons chopped parsley

Salt and pepper

¼ teaspoon saffron threads

½ teaspoon ground turmeric

1 tablespoon caraway seeds

3 lemons

Sprigs of fresh parsley and rosemary for garnish

In a large stewpot, brown the lamb well in 1½ teaspoons butter (you may need to add a little extra butter if the lamb is very lean).

While the meat is browning, bring the stock to a boil. Turn off the fire, leaving the pot, covered, on the burner to keep warm.

Remove the meat and set aside. In the same pot, melt 2 tablespoons butter and sauté the onion and garlic until they start to color. Add the rice and stir briefly to coat it with the butter.

Set aside ½ cup of the warm stock; add the rest to the rice, with the mace, ground cloves, herbs, and salt and pepper to taste. Stir well.

Add the meat and bring to a boil. Reduce the heat, cover, and simmer 45 minutes to 1 hour (or until the meat and rice are tender).

While the pilaff is simmering, set the saffron and turmeric to steep in the reserved stock.

Remove the lamb and keep it warm. You may also want to remove the garlic—if you can find it.

In a small pan over high heat, fry the caraway seeds in 1 teaspoon butter. Stir the seeds into the rice. Reserve 2½ cups of rice; mound the rest in the center of a warmed serving dish.

Return the reserved 2½ cups rice to the pot and stir in the saffron mixture. Cook over a low fire for 1–2 minutes, or until the liquid is absorbed and the rice is a lovely golden yellow.

Arrange the yellow rice in a ring around the mound of rice in the dish. Arrange the lamb over the white rice in the middle.

Squeeze the juice from 1 lemon and sprinkle it over the pilaff. Slice the other 2 lemons about ¼ inch thick and arrange the slices around the lamb. Garnish with a few sprigs of parsley and rosemary.

Note: We make the stock out of the bones and trimmings from the lamb, boiled up with an onion, a carrot, a rib of celery, salt and pepper, and a few pieces of Portable Soup (p. 240)—but any good stock will serve the purpose.

Serves 8

Lacquered Duck Bathed in Rich Sauce

A lovely rounded creature with golden hair treated him with the attentive respect due to his uniform, urging him to try a little more of this lacquered duck....

'A most capital dinner, upon my word. The duck was the best I have ever tasted.'

'I was sorry to see you help yourself to him a fourth time: duck is a melancholy meat. In any case the rich sauce in which it bathed was not at all the thing for a subject of your corpulence. Apoplexy lurks in dishes of that kind. I signalled to you, but you did not attend.' —H.M.S. Surprise, *277–8*

(For information on spit-roasting, see "About Roasting," p. 282.)

1 duck, about 5 pounds

Marinade:
3 star anise
1 teaspoon Szechuan peppercorns
1 teaspoon fennel seed
4 pieces dried tangerine peel
10 cardamom seeds
4 whole cloves
¼ teaspoon Chinese five-spice powder

2 tablespoons dry sherry
2 large knobs fresh ginger
4 scallions
¼ cup soy sauce
1 teaspoon sugar

Lacquer:
½ cup hot water
2 tablespoons red wine vinegar
1 tablespoon white vinegar
1 tablespoon honey

Sauce:

3 tablespoons tomato
   ketchup
1 tablespoon Worcestershire
   sauce
1 tablespoon soy sauce
¼ cup stock

¼ teaspoon Chinese five-spice
   powder
2 tablespoons dry sherry
2 teaspoons sugar
1 teaspoon hoisin sauce
1 teaspoon cornstarch mixed
   with 1 teaspoon water

Rinse the duck and pat dry inside and out. Sew the neck opening together as securely as possible. Combine the marinade ingredients and spoon them into the cavity. Sew the cavity shut.

Tie a heavy piece of string around the legs of the duck, making a loop so that it can be hung.

Combine the lacquer ingredients and brush onto the skin of the duck.

Hang the duck (over a drip pan) in a cool dry place for 6–8 hours or overnight.

Untie the duck and center and secure it on the spit. Set it to roast before a clear fire, basting occasionally with the lacquer mixture, for about 1½ hours, or until the skin is crisp and the juices run clear.

In a small saucepan, combine all the sauce ingredients except the cornstarch paste. Bring to a boil, reduce heat slightly, stir in the cornstarch paste, and cook gently until the sauce is thick and glossy.

Serves 4

Plum-Cake

A moment later Jack came in, followed by his steward bearing a plum-cake the size of a moderate cart-wheel and by two powerful hands with a hamper that clanked glassy as they set it down, while the pitter of hoofs overhead and a melancholy baa told of the presence of at least one devoted sheep.
—The Surgeon's Mate, 200–1

In the latter part of the eighteenth century, richer and more elegant Plum-Cakes were raised with eggs alone, but a common Plum-Cake still called for the more economical yeast and resembled a sweetened and enriched bread. Earlier Plum-Cakes contained many different kinds of dried fruits ("plum" being a generic term for anything of the kind), but by Jack's time raisins or currants were often the only fruit used. This cake is large enough to be the wheel of a *very* small cart; nevertheless we found that it fed, and pleased, an extraordinary number of people. It keeps very well for a number of weeks.

½ cup warm water	½ cup brandy
1 ounce compressed (or	¼ teaspoon rose water
1½ teaspoons active dry)	6 cups flour
yeast	Zest of 1 large lemon, finely
6 eggs	grated
½ pound (2 sticks) butter	5 cups dried currants
1 cup sugar	½ teaspoon salt
½ cup heavy cream	Icing (p. 272)

Put the water in a bowl, crumble the yeast into it, then cover with a damp cloth and set in a warm place until it bubbles (15–30 minutes).

Separate the eggs, reserving 3 whites for the cake and 2 for the icing.

Cream the butter and sugar together, add the egg yolks, and stir well.

Warm the cream and stir it into the yeast mixture with the brandy and rose water. Add the resulting liquid to the butter mixture.

Beat 3 of the egg whites to stiff peaks and fold into the butter mixture.

In a separate bowl, mix the flour, lemon zest and salt. Stir in the currants, breaking them apart (the flour will coat them and keep them from clumping together). Combine gently but thoroughly with the butter mixture.

Cover the bowl with a damp cloth and set to rise in a warm place for 2 hours.

Preheat oven to 375°.

Scrape the batter into a large, well-buttered springform pan. Bake 45 minutes. Turn the oven down to 325° and bake 15 minutes, or until a toothpick inserted in the center comes out clean.

Let the cake cool slightly, remove it from the pan, and set it on a rack until it has cooled completely.

Preheat oven to 200°.

Set the cake on a heatproof serving plate. Spread it with Icing and set in the oven to harden, about 10 minutes.

Decorate to your taste with cochineal-tinted Icing.

Serves 20

Jam Roly-Poly

'You may say what you please,' said Jack, 'but I have eaten roly-poly within the Arctic Circle, damned nearly within the Antarctic, and now under the equator, and I am of opinion that it has not its equal.'
'Except, perhaps, for spotted dog.'
'Ah, you have a point there, Stephen.' —The Thirteen-Gun Salute, *269*

The traditional jams for Roly-Poly are raspberry, strawberry, or apricot. It is a difficult choice, but we must give the preference to raspberry, by a narrow margin.

(For information on preparing and cooking puddings, see "About Puddings," p. 273.)

½ pound suet, finely grated	½ teaspoon salt
4 cups flour	Ice water
¼ cup sugar	12 ounces jam

Mix the suet, flour, sugar, and salt in a large bowl. Work in 1–2 tablespoons ice water. Continue gradually adding ice water until you have a stiff paste (it will probably take about a cup of water, but this will vary depending on temperature, humidity, the dryness of your flour, etc.). Work it with your hands until it forms a ball. Turn it out onto a well-floured board. Cover with a damp cloth and let rest for 5 minutes.

Knead the dough until it is shiny and elastic (6–8 minutes), cover again, let rest another 5 minutes, then knead again for 1–2 minutes. Roll out the dough (reflouring the board and the rolling pin as needed) into a rectangle about ¼ inch thick.

Spread the jam evenly over the dough, leaving a jamless border about 1 inch wide to allow for oozing as the pudding is rolled. Moisten three of the edges with water. Starting at the fourth edge, roll up the pudding, sealing the edges as you go. Seal the final edge to the pudding by pinching the dough together with your fingers to form a seam.

Wrap the pudding tightly in a well-floured cloth. Tie securely at both ends and in the middle. Immerse the pudding in a pot of rapidly boiling water and cook for 2½ hours, replenishing the water as necessary.

To serve: Untie and unroll the cloth. Turn the pudding out, seam-side down, onto a board or platter. Serve hot, accompanied by Custard Sauce (p. 264).

Serves 12–16

Variation: Treacle Roly-Poly: Substitute the filling from Treacle-Dowdy (p. 84) for the jam.

Boiled Sago Pudding

'They have traded six nine-pounders . . . for food, mostly sago. How sick of sago they will become, long before the Salibabu Passage, ha, ha, ha!'
'Do you really believe that an armed and desperate ship will confine itself to sago, Wan Da?'
'Not if it can possibly meet a weaker ship in some far corner of the sea.'
—The Nutmeg of Consolation, *61*

They were allowed pudding, but only apologetical fancies such as sago, summer's pudding made with what Peru could afford, and mere rice, rather than those true puddings based on suet.   —The Wine-Dark Sea, *196*

The sago used for pudding is the pith of the sago palm, and in its processed form it is very much like tapioca. The pudding, too, is very much like tapioca, and we cannot pretend to admire it. We are inclined to agree with Stephen's remark in *The Nutmeg of Consolation:* "the boiled sago God preserve them."

(For information on preparing and cooking puddings, see "About Puddings," p. 273.)

½ cup sago	Pinch of nutmeg
3½ cups milk	¼ cup sugar
½ cup heavy cream	3 eggs, lightly beaten
1 stick cinnamon	
Zest of ½ lemon, in large strips	

Put everything except the eggs in a heavy saucepan, bring to a boil, reduce heat, and simmer, stirring frequently, until the mixture thickens (about 15 minutes). Let cool about 30 minutes. Remove and discard the lemon zest and cinnamon, and stir in the eggs.

Pour the mixture into a buttered 6-cup pudding-basin. Tie a well-floured cloth over the pudding, place the basin in a pot of rapidly boiling water, cover, and steam for 1½ hours. Remove the pudding from the boiling water. Untie and remove the cloth.

To serve hot, spoon directly from the basin. To serve cold, refrigerate until set (at least 3 hours, and even then do not expect it to be very firm), and unmold onto a serving dish.

Serve with Sherry Sauce (p. 266) or stewed fruit.

Serves 8–10

Cabinet Pudding

A week later the Governor of the Cape also honoured the Commodore with a feast. It consisted of game—blauwbok, springbok, steinbok, klipspringer, hartebeest, wildebeest, the black and the blue—no lobster at all, and it took even longer to eat; but this was as far as the Governor's originality could take him; once more the meal ended with cabinet pudding, and once more the guests drank their port wishing that Jack might thump them again and again. —The Mauritius Command, *163*

We had hoped to reproduce this feast in its entirety; but alas, we were unable to procure blauwbok or indeed any kind of -bok or -beest. (The one item we could get easily, lobster, is of course the only one *not* on the menu.) The Cabinet Pudding, however, was a feast in itself.

(For information on preparing and cooking puddings, see "About Puddings," p. 273.)

½ pound (about 1 dozen) Savoy Biscuits (p. 271)	4 eggs
	1 pint heavy cream
4 ounces dried pitted cherries	2 tablespoons sugar
1 tablespoon grated lemon zest	

Split the biscuits lengthwise, cutting along the edges to make two flat halves.

Generously butter a 6-cup pudding-basin (we really mean *generously:* you should have a visible layer of butter spread smoothly over the inside of the basin). Arrange some of the dried cherries in attractive patterns in the bottom and up the sides of the basin, pressing them gently into the butter to hold them in place.

Sprinkle a small amount of lemon zest over the cherries in the bottom of the basin. Place a layer of biscuit halves in the basin. Distribute a handful of cherries over the biscuit.

Continue to build the pudding in alternating layers until the cherries, lemon zest and biscuit halves are used up (ending with a layer of biscuit).

In a separate bowl, beat the eggs, add the cream and sugar, and mix well. Pour the mixture into the pudding-basin. Cover with a plate and let stand 1 hour, to let the custard saturate the biscuits.

Remove the plate, tie a well-floured cloth over the pudding, place the basin in a pot of rapidly boiling water, cover, and steam for 1 hour. Remove the pudding from the boiling water. Untie and remove the cloth and let the pudding rest for 30 minutes or longer.

To serve: Run a thin sharp knife around the sides of the pudding to release it from the basin, and unmold onto a serving dish. Serve hot or cool, accompanied by Lemon Sauce (p. 265).

Note: While Savoy Biscuit is the cake of choice for this pudding because of its texture and its lemon flavor, you can reasonably substitute sponge cake, ladyfingers, or slices of what the cooks of Aubrey's time called a "French Role": brioche.

Serves 8–10

Heart of Oak

Come, cheer up, my lads, 'Tis to glo ry we steer, to add some-thing more to this
won- der- ful year; To hon- our we call you, as free men, not slaves, for
who are so free as the sons of the waves? Heart of
oak are our ships, jol- ly tars are our men: We al- ways are rea- dy,
Stea- dy, boys, stea- dy, We'll fight and we'll con- quer a- gain and a- gain.

We ne'er see our foes but we wish them to stay;
They never see us but they wish us away:
If they run, why, we follow, and run them ashore,
For, if they won't fight us, what can we do more?
       Heart of oak, &c.

We'll still make them fear, and we'll still make them flee,
And drub'em on shore, as we've drubb'd'em at sea:
Then cheer up, my lads, with one heart let us sing.
Our soldiers, our sailors, our statesmen, our king.
       Heart of oak, &c.

They swear they'll invade us, these terrible foes;
They frighten our women, our children and beaux;
But, should their flat bottoms in darkness get o'er,
Still Britons they'll find to receive them on shore.
       Heart of oak, &c.

We'll still make'em run, and we'll still make'em sweat,
In spite of the devil, and Brussels Gazette:
Then cheer up, my lads, with one heart let us sing.
Our soldiers, our sailors, our statesmen and king.
       Heart of oak, &c.

CHAPTER TWO

The Wardroom &
the Gunroom

'I dine with the gunroom on Sunday. It is the custom.'
'But surely, Captain, surely no previous engagement can stand in the way—His Majesty's direct representative!'
'Naval custom is holy at sea, Mr Atkins,' said Jack, turning away.
                                                      —H.M.S. Surprise, *104*

The Surprise *had not run off a thousand miles before the unvarying routine of the ship's day, from the piping up of the hammocks to the drumbeat of 'Heart of Oak' for the gunroom dinner, . . . obliterated both the beginning of the voyage and its end.*   —H.M.S. Surprise, *163–4*

Stephen walked into the wardroom, a fine long room with a fine long table down the middle, lit by a great stern-window right across its breadth, a room which, despite the lieutenants' cabins on either side, offered plenty of space for a dozen officers, each with a servant behind his chair, and as many guests as they chose to invite.
                                              —The Ionian Mission, *33–4*

The dinner ran its course, the wine did its cheerful work, and by the time the port was on the table the wardroom was filled with the comfortable noise of a party going well, laughter and a great deal of talk; the young officers had found their tongues—a decent loquacity—and riddles were

*propounded; Mowett obliged the company with a piece about dealing
with light airs abaft the beam, beginning:*

    With whining postures, now the wanton sails

    Spread all their charms to snare th'inconstant gales.

    The swelling stud-sails now their wings extend,

    The staysails sidelong to the breeze ascend.

—The Ionian Mission, *85*

Depending on the ship, Jack's officers returned his hospitality in either the wardroom or the gunroom. In a larger ship like the *Worcester,* the senior officers messed, and entertained their captain, in the wardroom; while the sub-lieutenants and midshipmen were relegated to the gunroom, on the lower gundeck. The *Surprise,* however, "a trim, beautiful little eight-and-twenty," was too small to have a wardroom, so the gunroom became the senior officers' mess. Except that the quarters were somewhat more cramped, it was a distinction without a difference where the food and the entertainment were concerned.

Turtle Soup

*Jack sat at Blaine's right hand in a pleasant state of mind and a lively anticipation of the turtle soup that his practised nose had long since detected.
The Bishop said grace; the promise became reality, green calipash and
amber calipee swimming in their juice; and after some moments Jack said
to Blaine, 'These classical fellows may prate about ambrosia till they go
black in the face, but they did not know what they were talking about. They
never ate turtle soup.'*   —The Letter of Marque, *214*

Turtle Soup was comparatively rare and exotic even in the eighteenth century—it was the province of the rich and well-staffed, and conferred great prestige on both those who served it and those who partook of it. Among those who couldn't find or afford real turtle, Mock Turtle Soup, an equally convoluted preparation made out of a calf's head and a large amount of Madeira, became very popular.

Even had we been able to find one, the preparation of a four-hundred-pound turtle was more than we felt we could undertake. If you read Hannah Glasse's recipe for Turtle Soup, we do not think you will blame us for failing to make the attempt.

To dress a Turtle the West Indian Way

Take the Turtle out of the Water the Night before you intend to dress it, and lay it on its Back, in the Morning cut its Throat or the Head off, and let it bleed well; then cut off the Fins, scald, scale and trim them with the Head, then raise the Callepy (which is the Belly or Under-shell) clean off, leaving to it as much Meat as you conveniently can; then take from the Back-shell all the Meat and Intrails, except the Monsieur, which is the Fat, and looks green, that must be baked to and with the Shell, wash all clean with Salt and Water, and cut it into Pieces of a moderate Size, taking from it the Bones, and put them with the Fins and Head in a Soop-pot, with a Gallon of Water, some Salt, and two blades of Mace. When it boils skim it clean, then put in a bunch of Thyme, Parsley, Savoury and young Onions, and your Veal Part, except about one Pound and a half, which must be made Forcemeat of as for Scotch Collops, adding a little Cayan Pepper; when the Veal has boiled in the Soop about an Hour, take it out and cut it in Pieces and put to the other Part. The Guts (which is reckoned the best Part) must be split open, scraped and made clean, and cut in Pieces about two Inches long. The Paunch or Maw must be scaled and skinned, and cut as the other Parts, the Size you think proper; then put them with the Guts and other Parts, except the Liver, with half a Pound of good fresh Butter, a few Shalots, a Bunch of Thyme, Parsley, and a little Savoury, seasoned with Salt, white Pepper, Mace, three or four Cloves beaten, a little Cayan Pepper, and take care not to put too much; then let it stew about half an Hour over a good Charcoal Fire, and put in a Pint and a Half of Madeira Wine and as much of the Broth as will cover it, and let it stew till tender. It will take four or five Hours doing. When almost enough, skim it, and thicken it with Flour, mixt with some Veal Broth, about the thickness of a Fricasey. Let your Force-meat Balls be fried about the Size of a Walnut, and be stewed about half an Hour with the Rest; if any Eggs, let them be boiled and cleaned as you do Knots of Pullets Eggs; and if none, get twelve or fourteen Yolks of hard Eggs: then put the Stew (which is the Callepash) into the Back-shell, with the

Eggs all over, and put it into the Oven to brown, or do it with a Salamander.

The Callepy must be slashed in several Places, and moderately seasoned, with Pieces of Butter, mixt with chopped Thyme, Parsley and young Onions, with Salt, white Pepper and Mace beaten, and a little Cayan Pepper; put a Piece on each Slash, and then some over, and a dust of Flour; then bake it in a Tin of Iron Dripping-pan, in a brisk Oven.

The Backshell (which is called the Callepash) must be seasoned as the Callepy, and baked in a Dripping-pan, set upright, with four Brickbats, or any Thing else. An Hour and a half will bake it, which must be done before the Stew is put in.

The Fins, when boiled very tender, to be taken out of the Soop, and put into a Stew-pan, with some good Veal Gravy, not high-coloured, a little Madeira Wine, seasoned and thickened as the Callepash, and served in a Dish by itself.

The Lights, Heart and Liver, may be done the same Way, only a little higher seasoned; or the Lights and Heart may be stewed with the Callepash, and taken out before you put it in the Shell, with a little of the Sauce, adding a little more Seasoning and dish it by itself.

The Veal Part may be made Friandos, or Scotch Collops of. The Liver should never be stewed with the Callepash, but always drest by itself, after any manner you like; except you separate the Lights and Heart from the Callepash, and then always serve them together in one Dish. Take care to strain the Soop, and serve it in a Turreen, or clean china Bewel.

Dishes.
A Callepy,
Lights, &c.—Soop—Fins
Callepash

N. B. In the West Indies they generally souse the Fins, and eat them cold, omit the Liver, and only send to the Table the Callepy, and Soop. This is for a Turtle about sixty Pounds Weight.

—Hannah Glasse, *The Art of Cookery made Plain and Easy* (1747)

Goose and Truffle Pie

'Here you are, Doctor,' cried Pullings, shaking his hand. 'On time to the second. . . . Come, . . . I have a surprise for you, and I long to show it. I fairly gripe to show you my surprise.' . . .

Pullings hurried them away to table, took his place at the head, dashed through his soup—the usual wardroom soup, Stephen noticed, quite useful for poultices . . .—and then called out to the steward, 'Jakes, is it done?'

'Done, sir, done to a turn,' came the distant answer, and a moment later the steward raced in from the galley with a golden pie.

Pullings thrust in his knife, thrust in his spoon and his anxiety gave way to triumph. 'There, Doctor,' he said, passing Stephen his plate. 'There's my surprise—there's your real welcome aboard!'

'Bless me,' cried Stephen, staring at his goose and truffle pie—more truffle than goose—'Mr Pullings, Joy, I am amazed, amazed and delighted.'

'I hoped you might be,' said Pullings, and he explained to the others that long ago, when first made lieutenant, he had seen that the Doctor loved trubs, so he had gone out into the forest, the New Forest, where he lived by land, and had dug him a basket, by way of welcome aboard: and Mowett had composed a song.

'Welcome aboard, welcome aboard,' sang Mr Mowett
'Sober as Adam or drunk as a lord
Eat like Lucullus and drink like a king,
Doze in your hammock while sirens do sing
Welcome, dear Doctor, oh welcome aboard
Welcome aboard,
Welcome aboard.'

—The Ionian Mission, *34–5*

This pie is loosely based on Hannah Glasse's recipe for "A Goose-Pye," and if it seems extravagant we can only assure you that it is positively meagre in comparison with her Yorkshire Christmas-Pye, built on similar principles, which calls for "a Turkey, a Goose, a Fowl, a Partridge, and a Pigeon," not to mention "a Hare . . . Woodcock, more Game, and what Sort of wild Fowl you can get . . . at least four Pounds of Butter" and "a Bushel of Flour."

This kind of concentric pie construction (shades of Winston Churchill's "riddle wrapped in a mystery inside an enigma") was not at all uncommon in Jack's day; and according to Hannah Glasse such pies were "often sent to London in a Box as Presents."

Since we cannot boast Pullings's resources, our relatively modest version is admittedly more goose than truffle rather than the other way round. If you are blessed with access to an abundance of "trubs," by all means vary the proportions accordingly.

(For information about preparing raised pies, see "About Raised Pies," p. 279.)

1½ recipes (6¾ pounds) Hot Water Paste (p. 269)	¼ pound stale French bread, coarsely crumbled (about 1½ cups)
1 goose, about 10 pounds	
1 chicken, about 3½ pounds	¼ pound suet, finely grated
1 large onion, peeled	2 tablespoons chopped fresh parsley
1 carrot, peeled and cut in half	
1 rib celery with leaves	Large handful of fresh sage, coarsely chopped
1 teaspoon peppercorns	
Salt and pepper	2 eggs
6 ounces truffles (more if you can afford them)	1 pound bacon
	1 tablespoon butter
½ pound ham, coarsely chopped	2 tablespoons brandy

Put one-quarter of the Hot Water Paste in a bowl, cover with a damp cloth, and set aside in a warm place.

Form the remaining dough into a ball and place on a large well-greased pan. Working quickly while the dough is warm, begin to raise an oblong coffin, continuing in stages until it is about 10 inches wide by 13 inches long by 3½ inches high (these measurements are approximate; the coffin should be big enough to hold your goose). Chill the coffin for at least an hour, or until it is firmly set.

Bone the goose and the chicken. Place the bones and the giblets (re-serve the liver for your own nefarious delectation) in a pot with the onion, carrot, celery, peppercorns, salt to taste, and water to cover. Bring to a boil, reduce heat, and simmer, covered, 1 hour.

Strain the stock, discarding the bones but reserving the giblets, and return it to the pot. Bring it to a simmer over low heat. Put in the goose, cover, and stew gently for about 20 minutes (this will firm up the flesh and melt most of the fat).

Peel or scrape the black skin off the truffles. Chop the peelings. Cut the peeled truffles into slices about ⅛ inch thick.

Make a forcemeat by combining the truffle peelings, ham, bread, suet, parsley, 1 teaspoon of the sage, 1 egg, and salt and pepper to taste.

Remove the goose from the pot and let it rest until it is cool enough to handle. Skim the fat from the stock. Reduce the stock by letting it boil gently, uncovered, while you assemble the pie.

Line the coffin with bacon, laying out the strips so that they radiate from the center and the outer ends are draped over the sides. Sprin-kle with pepper.

Lay the goose, skin side down, on a flat surface. Line with truffle slices and sage, reserving some of each for final assembly (we put truffle slices wherever we can find room for them, including the wings and legs of the birds). Place the chicken, skin side down, on the goose. Spoon the forcemeat onto the chicken (you will probably have more forcemeat than will fit in the chicken), and fold the chicken into a tight package enclosing the forcemeat. Fold the goose into a tight package enclosing the chicken. Using stout cotton string, tie the goose as necessary to keep it from unrolling.

Place the goose, seam side down, in the coffin. Scatter the remaining forcemeat, truffle slices, and sage wherever you can. Bring up the ends of the bacon slices to cover the goose.

Preheat oven to 450°.

In a small bowl, beat the remaining egg with 1 teaspoon water.

On a floured board, roll out the remaining pastry until it is about 3/16 inch thick. Cut it slightly larger than the dimensions of the coffin. Place the top crust over the pie. Moisten the edges of the two crusts with the egg wash and seal them tightly together by crimping with your fingers.

Cut one or two ½-inch holes in the top crust.

Cut decorative shapes (leaves, anchors, knots) from the pastry scraps and arrange them on the top crust, cementing them in place with the egg wash. Brush a thin layer of the remaining egg wash over the top of the pie.

Remove the reduced stock from the fire. Take 1 cup of the hot stock, add the butter and the brandy, and stir until the butter is melted.

Using a small funnel, carefully pour as much stock as you can through the holes in the crust. Place the pie in the oven *immediately* (if you wait, the hot stock will begin to melt the coffin).

Bake 15 minutes at 450°, turn the oven down to 300°, and bake 2½ hours. Let rest at least an hour (or refrigerate 30 minutes) before serving.

Note: If possible, remove the string from each slice before serving.

Serves 10–12

Haggis

The wardroom's dinner to the Captain was indeed heavy going at the start. . . . Perhaps haggis was not quite the dish for the occasion.
　　　　　　　　　　　　　　　　　　　—Desolation Island, *143*

With all due respect to its noble history, it seems to us entirely likely that Haggis was not the dish for the occasion. We have discussed our experience with others who have made or eaten it, and a pattern has begun to emerge. Those who enjoy eating it have never had a hand in its preparation; those who have cooked it are unwilling if not unable to consume it.

The making of Haggis requires a strong stomach—and a great deal of courage.

(Speaking of courage, the pluck or "gather" of an animal is defined as the heart, liver, and lungs, so called—speculates one source quoted in the *Oxford English Dictionary*—because they are the three organs that can be plucked out simultaneously with one hand. But the word also means "the inward part, or essence"—and "the heart as the seat of courage; courage, boldness, spirit; determination not to yield but to keep up the fight in the face of danger or difficulty." So "pluck" and "guts" follow parallel courses and are synonymous, both literally and figuratively.)

Paunch and pluck of a sheep
1 cup steel-cut oats
½ pound suet (mutton if possible), finely grated
2 medium onions, peeled and finely chopped
2 teaspoons salt

Juice of ½ lemon
Freshly ground pepper
Cayenne
½ cup rich brown stock (or reconstituted Portable Soup, p. 240)
Whiskey

Soak the paunch overnight in salted water.

Preheat the oven to 300°.

Rinse and trim the guts and place them in a large nonreactive pot with water to cover. The lights (lungs) should be at the top of the pile with the windpipe hanging over the edge of the pot. Place a bowl beneath the windpipe to catch the horrid impurities that will drip forth. Cover loosely, bring to a boil, and simmer for 1½ hours.

Put the oats in a shallow pan and toast them in the oven for 30 minutes.

Scrape the paunch inside and out and rinse it thoroughly in cold water.

When the pluck has finished cooking and is cool enough to handle, cut away the windpipe and any black or gristly bits. Mince it all finely (some cooks use only half the liver; frankly, it doesn't make much difference) and combine with the oats, suet, onions, salt, lemon juice, a large amount of pepper, and a considerable dash of cayenne. Stir in the stock.

Pour the mixture into the paunch, filling it a little over half full. Sew up the bag securely with stout thread. Though it isn't traditional, we strongly suggest tying the haggis up in a pudding cloth wrung out in hot water.

Place in a large nonreactive pot with boiling water to cover. Cook for 3 hours, pricking occasionally to keep it from bursting, and replenishing the water as necessary.

Remove from the pot, untie the cloth (if used), and set the haggis on a serving dish. Cut a cross in the top, peel back the bag, and sprinkle copiously with whiskey.

Serves 8

Bashed Neeps (Neeps Hackit with Balmagowry)

'Cucumbers, aye,' said Graham. . . . 'Just cast a wee glippet on this listie. . . .'

'Sure, you will like your dinner once you are well set to it,' said Stephen, looking at the bill of fare. 'What are bashed neeps?'

'Neeps hackit with balmagowry.'   —Treason's Harbour, 74

Bashed Neeps (sometimes called Neep Purry, or purée) are the classic accompaniment for Haggis (p. 68), but they also go beautifully with boiled Leg of Mutton (p. 191)—in fact, they benefit from being boiled in the same pot. We cannot be sure that the ginger is strictly traditional (it does not appear in most of our Scottish sources, though we have run across it in some Elizabethan recipes), but it is a nice touch, and is strongly recommended by Meg Dods, who avers that it "corrects the flatulent properties of this esculent."

2 large yellow turnips, about 1½ pounds each, peeled and quartered	½ cup Balmagowry (recipe follows)
2 tablespoons butter	Salt and pepper
½ teaspoon ground ginger (optional)	

Boil the turnips in salted water for 1½ to 2 hours. Drain and mash with the butter, ginger, Balmagowry, and salt and pepper to taste.

Serves 6

Balmagowry

We have found no reliable evidence as to the derivation of this word for slightly sour cream. The most likely suggestion we have run across is that, like Blairgowrie and the Carse o' Gowries apple, it takes its name from the Gowrie region of Scotland, just north of the Tay. "Balm o' Gowrie"—it tastes plausible to us.

⅔ cup heavy cream   ⅓ cup buttermilk

Put the cream in a warm place, uncovered, for 24 hours, or until it thickens and sours slightly. Skim off the butterfat that has risen to the surface.

Set the buttermilk to drain in a jelly bag or a cloth-lined strainer for 2 hours. Discard the whey.

Combine the soured cream with the drained buttermilk.

Makes about 1 cup

Steak and Kidney Pudding

'What shall you eat?'

'Steak and kidney pudding, without the shadow of a doubt: I slaver at the very words. . . .'

They moved on to the already well-filled supper-room, and for some time they ate seriously, with few more words than 'How is . . . your pudding?' 'A fine honest piece of work,' said Stephen, taking a little wishbone from his mouth. . . . And this, for example, is the true skylark, Alauda arvensis, not one of the miserable sparrows you find in certain establishments.'   —The Yellow Admiral, *171*

Of the three Steak and Kidney Puddings in the Aubrey novels, this was the first that explicitly demanded larks. We had been dreading such a moment, for larks, alas, are unobtainable in this country. So our pudding, though delicious and quite genuine, is entirely larkless.

(For information on preparing and cooking puddings, see "About Puddings," p. 273.)

½ pound suet, finely grated
4 cups flour
1 teaspoon salt
½ teaspoon pepper
  Ice water
  Flour for rolling and dredging
1 veal kidney (about ½ pound)
1½ pounds beef, not too lean, preferably shoulder or chuck

¼ pound mushrooms, quartered
1 large onion, peeled and cut into ½-inch pieces
2 tablespoons finely chopped fresh parsley
2 tablespoons Mushroom Ketchup (optional—p. 269)
  Salt and pepper
  Boiling water

Mix the suet, flour, teaspoon salt, and ½ teaspoon pepper in a large bowl. Work in 1–2 tablespoons ice water. Continue gradually adding ice water until you have a stiff paste (it will probably take about a cup of water, but this will vary depending on temperature, humidity, the dryness of your flour, etc.). Work it with your hands until it forms a ball. Turn it out onto a well-floured board. Cover with a damp cloth and let rest for 5 minutes.

Knead the dough until shiny and elastic (6–8 minutes), cover again, let rest another 5 minutes, then knead again for 1–2 minutes. Cut off one-quarter of the dough and set it aside for the top crust. Roll out the remaining dough (reflouring the board and the rolling pin as needed) until it is about ¼ inch thick. Line a well-greased 6-cup pudding-basin with the sheet of pastry, pleating as necessary to make it fit snugly. (You may have to cut a couple of these wedge-shaped pleats out of the pastry. To join the cut edges, moisten them thoroughly with cold water and press them together firmly with your fingers.)

Peel the kidney, if necessary. Trim the fat from the kidney and the beef, cut them into ¾-inch dice, and dredge them in flour. Mix with the mushrooms, onions, parsley, Mushroom Ketchup, and salt and pepper to taste.

Put a large pot of water on to boil (you will need about a cup for the gravy—the rest will be used to steam the pudding).

Roll out the reserved dough into a circle about ¼ inch thick.

Fill the pastry-lined basin with the meat mixture. Trim the excess pastry around the edge of the basin. Pour in boiling water almost to the top of the basin (about 1 cup, depending on how tightly the filling is packed).

Place the top crust over the pudding and trim it to fit. Moisten the edges with cold water, and pinch with your fingers to seal them tightly together.

Tie a well-floured cloth over the pudding, place the basin in a pot of rapidly boiling water, cover, and steam for three hours. You will probably need to add more boiling water as it cooks.

To serve: Take the pudding out of the pot and place it, basin and all, on a serving dish. Untie and remove the cloth. Wipe the outside of the basin and wrap a large napkin around it. With a sharp knife, cut a small hole in the center of the top crust. Serve it forth steaming.

Serves 4–6

PIG'S PETTITOES, TWO WAYS

The midshipmen's berth was rounding out their pease-pudding and pig's trotters with toasted bloaters. . . .   —The Ionian Mission, *265*

The boar emerged, standing motionless, its square snout twitching from side to side; with a detached, clinical look on his face Stephen dropped it dead and climbed down from the tree.

* . . . Stepping back he surveyed the boar with real satisfaction: . . . there were few dishes Jack Aubrey preferred to soused pig's face, while for his own part he was fond of a pair of cold crubeens.*

    —The Nutmeg of Consolation, *13–14*

For artistic and logistical reasons we have found it expedient to promote the midshipmen's Trotters (typically eaten pickled) to the gunroom for the moment, so that we could present them side by side with their cousins, the Crubeens of Stephen's imagination.

Trotters, of course, are pig's feet—specifically, for culinary purposes, the meaty long-cut hind feet.

Pig's Trotters

4 pig's trotters, cleaned, split
   and washed
4 large bay leaves
4 slices bacon
1½ cups water
1½ cups white wine vinegar
1½ cups white wine
½ teaspoon peppercorns
½ teaspoon whole coriander
½ teaspoon salt

¼ teaspoon mace
8 whole cloves
4 small onions, peeled
1 inch-long knob fresh ginger,
   slightly crushed
   Small handful of fresh sage
1 tablespoon chopped fresh
   savory
1 teaspoon chopped fresh
   parsley

Fold one slice of bacon over each bay leaf, and place it between the two halves of each trotter. Tie the halves together tightly with two or three pieces of stout string.

Place the feet in a heavy pot with the remaining ingredients. Cover and bring to a boil, then reduce heat and simmer for 2 hours. (You may have to add another cup of water.)

Remove from the fire and put the feet and onions in an earthen pot. Strain the broth and skim off the fat. Pour the broth over the feet and refrigerate, covered, until needed.

Serves 4

A Pair of Cold Crubeens

2 pig's trotters, cleaned and
   split
1 large carrot, peeled and cut
   in 1-inch pieces
1 medium onion, peeled and
   scored with a deep "X" at
   the root end
2 bay leaves

   Small handful of fresh parsley
   Small handful of fresh
   thyme
   Small handful of fresh savory
1 teaspoon salt
½ teaspoon peppercorns

Rinse the trotters and place them in a large pot with the carrot, onion, bay leaves, parsley, thyme, savory, salt, pepper, and water to cover. Bring to a boil, covered, and cook over medium heat for 3 hours. Remove the bay leaves.

Crubeens can be served hot or cold, either with the broth from the pot (when cold, the broth sets to a thick jelly) or with a sauce like the one that follows.

Serves 1

Michael Kelly's Sauce

When Stephen was hunting his boar and dreaming of crubeens, this sauce probably had not yet been invented; since its creator, born in 1790, would have been barely in his twenties. For that matter, it is not likely that many of the ingredients would have been available to him on a desert island in the South China Sea. Nevertheless, the sauce has since become a traditional accompaniment for the dish, and the combination is good enough to warrant a slight suspension of disbelief.

½ teaspoon dry mustard	1 tablespoon cider vinegar
½ teaspoon brown sugar	¼ cup melted butter
½ teaspoon pepper	
1 small clove garlic, peeled and finely chopped	

Combine the mustard, sugar, pepper, garlic and vinegar, and blend thoroughly. Gradually stir the mixture into the butter. Serve warm.

Makes enough for 1 pair of Crubeens

Roast Buffalo

'Yorke gave us a capital dinner, with roast buffalo, a pair of ducks, a ragoo, and a roly-poly pudding; and he and Stephen got along famously, as I hoped they should.   —The Fortune of War, 57

'Come, this is altogether snugger and more homely,' said Jack, smiling at the friendly faces, eight of them tight-packed round the gunroom table....

The fare was homely too, the main dish being the roast beef of Old Cal-
abria, a great piece of one of those Italian buffaloes known as grey friars in
the Navy and shipped to Malta when they were quite past work; and this
was followed by figgy-dowdy.

  'Now that is what I call a really good basis for literature,' said Jack.

—The Ionian Mission, *268–9*

Which you can't get real Italian buffalo (or even Pacific water buffalo, which is what Yorke would have served) in the United States, so we took a slight liberty and substituted American bison—and very good it was.

(For information on spit-roasting, see "About Roasting," p. 282.)

1 boneless buffalo roast, about 4 pounds, at room temperature	Suet for barding (you will need a large block, about ½ pound)
1 teaspoon pepper	Flour for dredging

Rub the roast with pepper.

If the suet has been frozen, make sure it is fully defrosted; otherwise it will tend to crumble as you cut it. Slice it into thin sheets (about ¼ inch thick) and tie them securely around the roast with several pieces of stout string.

Center the meat on the spit and set it to roast before a clear fire. After it has been cooking about 1½ hours, carefully cut the strings and remove the barding. Lightly sprinkle the meat on all sides with flour, baste it with some of the pan drippings, and roast it close to the fire for another 30 minutes. Like beef, buffalo will be rare when it reaches an inside temperature of 135°, well done at 165°.

Remove the meat from the spit, place it on a platter, cover it loosely, and let it rest at least 15 minutes before carving. You may want to serve it with Wine Sauce (p. 264) or Brown Onion Sauce (p. 263), though we prefer it with nothing but its own pan juices.

Serves 8–10

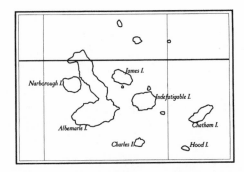

FLOATING ARCHIPELAGO IN THE SHAPE OF THE GALAPAGOS

. . . a most uncommonly splendid pudding brought in with conscious pride and welcomed with applause.

'What, what is this?' cried Jack.

'We thought you would be surprised, sir,' said Mowett. 'It's a floating island, or rather a floating archipelago.'

'It is the Galapagos themselves,' said Jack. 'Here's Albemarle, here's Narborough, here's Chatham and Hood . . . I had no idea there was anyone aboard capable of such a thing: a masterpiece, upon my word and honour, fit for a flagship.'

'One of the whalers made it, sir. He was a pastrycook in Danzig before he took to sea.'

'I put in the lines of longitude and latitude,' said the master. 'They are made of spun sugar; so is the equator, but double thick and dyed with port.'

'The Galapagos,' said Jack, gazing down on them. 'The whole shooting-match: there's even the Redondo Rock and Cowly's Enchanted Isle, laid down exactly.' . . .

'Will you not take some Galapagos, sir, before it comes adrift?' said Mowett.

'I hesitate to spoil such a work of art,' said Jack. 'But unless we are to go without our pudding'—this with a pretty knowing look as he poised his spoon above the pastry-cook's equator—'I believe I must cut the Line.'

—The Far Side of the World, 253–4

Just at the critical time when it crossed Jack Aubrey's path, Floating Island was undergoing a sea-change; and there is some question as to which form it might have taken when it appeared in the

Aubrey/Maturin novels. The Floating Island of eighteenth-century England was an elaborate affair of cake, jellies, and whimsical decorations, towering over a sea of cream or custard. The French *Ile Flottante* of the same period was closer to the Floating Island of today, a large molded Italian meringue surrounded by custard or cream. (And neither of them is to be confused with *Oeufs à la Neige,* which today is frequently—and mistakenly—also referred to as Floating Island.)

Judging from the cookery books of the period, it appears that the recipes crossed the Channel in both directions, and that during Jack's time there were several hybrid versions adding to the confusion. Since the pastrycook in *The Far Side of the World* was from Danzig, it is reasonable to suppose that he inclined toward the Continental, or meringue, side of the question. On the other hand, it is dreadfully difficult to make the Galapagos in meringue, and much less so to perform the operation with cake and jelly. We have tried both, and we felt it would be only fair to offer a choice.

Floating Archipelago

(The cake in this first version is virtually the same as Savoy Biscuit, except for the extra egg white.)

Scale: 1 inch = 10 nautical miles

3 egg yolks
¾ cup plus 2 teaspoons sugar
2 teaspoons grated lemon zest
2 teaspoons lemon juice
¼ teaspoon salt
4 egg whites
1½ cups flour
¾ cup currant jelly
¾ cup Calf's Foot Jelly (p. 268)
1 cup heavy cream
Bits of edible greenery such as tips of rosemary sprigs, etc.
Comfits (p. 39) or candied flowers (optional)
1 recipe (about 1½ cups) Custard Sauce (p. 264)
Spun Sugar (p. 81)

Preheat the oven to 350°.

Beat the egg yolks until they are smooth. Continue to beat, gradually adding the ¾ cup sugar. Add the lemon zest, lemon juice, and salt.

In a separate bowl, beat the egg whites until they form soft peaks. Fold them into the egg yolk mixture.

Sift the flour into the egg mixture and stir gently until smooth.

Pour the batter into a well-greased 10 × 15-inch jelly-roll pan. Bake 12–15 minutes, or until just golden brown at the edges. Turn out onto a rack to cool.

Using a small knife or a sharp scissors, cut the cake into Galapagos shapes, making 3 copies of each island.

Spread 1 set of islands with currant jelly. Lay them out on a large shallow platter, beginning with Albemarle and Narborough, and arrange them into their proper geographical relationship.

Place the second set of islands over the first. Spread this layer with Calf's Foot Jelly, then top with the final set of islands.

Cut volcanoes and other geological formations out of the cake scraps.

Whip the cream with the 2 teaspoons sugar until it is fairly stiff. Cement each volcano in its appropriate geographical position with a dab of whipped cream. Spread the rest of the whipped cream over all the islands, and landscape with bits of greenery (rosemary sprigs make very good palm trees) and Comfits.

Pour the Custard Sauce carefully around the islands. Decorate with lines of latitude and longitude made from Spun Sugar.

Serves 4–6

Archipel Flottant

(This recipe calls for 4 egg whites, and the Custard Sauce uses 4 yolks—most convenient.)

4 egg whites, at room temperature
  Pinch of salt
½ cup superfine sugar
  Butter for greasing
  Granulated sugar
3 tablespoons crushed Almond
   Comfits for garnish (optional—p. 39)

  Hot water for water bath
1 recipe (about 1½ cups) Custard Sauce (p. 264),
   chilled
  Spun Sugar (recipe follows)

Preheat oven to 300°.

Whip the egg whites until they begin to foam. Add the salt and continue beating until the whites form soft peaks. Still beating, gradually add the superfine sugar, until the mixture is stiff and shiny.

Lightly butter and sugar (and sprinkle with crushed Almond Comfits, if you are using them) the insides of a set of copper Galapagos molds (if you don't have molds in the shape of the Galapagos you can always fall back on 1-cup molds shaped like fish, shrimp, scallops, etc.). Gently tap the molds to shake out the excess sugar.

Fill the molds with the meringue mixture, and set them in a shallow pan. Carefully pour hot water into the pan until it comes about halfway up the outsides of the molds.

Place the pan in the oven and cook about 40 minutes (the meringue is done when it pulls away a little from the edge of the mold). Remove the molds from the hot water bath and set them on racks to cool.

When the meringues have cooled to room temperature, unmold them (you may need to loosen the edges first with a small knife) onto a large shallow platter. Arrange them into either their proper geographical relationship or an artistic pattern, as the case may be.

Pour the Custard Sauce around the islands (or fish). Decorate with lines of latitude and longitude (or seaweed) made from Spun Sugar (recipe follows).

Serves 4–6

Variation: Floating Island as served by Captain Dawson:

His cook had been ill, 'struck down by a treacherous crab he had ate last thing in Valletta. He is recovered now, I am happy to say. . . .'
    Recovered he had, but he had celebrated the event by getting drunk, and the meal followed a strange chaotic course with very long pauses and then the sudden appearance of five removes all together, and eccentricities such as floating island with an uncooked carrot in it.
        —Treason's Harbour, *316–7*

Make either version given above, and set an uncooked carrot adrift somewhere between Chatham and Hood.

Spun Sugar

½ cup sugar
3 tablespoons water
½ teaspoon grated beeswax (see note)

1 tablespoon port for coloring the equator

Spread the floor liberally with newspapers. This is a very messy business.

Combine the sugar and the water in a small heavy saucepan, and stir to dissolve. Bring to a boil over high heat, add the beeswax, and continue to cook until the syrup turns a light golden color.

For lines of latitude and longitude:
Let the syrup cool until it is fairly thick but not hard (the timing is a bit tricky, but if you miss your chance you can reheat the syrup and try again). Dip a cooking fork into the syrup and slowly, slowly, slowly pull it up, forming a thick thread. When the thread is long enough,

cut it off with scissors (do not touch it with your fingers until you are sure it is cool!) and lay it carefully on a flat surface.

To make the equator, reheat the syrup until it melts, add the port, and repeat the process (unless your port is very dark indeed, the difference will not be particularly noticeable; we have tried adding cochineal to darken it, and we cannot recommend the practice).

For seaweed:

Oil a belaying pin (or a dowel or broomstick). Let the syrup cool very slightly. Holding the belaying pin in one hand, with the other dip a cooking fork into the syrup, then wave it carefully back and forth above the belaying pin. The syrup will form cobwebby threads, most of which will fall over the pin. Gather the threads while they are still soft and shape them into attractive clumps of seaweed.

Note: The use of beeswax is an old pastry-cook's trick to keep spun sugar from melting as soon as it comes into contact with liquid. Even with the wax, spun sugar will not hold together for long once it is afloat in a sea of custard, so do not lay out your lines or seaweed until just before serving the archipelago.

Fu-Fu

. . . one of the Commodore's favourite forecastle dishes, fu-fu, ordinarily made of barley and treacle, but now with honey and cognac. . . .
—The Commodore, *270*

In *The Sailor's Word Book,* Fu-fu is described as "a well-known sea dish of barley and treacle" that was especially popular in merchant ships. The original Fu-fu (which also has cousins called cou-cou and tou-tou) is a basic mush made from yams or from starches such as rice, cassava, and corn. Since it is common both in West Africa and in the Caribbean, we have hazarded an educated guess that the merchant ships in question were engaged in the slave-trade. English sailors, as a rule, would not have had yams, so barley must have seemed a reasonable alternative.

But Fu-fu made from barley meal is—it pains us to have to say this—an insipid mess. We tried any number of variations. Nothing helped.

| 1 cup barley meal | 1½ tablespoons treacle |
| 4 cups water | 3 tablespoons sugar |

In a heavy saucepan, thoroughly combine the barley meal and 1 cup water. In another pot or kettle, bring the remaining 3 cups water to a boil. Gradually pour the boiling water into the barley mixture, stirring briskly to keep lumps from forming.

Bring the mush to a boil and cook 2 minutes over medium heat, stirring all the while. Cover and simmer 15 minutes over the lowest possible heat.

Remove from heat and stir in treacle and sugar.

Serves 8–10

Variation: Substitute 2 tablespoons honey and 2 tablespoons brandy for the treacle and sugar.

Naples Biscuits

'You must allow me to warn you against any indulgence in lowness,' he said. 'Were you to give way to melancholy, you would certainly pule into a decline.'

She managed a smile, and said, 'Perhaps it is no more than the effect of Naples biscuits, sir. I must have eaten a thousand, at least.'

'Unrelieved Naples biscuit? Do they not feed you at all?'

'Oh yes, and I am sure I shall come to relish it soon. Pray do not think I complain.' —Desolation Island, *109*

One can understand that an exclusive diet of Naples Biscuit might have sent Mrs. Wogan, or indeed anyone, puling into a decline. Eaten in reasonable numbers, though, they are pleasant if not exciting, and useful as a basis for various other sweet dishes—rather like today's ladyfingers.

3 eggs, separated	¼ teaspoon salt
⅓ cup superfine sugar	¾ cup flour
⅛ teaspoon rose water	

Preheat oven to 350°.

Whip the egg whites until doubled in volume. Continue to whip, gradually adding the sugar, until the whites are smooth and glossy.

Beat the yolks and stir in the rose water and salt. Fold into the egg-white mixture. Sift the flour into the egg mixture and stir gently to combine.

Using a spoon or a pastry bag, shape batter into "fingers" on lightly greased cookie sheets. Bake 10 minutes.

Makes about 30 biscuits

Treacle-Dowdy

'My compliments to Mr Whiting, and he may make sail to close the Dryad, *if* Dryad *she be. I shall come on deck after dinner.' And in an aside to Pullings he added 'It would be a pity to waste a crumb of this glorious treacle-dowdy.'* —The Ionian Mission, *171*

A dowdy, generally speaking, is a boiled or steamed pudding in which the dough (or "dow," as it was called in the seventeenth century—hence "dowdy") lies on top of the filling (for a notable exception, see "Figgy-Dowdy", p. 86). The baked version is known as pandowdy in the United States, where it is almost invariably made with apples. The dough-on-top-of-filling theme is echoed repeatedly in this variation, producing a pretty striped pattern when the Treacle-Dowdy is sliced.

(For information on preparing and cooking puddings, see "About Puddings," p. 273. For information on treacle, see "Treacle Pudding," p. 138.)

Pastry:
½ pound suet, finely grated
4 cups flour
¼ cup sugar
½ teaspoon salt
   Ice water

Filling:
¼ cup treacle
¼ cup sugar
   Juice and grated zest of ½ lemon
1 large knob (about 1½ inches long) fresh ginger, peeled and grated

Mix the suet, flour, sugar, and salt in a large bowl. Work in 1–2 tablespoons ice water. Continue gradually adding ice water until you have a stiff paste (it will probably take about a cup of water, but this will vary depending on temperature, humidity, the dryness of your flour, etc.). Work it with your hands until it forms a ball. Turn it out onto a well-floured board. Cover with a damp cloth and let rest for 5 minutes.

Knead the dough until it is shiny and elastic (6–8 minutes), cover again, let rest another 5 minutes, then knead again for 1–2 minutes. Cut off one-third of the dough and roll it out (reflouring the board and the rolling pin as needed) until it is about ⅛ inch thick. Line a well-greased 6-cup pudding-basin with the sheet of pastry, pleating as necessary to make it fit snugly. (You may have to cut a couple of these wedge-shaped pleats out of the pastry. To join the cut edges, moisten them thoroughly with cold water and press them together firmly with your fingers.)

Roll out the remaining pastry until it is about ⅛ inch thick. Cut the sheet of pastry into pieces of approximately the same size and shape as the diameter of the basin.

Combine the treacle, sugar, lemon juice and zest, and ginger. Spoon a thin layer of the filling into the bottom of the basin. Place a piece of pastry over the filling, pressing the edges gently into the pastry lining the basin walls. Continue in alternating layers until both are used up, finishing with a layer of pastry. Moisten the edges with cold water, and pinch with your fingers to seal them tightly together. (The pudding will not quite fill the basin, but it will swell during cooking.)

Tie a well-floured cloth over the pudding, place the basin in a pot of rapidly boiling water, cover, and steam for two hours.

Remove the pudding from the pot, untie the cloth, and unmold onto a serving dish. Cut into thin wedges, and serve with Custard Sauce (p. 264) or Lemon Sauce (p. 265).

Serves 8

Figgy-Dowdy

'Now, sir,' said Jack to Canning, 'we have a Navy dish that I thought might amuse you. We call it figgy-dowdy. You do not have to eat it, unless you choose—this is Liberty Hall. For my part, I find it settles a meal; but perhaps it is an acquired taste.'

Canning eyed the pale, amorphous, gleaming, slightly translucent mass and asked how it was made; he did not think he had ever seen anything quite like it.

'We take ship's biscuit, put it in a stout canvas bag—' said Jack.

'Pound it with a marlin-spike for half an hour—' said Pullings.

'Add bits of pork fat, plums, figs, rum, currants,' said Parker.

'Send it to the galley, and serve it up with bosun's grog,' said Macdonald.

—Post Captain, *269*

The Sailor's Word Book defines "figgie-dowdie" as "a cant West Country term for plum pudding," which it says is "made of raisins and dough." The Cornish, as a rule, say "fig" where the English would say "plum"—and it is well known that when the English say "plum" what they actually mean is "raisin" or in some cases "currant."

Fruit nomenclature aside, the passage above is a perfectly clear blueprint for the dish, and it would be folly to deviate from it more than strictly necessary. A raisin by any other name . . .

(For information on preparing and cooking puddings, see "About Puddings," p. 273.)

1 pound Ship's Biscuit (p. 102), or enough to make about 4 cups crumbs	¾ cup dried currants
	¾ cup raisins
	½ pound pork fat (or suet), finely grated
½ cup flour	2 teaspoons freshly grated ginger
¼ cup sugar	
½ teaspoon ground nutmeg	3 eggs, lightly beaten
½ teaspoon salt	¼ cup rum
¾ cup coarsely chopped figs	¾ cup water

Pound the biscuit into fine crumbs with a marline-spike or belaying pin. Put the crumbs in a large bowl, add the flour, sugar, nutmeg, and salt, and stir to combine. Stir in the figs, currants, and raisins, breaking them apart (the flour and crumbs will coat them and keep them from clumping together). Mix in the fat. Add the ginger, eggs, rum, and water, and work the mixture thoroughly with your hands.

Tie tightly in a well-floured cloth. Place in a large pot with boiling water to cover. Cover, bring to a boil, and cook rapidly for 3 hours (you may need to replenish the water as it cooks).

Remove the pudding from the pot, untie it, and turn out into a serving dish. Slice into thin wedges and serve with Custard Sauce (p. 264).

Serves 10–12

A Long Grey Pudding, Made with Sea-Elephant Suet and Studded with Juan Fernandez Berries

Presently the purser, the chaplain and the surgeon were left to themselves with the greater part of a long grey pudding, made with sea-elephant suet and studded with Juan Fernandez berries, and Stephen observed, 'I have seen many examples of the seaman's volatility, but none equal to this. When you recall the last week, . . . the collective sense of impending, ineluctable doom, and when you compare that with today's brisk gaiety, the lively eye, the hop, skip and jump, why, you are tempted to ask yourself whether these are not mere irresponsible childish fribbles . . .'

* 'Fribble yourself,' murmured the gunroom steward the other side of the door, where he was finishing the officers' wine with Killick.*

—The Far Side of the World, 233

Make Drowned Baby (p. 92), substituting sea-elephant suet for the beef suet and Juan Fernandez berries for the raisins.

Clarissa Oakes's Bridal Dinner

Swordfish Soup   Swordfish Fritters   Swordfish Steaks

Dried Peas Beaten into a Paste with a Marline-Spike
and Flavoured with Turmeric

White Sauce Beautified with Cochineal

Drowned (Boiled) Baby

from *The Truelove*, 89–110

'The ship's side has been pierced below the waterline. . . .'

'It was a swordfish, and his sword is still plugging the hole.' . . .

'He is one of the histiophori,' said Stephen, standing there in his night-shirt. 'Probably pulchellus.'

'Can he be ate?' asked Pullings.

'Of course he can be ate. He eats better by far than your common tunny.'

'Then we shall be able to have our feast at last,' said Pullings. 'I have been growing so shamefaced this last fortnight and more I could hardly meet her eye, a bride and all. . . .'

The sound of chairs being drawn in, the arrival of the swordfish soup and the ladling of it out filled the gunroom with the pleasant confusion of sounds usual at the beginning of a feast; . . .

Swordfish Soup

4 pounds swordfish bones and scraps
2 large onions, peeled and cut in half
2 large carrots, peeled and cut in half
1 large bay leaf
1 teaspoon peppercorns
2 cups white wine
Salt
1 large lemon
½ teaspoon saffron threads
2 pounds swordfish steaks

Put the bones, onions, carrots, bay leaf and peppercorns in a large stockpot with water to cover. Add the wine.

Bring to a boil. Add salt to taste. Reduce heat, cover, and simmer 1 hour.

Strain the stock, reserving the carrots.

Return the stock to the pot. Cut the lemon in half and squeeze about half the juice from each half into the stock. Slice the lemon halves about ¼ inch thick and add the slices to the stock. Add the saffron.

Bring to a boil. Cut the carrot and the swordfish steaks into ½-inch pieces. Add them to the soup and simmer about 5 minutes.

Ladle into bowls and float one of the lemon slices in each bowl.

Serves 8

There was the relief of taking soup plates away with a fine mess-deck clatter and bringing on the swordfish fritters, . . .

Swordfish Fritters

2 pounds swordfish, skin removed
Lard or oil for deep-frying, about 3 cups
2 eggs
1 tablespoon butter, melted
1 cup flour, sifted
1 teaspoon salt
⅔ cup cold water

Cut the swordfish into 1-inch cubes. Pat them dry.

In a heavy saucepan or deep-fryer (we like a wok because it requires less oil), heat the oil to about 370°, or until it will brown a ½-inch cube of bread in 20 seconds.

Whisk the egg to a fine froth and add the melted butter. Stir in the flour and salt. Gradually add the water, whisking all the while until the batter is smooth.

Dip a few pieces of swordfish in the batter, turning them so that they are coated on all sides. Drop them gently into the hot fat, stir briefly to make sure they do not stick together, and fry them until they are a lovely golden brown. Remove with a runcible spoon, drain briefly and keep warm. Repeat with the remaining fish.

Serve with Mayonnaise (p. 262) seasoned to taste with lemon juice or hot pepper sauce.

Serves 8 as a first course

'Sir,' whispered the gunroom steward in Pullings' ear, 'cook says if we don't eat our swordfish steaks this selfsame minute he will hang himself.'

Swordfish Steaks

8 swordfish steaks, ¾ inch   Slush for frying
       thick, about ½ pound each
   Flour for dredging, seasoned
       to taste with salt and pep-
       per

Pat the steaks dry and dredge them lightly in the seasoned flour. Heat 2 (or more, if necessary to hold all the steaks without crowding) large frying pans over high heat. Put in enough slush to coat the pans. When the slush sizzles, put in the steaks and brown them well, 2–3 minutes on each side, or until cooked to your liking.

Serves 8

The steaks arrived in style, the dishes covering the middle of the table, while in the intervals and at the corners there were small bowls of such things as dried peas beaten into a paste with a marline-spike and flavoured with turmeric, and white sauce beautified with cochineal.

Dried Peas Beaten into a Paste with a Marline-Spike and Flavoured with Turmeric

1 cup whole dried peas	½ teaspoon turmeric
3 cups cold water	Salt

Beat the peas to a fine meal with a marline-spike or a like implement. Put in a pot with the water and stir thoroughly. Bring gradually to a boil, stirring constantly. Reduce heat and cook very gently for 1 hour. Add the turmeric and salt to taste.

Serves 8 as a side dish

White Sauce Beautified with Cochineal

¼ teaspoon cochineal	1½ cups veal or chicken stock
1 teaspoon hot water	¼ cup heavy cream
2 tablespoons butter	Juice of ½ lemon
2 tablespoons flour	Salt and pepper

Pound the cochineal to a fine powder and set it to steep in the hot water.

Melt the butter in a small saucepan. Add the flour, stirring frequently until the flour is thoroughly cooked, but not brown. Stirring constantly, gradually add the stock, the cream, and the lemon juice. Season to taste.

Strain the cochineal solution. Stir about ¼ teaspoon of the liquid into the sauce. If the color does not please you, add more, drop by drop, until the sauce is sufficiently beautified.

Makes about 1½ cups

'It seemed to me to express the state of mind of a deeply injured furious duellist when he plunges his sword into the opponent's bowels.'

'May I cut you a trifle of pudding, ma'am?' asked Pullings, moved by the association of ideas.

It is the association of ideas that moved us to insert Boiled Baby at this point. There must, of course, be a pudding at the end of Clarissa's dinner—we cannot be sure which pudding it was, for the text does not specify; but since Boiled Baby was Jack's own suggestion for the feast (in his letter to Sophie), it seemed a logical choice.

Drowned (Boiled) Baby

The gunroom's feast for the Captain was if anything more copious than that of the day before: . . . the gunroom cook, by means known to himself alone, had conserved the makings of a superb suet pudding of the kind called boiled baby in the service, known to be Jack Aubrey's favourite form of food, and it came in on a scrubbed scuttle-cover to the sound of cheering.

—The Nutmeg of Consolation, *227*

Jack reached the galley, inspected the coppers, the harness-casks, the slush-tubs, the three hundredweight of plum-duff preparing for Sunday dinner; and with some satisfaction he noticed his own private drowned baby simmering in its long kettle. But this satisfaction was as private as his pudding.

—The Ionian Mission, *136*

(For information on preparing and cooking puddings, see "About Puddings," p. 273.)

4 cups flour	1½ cups raisins
¼ cup sugar	½ pound suet, finely grated
½ teaspoon salt	Ice water
1 teaspoon ground cinnamon	

In a large bowl, mix the flour, sugar, salt, and cinnamon. Stir in the raisins, breaking them apart (the flour will coat them and keep them from clumping together). Mix in the suet.

Work in 1–2 tablespoons ice water. Continue gradually adding ice water until you have a stiff paste (it will probably take about a cup of water, but this will vary depending on temperature, humidity, the dryness of your flour, etc.). Work it with your hands until it forms a ball. Turn it out onto a well-floured board. Cover with a damp cloth and let rest for 5 minutes.

Knead the dough until it is shiny and elastic (6–8 minutes), cover again, let rest another 5 minutes, then knead again for 1–2 minutes.

Shape the dough into a nice, fat, vaguely cylindrical lump. Wrap the pudding fairly loosely in a well-floured cloth. Tie securely at both ends (we usually also tie a string loosely around the middle, to keep the cloth from gaping). Immerse the pudding in a pot of rapidly boiling water and cook for 2½ hours, replenishing the water as necessary.

To serve, untie and unroll the cloth. Turn the pudding out onto a board or platter. Serve hot, accompanied by Custard Sauce (p. 264).

Serves 12–16

Spanish Ladies

Fare- well and a- dieu to you Span- ish la- dies! Fare-

well and a- dieu to you, la- dies of Spain! For we've re- ceived or- ders to

sail for old Eng- land, And per- haps ne- ver more we shall see you a- gain.

Chorus: *We'll rant and we'll roar like true British sailors;*
We'll rant and we'll roar all on the salt seas;
Until we strike soundings in the channel of England;
From Ushant to Scilly 'tis thirty-five leagues.

We hove our ship to, with the wind at sou' west, boys,
We hove our ship to, for to strike soundings clear.
Then we fill'd our main topsail, and bore right away, boys,
And straight up the Channel our course we did steer.
We'll rant and we'll roar, &c.

Now the first land we made it is called the Deadman,
Next Rams Head, off Plymouth, Start, Portland, and Wight:
We sailed by Beachy, by Fairlee and Dungeness,
And then bore away for the South Foreland Light.
We'll rant and we'll roar, &c.

Now the signal was made for the Grand Fleet to anchor,
And all in the Downs that night for to meet.
Then it's stand by your stoppers, let go your shank painters,
Haul up your clew garnets, stick out tacks and sheets.
We'll rant and we'll roar, &c.

Now let ev'ry man toss off a full bumper,
Now let ev'ry man take off his full bowl.
For we will be jolly and drown melancholy,
With a health to each jovial and true-hearted soul.
We'll rant and we'll roar, &c.

CHAPTER THREE

The Seamen's Mess

*A*t this moment hands were piped to dinner, and the berth-deck, the long space behind the canvas screen that Stephen had had set up to protect the sick-bay a little, was filled with a tumult of hungry men. An orderly tumult, however: each mess of eight men darted to its particular place, hanging tables appeared, dropping instantly from the beams, wooden kids filled with salt pork (another proof that it was Thursday) and peas came from the galley, and the grog, which Mr Pullings had just mixed at the scuttle-butt by the mainmast, was carried religiously below, everyone skipping out of its way, lest a drop should fall. —Master and Commander, *196*

'And yet as I am sure you have noticed, the ordinary work of the ship carries on as it were by its own momentum: the glass is turned, the bell is struck, the watch is relieved; when a brace is required to be adjusted, or rounded-in, as we say, the hands are there; the salt pork is already in its steep-tubs, growing a little more nearly edible; and I have no doubt that at eight bells it will be eaten.' —The Nutmeg of Consolation, *131–2*

The sailors' diet was monotonous at best, unhealthy as a rule, and frequently quite revolting. Such as it was, however, it was at least regular and comparatively plentiful, which was more than most sailors could hope for on land.

There was little scope for imagination in the weekly menu, as shown in the following excerpts from William Falconer's *Marine Dictionary,* based on the 1797 regulations of the Victualling Office:

PROVISIONS, those articles of food and sustenance which are served out daily to each person on board his Majesty's ships, under the superintendance of the purser, and consist of such as are undermentioned:

TABLE OF THE DAILY PROPORTION OF PROVISIONS
ALLOWED TO EVERY PERSON ON BOARD
HIS MAJESTY'S SHIPS.

	SUN.	MON.	TUE.	WED.	THU.	FRI.	SAT.	TOT. PR. WK.
Bread, lbs.	1	1	1	1	1	1	1	7 lbs.
Beer galls.	1	1	1	1	1	1	1	7 galls.
Beef, lbs.			2				2	4 lbs.
Pork, lbs.	1				1			2 lbs.
Pease, pts.	½			½	½	½		2 pts.
Oatmeal, pt.		½		½		½		1½ pts.
Sugar, oz.		2		2		2		6 oz.
Butter, oz.		2		2		2		6 oz.
Cheese, oz.		4		4		4		12 oz.

together with an allowance of vinegar, not exceeding half a pint to each man per week. There is cocoa with sugar allowed for breakfast, as a substitute for butter or oatmeal, and lime-juice with sugar, as a beverage, when subsisting on salt provisions.

When the beer is expended, a pint of wine, or half a pint of rum, brandy, or other spirits is allowed daily, the spirits being always mixed with water, to each person, instead. . . .

Captains may shorten this allowance, if necessity requires it, taking due care that the men be paid for the deficiency; nor is any officer to have whole allowance while the company is at short. . . .

Beef is cut into four pound pieces, and pork into two, and every cask is to have its contents marked on the head. . . .

One day in every week there shall be issued out a proportion of flour and suet in lieu of beef, but this is not to extend beyond four months victualling at one time.

Only three months butter and cheese shall be supplied for foreign voyages, the remainder to be made up in olive oil.

Fresh meat is to be allowed every day (when it can be conve-

niently done), instead of salt meat; three pounds of mutton ac-
counted for a four pound piece of beef, or a two pound piece of
pork with pease.

The meat itself was of questionable origins—the salt beef was often
called salt horse because it was suspected of being exactly that; John
Masefield, among others, tells tales of horseshoes being found at the
bottom of beef casks.

And the poor quality of the meat is also legendary: not only did it
contain an inordinately high proportion of gristle to begin with; but
since old provisions left over from previous voyages were always used
before the newer ones, a cask was often several years old before being
opened. "The beef had been to the West Indies and back, and now, in
its raw state, it could be carved and filed into durable ornaments; and
even after some hours in the steep-tubs and the galley copper it still
retained something of its heart of oak" (*The Surgeon's Mate*, 196–7).

(Monday, Wednesday and Friday were known as banyan days, so
named for the Banyans of Western India, a Hindu caste whose reli-
gion forbade the eating of animal flesh. All things considered, one has
to wonder whether or not this was viewed as a privation.)

Furthermore, as a rule captains did indeed "shorten this allowance,"
as the regulations permitted them to do, so even the quantity was not
always as advertised.

Rather to our relief, we were unable to obtain—and we did not
have the resources to produce—anything so rancid and rocklike as the
rations of two hundred years ago; so we contented ourselves with a
symbolic substitution of corned beef and modern salt pork.

Dried Peas with Lumps of Pork

*The ceremony of the noon-observation went mechanically through its rit-
ual words and motions, at the end of which Jack, in a harsh official voice
said 'Make it twelve.' A few moments later eight bells was struck and
Rowan cried 'Pipe to dinner.'*

*The bosun piped, the men ran to their places, the cooks of each mess as-
sembled in the galley, where (though it seemed unbelievable) their lumps
of pork had been simmering for a great while, together with their dried
peas, this being Thursday.* —Treason's Harbour, *188*

2 pounds lean salt pork
2 cups whole dried peas

1 medium onion, peeled (op-
     tional)
   Salt and pepper

Soak the pork and the peas separately, in cold water to cover, for at least 12 hours.

Put the pork and the peas in a pot with 1½ quarts water. Bring to a boil, reduce heat, and simmer, covered, stirring occasionally, about 5½ hours. If you are so fortunate as to have an onion about you, adding it to the soup during the last hour or so will greatly improve the flavor. Season with salt and pepper to taste.

Serves 2 sailors or 8 lubbers

Dog's Body

See Pease-Pudding, Variation (p. 137).

Oatmeal

But there were few bellies that filled themselves heartily aboard the Sophie *that brilliant morning; a kind of impatient rigidity kept the oatmeal and hard-tack from going down regular and smooth.*

—Master and Commander, *234*

2 cups steel-cut oats
4 cups water

1 teaspoon salt
   Heavy cream (optional)

Gradually stir the oats into the water. Set over medium heat and bring to a boil. Reduce heat and simmer 15 minutes, stirring constantly. Remove from heat and add the salt. Serve with heavy cream, if possible.

Serves 4

Burgoo

'You will be there presently,' said Stephen, 'but none of your mainbrace, none of your nasty grog, my friend, until you learn to avoid the ladies of Portsmouth Point, and the fireships of the Sally-Port. No ardent spirits at all for you. Not a drop, until you are cured. And even then, you would be far better with mild unctuous cocoa, or burgoo.'

'Which she told me she was a virgin,' said the sailor, in a low, resentful tone. —Post Captain, *297*

Some of the Ariel's *people were badly frightened, as well they might be, and an appearance of order would comfort them, to say nothing of hot burgoo in their bellies.* —The Surgeon's Mate, *305*

Our recipe for Burgoo is taken almost verbatim from Falconer's *Marine Dictionary*, which describes it thus:

> BURGOO, a seafaring dish, made by gradually adding two quarts of water to one of oatmeal, so that the whole may mix smoothly; then boiling it for a quarter of an hour, stirring it constantly; after which, a little salt, butter, and sugar, is generally added. It is a cheap and strengthening diet, held by Cockburn very proper to correct that viscidity of humours and costiveness to which the other diet of sailors so much disposes them.

2 cups steel-cut oats	3 tablespoons butter
4 cups water	4 teaspoons sugar
1 teaspoon salt	

Gradually stir the oats into the water. Set over medium heat and bring to a boil. Reduce heat and simmer 15 minutes, stirring constantly. Remove from heat, add the salt, butter, and sugar, and stir to dissolve.

Serves 4

Ship's Biscuit (Hard Tack)

Ship's Biscuit was mass-produced by the bake-houses of the Royal Navy's victualling yards, and we cannot possibly improve upon Falconer's description of the process, so we offer it here in its entirety. We have, however, made our own hard tack (on a *much* smaller scale), and that recipe also follows.

> BISCUIT, Sea, is a sort of bread much dried, to make it keep for the use of the navy, and is good for a whole year after it is baked.
>
> The process of biscuit-making for the navy is simple and ingenious, and is nearly as follows: A large lump of dough, consisting merely of flower and water, is mixed up together, and placed exactly in the centre of a raised platform, where a man sits upon a machine, called a horse, and literally rides up and down throughout its whole circular direction, till the dough is equally indented, and this is repeated till the dough is sufficiently kneaded.
>
> In this state it is handed over to a second workman, who, with a large knife, puts it in a proper state for the use of those bakers who more immediately attend the oven. They are five in number; and their different departments are well calculated for expedition and exactness.
>
> The first man on the farthest side of a large table moulds the dough, till it has the appearance of muffins, and which he does two together, with each hand; and then delivers them over to the man on the other side of the table, who stamps them on both sides with a mark, and throws them on a smaller table, where stands the third workman, whose business is merely to separate the different pieces into two, and place them under the hand of him who supplies the oven, whose work of throwing or chucking the biscuits on the peel must be performed with the greatest exactness and regularity. The fifth arranges them in the oven, and is so expert, that though the different biscuits are thrown to him at the rate of seventy in a minute, the peel is always disengaged in time to receive them separately.
>
> So much critical exactness and neat activity occur in the exercise of this layout, that it is difficult to decide whether the palm of

excellence is due to the moulder, the maker, the splitter, the chucker, or the depositor; all of them, like the wheels of a machine, seeming to be actuated by the same principle. The business is to deposit in the oven seventy biscuits in a minute; and this is accomplished with the regularity of a clock; the clack of the peel, during its motion in the oven, operating like the pendulum. The biscuits thus baked are kept in repositories, which receive warmth from being placed in drying lofts over the ovens, till they are sufficiently dry to be packed into bags, without danger of getting mouldy; and when in such a state, they are then packed into bags, of an hundred weight each, and removed into store-houses for immediate use.

At Deptford the bake house belonging to the victualling-office has twelve ovens; each of which bakes twenty shoots daily; the quantity of flour used for each shoot is two bushels, or 112 pounds; which baked, produce 102 pounds of biscuit. Ten pounds are regularly allowed on each shoot for shrinkage, &c. The allowance of biscuit in the navy is, one pound for each man per day; so that, at Deptford alone, they can furnish bread, daily, for 24,480 men, independent of Portsmouth and Plymouth.

Ship's Biscuit for a Single Mess

Two weevils crept from the crumbs. 'You see those weevils, Stephen?' said Jack solemnly.

'I do.'

'Which would you choose?'

'There is not a scrap of difference. Arcades ambo. *They are the same species of curculio, and there is nothing to choose between them.'*

'But suppose you had to choose?'

'Then I should choose the right-hand weevil; it has a perceptible advantage in both length and breadth.'

'There I have you,' cried Jack. 'You are bit—you are completely dished. Don't you know that in the Navy you must always choose the lesser of two weevils? Oh ha, ha, ha, ha!'					—The Fortune of War, *54–5*

Ship's Biscuit is chiefly remarkable as a haven for weevils, politely known as bargemen. We were half-sorry, half-relieved to find that our

biscuit did not breed them. We went to some trouble, therefore, to locate weevils from other attractive sources, in a couple of different
sizes. Having laid in a plentiful supply . . . we did not choose to eat
them. Not even the lesser of the two.

4 cups flour	1–1½ cups water
1 teaspoon salt	

Preheat oven to 325°.

Stir the flour and the salt together. Add the water, stirring, until you
have enough to form a very stiff dough. Turn the dough out onto a
floured surface, cover it with a damp cloth, and let it rest for 10 minutes.

Knead the dough for a minute or two, until all the flour is absorbed.

Beat the dough with a mallet or rolling pin until it makes a flat sheet
about ½ inch thick. Fold it into several layers and beat again. Continue folding and beating until the dough is smooth and elastic (about
30 minutes).

Roll the dough into a rectangle about ½ inch thick. Cut it into 2-inch
squares. Prick the biscuits with a fork or toothpick. Place them on un-
greased cookie sheets and bake for 1 hour.

Cool on racks and store in barrels for many years. After a few weeks
at sea, check for bargemen.

Makes 1¼ pounds

Note: In direct contravention of all traditional methods, we have
discovered two excellent alternatives to the arduous process of beating the dough. One is to run it repeatedly through a hand-cranked
pasta machine; the other, much more exciting though a bit less
efficient, is to put it in a large stout bag and repeatedly drive a car
over it.

Plum-Duff

... Reflections upon their dinner, their Sunday dinner, the plum-duff that was simmering under the equatorial sun with no more than a glowing cinder to keep it on the boil. ... —H.M.S. Surprise, *116*

Every man aboard knew that ... he must make up his mind at once between fighting the ship in his best clothes and missing if not his beef then his double-shotted duff. Most plumped for the duff, which they ate on deck, by their guns, holding it carefully away from their snowy shirts, their silk neckerchiefs, and trousers beribboned at the seams.

—The Mauritius Command, *316*

He faintly heard the psalm; he was aware of the Sunday smells, pork and plum-duff, coming from the galley. —The Thirteen-Gun Salute, *125*

Fundamentally, duff is dough. In its plainest form it is no more than flour (half a pound per man) mixed with salt water, put in a bag, and boiled in the coppers with the meat for four or five hours. The next level of refinement calls for the addition of slush or bits of pork fat, and perhaps a little sugar. On Sundays plain duff is transformed into Plum-Duff by virtue of an ounce of mouldy raisins or currants—the opulence of "double-shotted" duff being achieved by a commensurate increase in the "plum" ration.

One bizarre seafaring legend depicts the distribution of plums as being much more a matter of chance: on duff day, it seems, the cook would climb to the maintop with the bag of raisins and throw them at a lump of dough held in the arms of a man on deck—the plumminess of the result being entirely dependent on the accuracy of his aim. Considering the value of plums and the likelihood of most of them going overboard, we are inclined to take this story with a great deal of salt.

4 pounds flour	1 quart water
2 pounds grated pork fat	1½ cups raisins or dried
1 cup sugar	currants

Mix all ingredients together and knead thoroughly (adding extra water if necessary) to make a stiff dough.

Divide into 8 equal portions and tie each snugly into a floured pudding bag or cloth. Put the bags in the coppers with the salt meat and boil for 4–5 hours.

Serves 8

Variation: For double-shotted duff, double the "plums."

Plum-Duff Another Way

Meanwhile, Plum-Duff on land was a different and rather more appetizing matter—oddly reminiscent of today's raisin bread. (Strictly speaking, it's out of place in the seamen's mess; but having tested the recipe and found it good, we felt it was a pity not to include it.)

1 ounce compressed (or 1½ teaspoons active dry) yeast	2 teaspoons freshly ground allspice
1 cup warm water	1 teaspoon ground cinnamon
½ cup sugar	1½ cups raisins
½ cup warm milk	4 cups flour
1 teaspoon salt	

Put the yeast in a large bowl with the water and 1 tablespoon of the sugar, stir briefly, then cover with a damp cloth and set in a warm place until it bubbles (about 15 minutes).

Stir in the remaining sugar, milk, salt, allspice, and cinnamon. Combine the raisins with the flour (to keep them from clumping together), and add to the yeast mixture. Stir to form a stiff dough. Cover once more with a damp cloth and set in a warm place to rise until doubled in bulk (about 1 hour).

Punch down the dough and turn it out on a floured board. Knead until smooth and elastic. Tie loosely in a well-floured cloth. Place in a large pot with boiling water to cover. Cover, bring to a boil, and cook rapidly for 1½ hours (you may occasionally need to replenish the water as it cooks).

Remove the pudding from the pot, untie it, and turn the duff out into a serving dish. Slice into thin wedges and serve with Custard Sauce (p. 264).

Serves 10–12

Drops of Brandy

CHAPTER FOUR

A Glass
of Wine with
You, Sir

Among the rest of the wine, twenty-one dozens of Margaux of '88, with the long cork, together with an almost equal quantity of Château Lafite. Sure, I cannot tell how we shall ever get through them all; yet it would be the world's shame to let such noble wine go back, and in these conditions another year must see it the mere ghost of itself.'

The claret never saw another year, however, nor did that splendid vintage go to waste: with steady application and with some help from Bretonnière and other guests from the gunroom Jack and Stephen drank almost every drop as the days went by.   —The Mauritius Command, 66

Sir Francis said, 'Aubrey, here's to your health and happiness.'

'And to yours, sir,' said Jack, savouring the fresh, flowerly, grateful wine. 'Lord, how well it does go down.'

'Don't it?' said the Admiral.   —The Far Side of the World, 35

Stephen . . . drank the wine that a heavily-breathing Marine poured into his glass, his brimming glass. It was the same sillery that Jack had drunk the day before and it went down even more gratefully. 'What delightful wine,' observed Stephen to nobody in particular. 'But it is by no means innocent,' he added, slowly drinking the rest of the glass.

—The Far Side of the World, 51

'The bubbly stuff is all very well,' said Jack, looking at the light through his glass, 'but for flavour, for bouquet and for quality, give me good sillery every time.'

—The Thirteen-Gun Salute, *88*

The wines and other drinks that appear in the novels range from the sublime to the ridiculous—from great historic clarets and lovely sillery to seven-water grog and strange poisonous compounds of dubious origins.

We cannot, of course, presume to write recipes for the wines and brandies, though we do list and describe them. But the mixed drinks and punches, the flips and shrubs, are fearfully and wonderfully made, and many of them both cheer and inebriate.

Admiral's Flip

'So here's to his health, sir, in admiral's flip,' cried Pullings, putting an ice-cold silver tankard into his hand.

'Admiral's flip, at this time of day?' said Jack, looking thoughtfully at Captain Pullings' round, happy face . . . the face of one who had already swallowed a pint of marsala . . . the face of an ordinarily abstemious man who was now in no state to drink champagne mixed with brandy half and half. . . .

'Come sir,' said Pullings reproachfully. 'It's not every day I wet the swab.' . . .

The admiral's flip did for poor Pullings even sooner than might have been expected.

—Treason's Harbour, *31–2*

Admiral's Flip is not a true "flip" in that it is not flipped. For a proper flipped flip, see "Flip" (p. 114).

The proportions for this drink seem to be somewhat arbitrary. We did not find the half-and-half combination especially palatable, but we do feel that the version given here (perhaps an ancestor of the modern Champagne Cocktail?) makes a highly appropriate beverage for swab-wetting purposes.

½ cup chilled brandy
2 tablespoons sugar

1½ cups champagne
1 whole nutmeg

Combine the brandy and sugar and stir well to dissolve. Add the champagne, dust with freshly grated nutmeg, and serve in ice-cold silver tankards.

Serves 4

WHAT'LL IT BE, SIR?

These three drinks appear—or rather, fail to appear—on various occasions in the Aubrey/Maturin novels; the first two are *not* what Jack drinks to wash down Stephen's enormous bolus, and all three are *not* what has made Bonden so happy in the aftermath of the *Shannon*'s victory over the *Chesapeake*.

'What'll it be, sir? Dog's nose? Flip? Come, sir,' he said, with the authority of the well over the sick in their care, or even out of it, 'What'll it be? For down it must go or it will miss the tide.' Jack thought he would like a little sherry. 'Oh no, sir. No wine. The Doctor said, No wine. Porter is more the mark.' —Post Captain, *390*

When Bonden . . . reported to the drawing-room for orders, his happiness owed little to dog's nose, flip, or raspberry shrub.

—The Surgeon's Mate, *107–8*

Dog's Nose

Dog's Nose is a direct descendant of Purl, described in the mid-seventeenth century as an infusion of bitter herbs in beer (one recipe lists the following: wormwood, gentian, calamus aromaticus, snake root, horse radish, dried orange peel, juniper berries, seeds of Seville oranges, and—optionally—galingale; substitute spirits for the beer and it becomes a recipe for Bitters). Purl itself remained popular well into the nineteenth century, but in the late eighteenth century it acquired the offshoot called Dog's Nose, in which most of the herbs had gradually faded away and a dash of gin had appeared in their place.

3 cups porter   2 tablespoons sugar
2 sprigs wormwood   ¼ cup gin
1 teaspoon freshly grated gin-   1 whole nutmeg
   ger (or more, to taste)

Combine the porter, wormwood, ginger and sugar in a saucepan. Bring to a boil. Remove from heat, stir in the gin, pour into tankards, and dust with freshly grated nutmeg.

Serves 2

Flip

1 egg   2 teaspoons sugar
1 pint dry sherry   1 teaspoon butter
½ teaspoon ground nutmeg

Have ready two large (about 1 quart) earthenware jugs or measuring cups. In one jug, beat the egg with 1 tablespoon of the sherry. Heat the remaining sherry in a saucepan with the nutmeg, sugar, and butter, until the mixture is nearly boiling. Gradually add the hot sherry mixture to the egg mixture, stirring rapidly to keep it from curdling. "Flip" the mixture by pouring it rapidly back and forth between the two jugs until it is creamy and well-frothed.

Serves 2

Variation: For a more plebeian but equally authentic Flip, substitute a good brown ale for the sherry. William Kitchiner, among others, calls this "A Yard of Flannel."

Raspberry Shrub

Bonden had other sources for his happiness; for those who don't, we recommend this drink—it is sufficient in itself.

1½ pints fresh raspberries   1 cup brandy
 ½ cup sugar   1 teaspoon lemon juice

Crush the raspberries and strain the juice through a jelly bag or a very fine strainer (you will have about 2 cups of juice). Add the sugar, brandy and lemon juice, and stir well. Bottle and set in a cool place. It will be fit for use in about a week, and it improves with longer keeping.

Makes about 3 cups

Arrack-Punch

'Killick!'

'Sir?' answered Killick, appearing within the second.

'Bring the Doctor the best punch-bowl and everything necessary. . . .'

'Punch-bowl it is, sir; and the kettle is already on the boil,' said Killick. . . .

'And Killick,' said Stephen, 'instead of the lemons, pray bring up the smaller keg from my cabin: you may take it from its sailcloth jacket.' . . .

'Which I never knew you had it,' said Killick with an odd mixture of admiration and resentment as he stood away from the barrel, oak with polished copper bands and on its head the stamp Bronte XXX *with an engraved plate below* To that eminent physician Dr Stephen Maturin, whose abilities are surpassed only by the gratitude of those who have benefited from them: Clarence.

'Bronte!' cried Jack. 'Can it be . . . ?'

'It can indeed. This is triple-refined Sicilian juice from his own estate,
a present from Prince William. I had meant to keep it for Trafalgar Day,
but seeing this is a special occasion perhaps we may draw off an ounce or
so and drink the immortal memory tonight.'

The steaming bowl, the melted sugar, the heady smell of arrack.

—The Nutmeg of Consolation, *196–7*

Ah, arrack. We searched and struggled long and hard.

According to the *Oxford English Dictionary,* arrack is "a name applied in Eastern countries to any spirituous liquor of native manu-
facture; especially, that distilled from the fermented sap of the
coco-palm, or from rice and sugar, fermented with the coco-nut
juice."

The arrack used in Arrack-Punch came chiefly from Batavia, having made its way to Europe via the East India trade. It was wildly
popular in both England and America well into the nineteenth century—in fact, it was the (ar)rack-punch at Vauxhall that so demoral-
ized Jack's contemporary, Jos Sedley, in *Vanity Fair.*

We have reason to believe that arrack was still available in the
United States as late as the 1960s. No longer. The term is still applied
to various liquors (including an anisette-flavored Israeli *eau-de-vie*),
but the true Batavia arrack has proved elusive. Not that we haven't
tried. Our agents in Sweden (where it is a component of Punsch, the
national drink) produced historical information but not a drop of the
actual stuff; our courier in Indonesia was even less successful.

Bound and determined to produce Arrack-Punch in some form,
we turned to Mary Randolph's *Virginia Housewife,* according to
which "a Substitute for Arrack" may be made by dissolving "two scruples flowers of Benzoin, in one quart of good rum." The search for arrack was at an end; the search for benzoin had begun. After many
vicissitudes and humiliations, we obtained (through means which we
dare not reveal) a small amount of tincture of benzoin—which we are
happy to report is not actually poisonous, though it does contain
traces of a few "controlled" substances.

Having no better rule to go by, we adopted Mrs. Randolph's mea-
surement and mixed our tincture with good rum at the rate of ¾ teaspoon (roughly equivalent to 2 scruples—or 1 drachm) to the quart.
It fizzed a bit, and produced exciting swirls and a most aromatic
brew.

If you cannot get benzoin, or are concerned about ingesting it, the closest approximation we can suggest is vanilla: 2 teaspoons added to a quart of rum produces an effect reminiscent of benzoin, which in turn is presumably reminiscent of arrack. Who knows?

A note about the apparent solecism of the lemon juice: it seems incongruous, at sea, to make punch with "concentrated" bottled lemon juice, when fresh lemons are actually available; but it is a measure of Stephen's generous affection for Jack that on the momentous occasion of selling him the *Surprise* he chooses to seal the bargain by sharing his precious legacy from Lord Nelson's lemon groves.

½ cup sugar
¼ cup water
   Zest of 1 large lemon
2 whole cloves
½ teaspoon whole coriander
   Juice of 2 large lemons (or 3
      tablespoons Bronte XXX
      Triple-Refined Sicilian
      Juice)

1 cup arrack
1 cup brandy
2 cups boiling water

In a small saucepan, stir the sugar into the ¼ cup water. Cook over medium heat until the sugar is completely dissolved.

Put the lemon zest and the spices into a bowl. Pour the sugar syrup over them and let them steep for a few minutes.

Add the lemon juice, arrack, brandy, and boiling water, and stir well. Strain.

Stephen and Jack quite often drink this iced, but it is also famous for being brewed with much ceremony and drunk hot; and very comfortable it is, on a cold evening. It can also be bottled and kept for future use.

Makes 1 quart

Claret-Cup

Raffles' hearers, ordinarily fed much earlier in the day, were hungry, clam-
mily hot and thirsty . . . any speech would have been too long for them; . . .
and when Reade turned pale the Governor came to an abrupt close, skip-
ping five paragraphs and drinking to their happy return in ice-cold claret-
cup, considered more healthy in this climate for invalids and the young.

—The Nutmeg of Consolation, 72

Aside from its use in flavoring this drink, borage is well worth growing for its edible flowers and its power to inspire courage and forget-
fulness in those who partake of it. If you cannot get borage, you may
substitute an equal amount of cucumber peel, but do not let it steep
more than 10 minutes, as the taste quickly becomes overpowering.

Zest of ½ lemon	1 cup soda water
3 teaspoons sugar	1 sprig fresh borage, lightly
Boiling water	crushed
1 pint claret	1 whole nutmeg
¼ cup brandy	Ice

Put the lemon zest and sugar in a jug. Add enough boiling water to
moisten thoroughly, stir, cover, and let steep for a few minutes.

Add the claret, brandy, soda water, and borage. Grate in a sprinkling
of nutmeg. Let it sit for 10 minutes. Add ice, stir well, and strain into
glasses.

Serves 4–6

Grog

'This grog is the vilest brew, even with my cochineal and ginger in it:
how I long for wine again . . . a good full-bodied red.'

—H.M.S. Surprise, 367

From *The Sailor's Word Book:*

> Grog: A drink issued in the navy, consisting of one part of spirits
> diluted with three of water; introduced 1740 by Admiral Vernon, as

a check to intoxication by mere rum, and said to have been named for his grogram coat. . . . The addition of sugar and lemon juice now makes grog an agreeable anti-scorbutic.

The *Oxford English Dictionary* quotes one Trotter (1781) as having written:

A mighty bowl on deck he drew,
   And filled it to the brink;
Such drank the *Burford*'s gallant crew,
   And such the gods shall drink.
The sacred robe which Vernon wore
   Was drenched within the same;
And hence his virtues guard our shore,
   And Grog derives its name.

Admiral Vernon's original formula is for "three-water" grog. At various points in the novels, Jack and crew are either so hard up as to be drinking four-water or well-enough-off for two-water; fortunately they are never reduced to the final ignominy of seven-water. In any proportion, grog was the high point of the seaman's diet. What it was that made Stephen's grog so "vile" that he felt compelled to disguise it with cochineal and ginger, one can only speculate.

½ cup rum	1 teaspoon ground ginger (optional)
1½ cups water	
2 tablespoons lemon juice	¼ teaspoon finely pounded
2 tablespoons sugar	cochineal (optional)

Mix all ingredients.

Serves 1

Milk-Punch

'Is there anything to eat or drink in the boat?'
'Which Killick put up some milk-punch and pickled seal, sir, in case you wasn't dead,' said Bonden. 'And we have our rations.'
'Tell him punch and seal, then.'   —The Far Side of the World, *287*

⅔ cup brandy	2 cups milk, warmed
1⅓ cups rum	3 cups water
Juice of 2 lemons	4 tablespoons sugar
Zest of 1 lemon	Pinch of ground nutmeg

Combine all ingredients and let stand 2 hours. Strain through a jelly bag until the liquid runs clear. Bottle and keep 2 weeks before drinking. This punch can become highly effervescent with long keeping, so open with great care.

Makes 1 quart

Negus

'Thank you, thank you, Mercy dear; I am infinitely obliged to you. Tell me, ... diga me, would you be a good creature, bona creatura, and fetch me some iced negus? Sangria colda? Thirst, soif, very thirst, I do assure you, my dear.'   —Master and Commander, *341–2*

Though Jack seems to have preferred it iced as a rule (understandable in the climate of Port Mahon), this lovely drink, named for its inventor, Colonel Francis Negus, was more often served hot.

1 pint medium-dry sherry or port	1 pint boiling water
2 tablespoons sugar	whole nutmeg
Juice and grated zest of 1 lemon	

Put the sherry, sugar, lemon juice and zest into a jug. Add the boiling water and stir until the sugar is dissolved. Pour into glasses or tankards and grate a little fresh nutmeg into each.

Serves 4

Lemon Shrub

'What the Doctor would say, was he here, I do not know,' said Killick.
'He would carry on something cruel about folk risking the pulmony: he
would say you ought to be in your cot.'
　　'Give me a glass of hot lemon shrub, will you, Killick?' said Jack. . . .
　　'I got to hang the wipes out first, ain't I?' said Killick.

—The Ionian Mission, *158*

Zest of 1 lemon	¾ cup sugar
½ cup lemon juice	2 cups rum

Combine all ingredients, stir well, bottle and set aside in a cool place.
It will be ready to drink after about a week.

To serve, mix 2–3 parts boiling water to 1 part Shrub.

Makes about 3 cups

Rum-Punch

The loyal toast being proposed, Canning leapt to his feet, struck his head
against a beam and collapsed into his chair as though pole-axed. . . . Jack
called for the punch, . . . and administered a tot with a medical air, ob-
serving, 'We are privileged to drink the King seated in the Navy, sir; we
may do so without the least disrespect. Few people know it however—
quite recent—it must seem very strange.'
　　'Yes. Yes.' said Canning, staring heavily straight at Pullings. 'Yes. I re-
member now.' Then, as the punch spread new life throughout his vitals he
smiled round the table and said, 'What a green hand I must look to all you
gentlemen.'　　　　　　　　　　　　　　　　　　—Post Captain, *270–1*

1 lemon	1 cup rum
1 sugar lump	¼ cup brandy
2 tablespoons sugar (or more,	2 cups boiling water
to taste)	

Rub the lemon with the sugar lump. Peel the zest and squeeze the juice from the lemon. Warm the lemon zest, brandy, rum, and all the sugar in a saucepan. Remove from heat, carefully set the mixture aflame and let it burn for 2 minutes, then cover tightly to extinguish the flames. Pour in the lemon juice and the boiling water and stir well. Cover and let stand 5–10 minutes. Serve hot, adding more sugar if necessary.

Serves 4

Iced Lemonade, Heightened with Marsala

Jack, listening with what attention he could spare from his tankard of iced lemonade heightened with marsala, heard of coral reefs running out as much as twenty miles on the east coast.   —Treason's Harbour, *48*

4 large lemons	1 quart boiling water
12 sugar lumps	¾ cup sweet marsala

Rub the lemons hard with one or two of the sugar lumps. Peel the zest from one lemon, squeeze the juice from all 4, and combine in a bowl with all the sugar. Pour in the boiling water and stir until the sugar is dissolved. Add the marsala. Cool, strain, and serve over ice.

Serves 4

Note: Our sugar lumps are the equivalent of 1 teaspoon apiece—if you are using a different size, adjust accordingly.

Under False Colours

They pledged one another in the sloe-juice, vinegar and sugar of lead that had been sold to Jack as wine.   —Master and Commander, *110*

. . . and then drank to him in the thin harsh purple liquid that passed for claret in the Worcester's *wardroom.*

Thin though it was, the claret was nothing like so disagreeable as the substance called port that ended the meal. This probably had the same basis of vinegar and cochineal, but Ananias, the Gosport wine-merchant, had added molasses, raw spirit, and perhaps a little sugar of lead, a false date and a flaming lie by way of a label. —The Ionian Mission, *36*

We did some experimenting along these lines, using the juice of un-ripe beach plums as a substitute for sloe-juice, and replacing the poisonous sugar of lead (lead acetate) with a more innocuous raw cane sugar. We did succeed in producing some very thin harsh purple liquids—but no amount of seasoning, flavoring, fermentation, or aging made any of them remotely drinkable. Even in the interests of pure research, we cannot bring ourselves to print a recipe for any of these dreadful concoctions. Our profound sympathy to Jack.

Bitters

'Killick,' he called, 'rouse out a glass of bitters, will you? And have one for yourself while you are about it.' The gunroom's dinner was earlier than Jack's usual hour, and he wanted to do honour to their feast.

'Which there ain't none left, sir,' replied Killick, pleased for the first time that day. 'Don't you remember the case dropped into the hold in consequence of the orlop-scuttle had been shifted, which they never told us, and was stove: so there ain't none left—all wasted, not even tasted, all gone into the bilge.'

'All wasted

Not even tasted

All gone into the bilge,' he repeated in a lugubrious chant.

—The Ionian Mission, *265*

Bitters could denote almost any combination of bitter herbs and aromatics infused in almost any kind of spirits. Used early as a tonic (to ward off fevers) and an anthelmintic (to kill worms), it later became popular for its stomachic properties; and was used both to stimulate the appetite before, and to settle the digestion after, a meal.

2 cups brandy (or whisky or
   gin)
3 dried juniper berries, crushed
   Pinch of cardamom seeds
   Pinch of coriander seeds
   Pinch of caraway seeds

Pinch of cochineal
Pinch of centaury
Pinch of dried chamomile
1 sprig fresh wormwood
1 sprig fresh rosemary
Zest of ¼ lemon

Combine all ingredients. Bottle and let steep for 2 months before
using.

Makes 1 pint

Wines and Liquors

Aguardiente
: Literally, burning (ardent) water—i.e., liquid containing enough alcohol to set aflame; a Spanish or Portuguese brandy, distilled from local red wine.

Banyuls
: From the Banyuls region of the Pyrénées-Orientales, a naturally sweet red or rosé wine made from the Grenache Noir grape. When it ages it develops a characteristic and highly prized flavor known as "rancio" among Catalan cognoscenti.

blackstrap
: Sailors' slang for the rough red wines ("fierce local wines") of the Mediterranean. John Masefield says "to be stationed in the Mediterranean was 'to be black-strapped.'"

Canary
: A light, sweet sack from the Canary Islands off the Northwest coast of Africa.

Chambertin
: Côte de Nuits (Burgundy), originally grown by one Bertin, at Gevrey-Chambertin, just outside Dijon—the name is a contraction of Champ de Bertin ("Bertin's field").

Chambolle-
Musigny
: Côte de Nuits (Burgundy) produced in the commune of Chambolle-Musigny, slightly south of

Gevrey-Chambertin. Musigny, dating back to the early twelfth century, is the most famous of its vineyards and produces its finest wines.

Château Lafite	One of the three greatest clarets (Bordeaux) of all, from the Pauillac commune in the Haut-Médoc.
Chian wine	Wine from the Greek Island of Chios, in the Eastern Aegean, celebrated in the works of Plutarch, Horace and Pomponius Mela.
Claret	The English name for the wines of Bordeaux—from the French *clairet,* "clear, light, bright." Originally referred to yellowish or light-red wines; by about 1600, it came to apply to red wines in general, then gradually narrowed to its present meaning.
Constantia	Constantia Berg—a sweet, heavy Muscat dessert wine from the western Cape province of South Africa. One of the most expensive and sought-after wines in the world during the nineteenth century.
Diamant	A medium-sweet white Rioja.
Fombrauges	One of the lesser-known Saint-Émilions.
Frontignan	(or Frontignac) A famous, intensely sweet and aromatic French Muscat wine, slightly fortified, from Hérault, just north of the Pyrenees.
Haut-Brion	One of the great clarets, the "uncrowned king of Graves."
Hermitage	A Côtes du Rhône, one of the foremost wines of France and a favorite at the Russian court; supposedly named for the hermit Henri-Gaspart de Sterimberg, who had brought the first Syrah vine from Persia on his return from the Albigensian Crusade.
Hollands	Also known as the Dutch gin *genever,* which in turn takes its name from the juniper berry from which it is distilled.
Latour	Another of the three greatest clarets of all, from the Pauillac commune in the Haut-Médoc.

Madeira	This name belongs to several fortified wines made on the island of Madeira. Smoky and rather sweet, they are famous for traveling extremely well. Unlike most wines, they actually benefit from the rigors (agitation and extremes of temperature) of a sea-voyage; the most desirable Madeiras were those which had been "sent round the Cape."
Malmsey	The earliest, rarest, sweetest, and traditionally considered the finest, of the Madeiras. Malmsey (of Duke of Clarence fame) is made from the Malvasia grape, which was brought to Madeira from Crete in the fifteenth century.
Margaux	The third of the three greatest clarets, from Margaux in the Haut-Médoc.
Marsala	A sweet Sicilian wine, first produced in 1775 for the English market by the Englishman John Woodhouse.
right Nantes or right Nantz	A brandy from Nantes in the Loire valley.
Pontet-Canet	A lesser claret, a fifth-growth Médoc from the Pauillac region.
Priorato	A dry Spanish table wine with a high alcohol content—named for the priors of a fifteenth-century Carthusian monastery on the east coast of Spain (there is also a sweet fortified Priorato, more like a port).
resiny wine	Presumably a Retsina, the resinated wine of ancient Greece, which originally acquired its taste from the pine-tarred amphorae in which it was stored.
Sillery	A dry white wine from the area around the village of Sillery in the Champagne region, in the Reims arrondissement of the Marne. The Marquis de Sillery, in the seventeenth century, was the first to ship sparkling Champagne to England; nevertheless Sillery itself is a still wine.

St.-Julien	Another claret from the Haut-Médoc, dark, full-bodied, and mellow.
Tavel	A Côtes du Rhône, much loved by the popes of Avignon, a light and aromatic wine. Philippe le Bel, in the early fourteenth century, said "the only good wine is from Tavel."
tent	A Spanish *vino Tinto,* deep red and low in alcohol, often used as a sacramental wine.
toddy	The sap from any of several types of palm trees, especially the wild date, the coconut, and the palmetto; also a wine distilled from the same sap.
Tokay	"King of wines, wine of kings"—Aszú or Szamorodni—the mystical dessert wine of Hungary, once served at the court of the Roi Soleil. According to Lord Dunsany *(My Talks with Dean Spanley)* "this rare wine, that until a little while ago was only uncorked by command of Emperors of Austria," could reveal the secrets of transmigration.

When the Stormy Winds do Blow

Ballad Broadsides; Loyal Songs, 1686

You Gen- tle- men of Eng- land. That live at home at ease. How lit- tle do you

think up- on The dan- gers of the seas. Give ear un- to the mar- i- ners. And

they will plain-ly show. All the cares and the fears When the storm-y winds do blow.

The sailor must have courage.
  No danger he must shun:
In every kind of weather
  His course he still must run:
Now mounted on the top-mast.
  How dreadful ' tis below:
Then we ride, as the tide.
    When the stormy winds do blow.

If enemies oppose us.
  And England is at war
With any foreign nation.
  We fear not wound nor scar.
To humble them. come on. lads.
  Their flags we' ll soon lay low:
Clear the way for the fray.
    Tho' the stormy winds do blow.

Sometimes in Neptune' s bosom
  Our ship is toss' d by waves.
And every man expecting
  The sea to be our graves;
Then up again she' s mounted.
  And down again so low.
In the waves. on the seas.
    When the stormy winds do blow.

But when the danger' s over.
  And safe we come on shore.
The horrors of the tempest
  We think of them no more:
The flowing bowl invites us.
  And joyfully we go.
All the day drink away.
    Tho' the stormy winds do blow.

CHAPTER FIVE

In the Heat of Battle (Dishes Eaten Cold)

He will spend the night plying to windward, while we lie to. His people will be worn out for the morning action. Ours must get all the rest we can manage: and food. Mr Stourton, since we have lost our purser, I must ask you to see to the serving-out of the provisions. Let the men make a good hearty supper—there are some hams in my store-room. Where is my steward? Pass the word for—'

'Here I am sir, and have been a-standing by the bitts this half-glass and more,' said Killick in his disagreeable injured whine, 'a-holding of this sanglewich and this here mug of wine.'

The burgundy went down more gratefully than any wine he had ever drunk, strengthening his heart, dispelling weariness.

—H.M.S. Surprise, *316*–7

Immediately afterwards the hands were piped to dinner, and at the same time the drum beat for the officers. This pleased Jack: Lambert meant to take advantage of the last minutes before the galley fires were put out in clearing the ship for action. He and Jack might differ about manoeuvring, but they were of the same mind about going into battle with a full belly.   —The Fortune of War, *109*

'What is that frightful noise, that great resounding crash?'
'We call it slapping. Some of our northern ships do it when they stem

these short hollow seas. It makes the Mediterranean builders laugh.'

'Perilous would it be, at all?'

Jack whistled. 'Why, as long as we do not spring a butt, we are not likely to founder. . . .'

He returned to the task of driving a heavy, partially-waterlogged and possibly disintegrating ship through a savage chaotic cross-sea, the Mediterranean at its sudden worst. . . .

At four bells Dr Maturin, changing into his old crusted black coat, crept down to make his rounds of the sick-bay: this was earlier than his usual time, but it was rare that a heavy, prolonged blow did not bring a fair number of casualties. . . .

'This will take us until after dinner, gentlemen,' he said. . . .

'In any case there will be nothing hot for dinner,' said Mr Lewis. 'The galley fires are out.'

'They say there are four feet of water in the hold,' said Mr Dunbar.

'They love to make our flesh creep,' said Stephen.

—The Ionian Mission, *249–51*

Jack may have felt strongly about going into battle with a full belly, but it wasn't always possible for the contents of that belly to be hot. When clearing for action, or when wallowing in gales and hurricanoes, it was vitally important to douse the galley fires, and there was not always time to prepare a hot meal before doing so. Men and officers alike made do with whatever cold provender was available; which might include leftover pudding, hard tack, raw meat, and the relatively newfangled "sanglewich."

A word about the possible origins of the "sanglewich": There is, of course, the popular story of its invention circa 1765 by the Earl of Sandwich, who supposedly could not bring himself to leave the gaming-table long enough to eat a proper meal, and sustained himself for twenty-four hours on nothing more than pieces of cold meat between two slices of bread. But there is earlier evidence of a sandwich-like phenomenon. Charles Carter, in 1730, gave a recipe for Travelling Loaves: ". . . take Fowl, Rabits, Neck of Lamb, roast it off cold, and stuff large French Loaves of three Pence apiece, or other

Bread, cut off the Top, scoop out most of the Crumb; you may then insert your Meat or a Sallad Mogundy, or sliced Tongue or Ham; and as you travel you may eat wherever on the Road, or in your Coach. . . ."

Actually, in 1810 one Alexander Hunter, in his *Culina Famulatrix Medicinae,* produced the earliest putative sandwich citation of all. According to his somewhat biased interpretation of Suetonius, when the emperor Claudius asked the Senate, *"Rogo vos, quis potest sine of-fula vivere?"* ("I ask you, who can live without tidbits?"), Hunter insists that the indispensable tidbit in question is actually an early sandwich. While taking his pronouncement with a healthy dose of skepticism, one must nevertheless admit that the combination of meat and bread has always been a practical and natural one.

A Cold Collation in the Gunroom

Potted Meat   Anchovies   Pickled Gherkins

The Doctor was already in the gunroom, and he and the other officers wel-comed Jack with potted meat, anchovies, hard-boiled eggs and ham, pick-led gherkins, onions, mangoes; they were as hospitable as could be.

—The Nutmeg of Consolation, *143*

Potted Meat

This method of preserving meat dates back to Elizabethan times and has not changed much since.

1 pound lean beef such as shoulder or round, cut in 2-inch cubes
¼ pound bacon, cut into small pieces
2 tablespoons water
2 tablespoons red wine

½ pound (⅛ recipe) Hot Water Paste (p. 269)
¼ teaspoon mace
   Dash cayenne
13 tablespoons clarified butter (approximately)
   Salt and pepper

Preheat the oven to 300°.

Put the beef, bacon, water and red wine into a crock. On a floured board, roll out the pastry slightly larger than the top edge of the crock. Lay the pastry over the crock and crimp it securely over the edges, sealing the crock as tightly as possible. Set in a shallow water bath and bake for 3 hours (replenishing the water periodically if necessary).

Take the crock out of the oven. Remove and discard (or eat) the crust. Strain the meat, reserving the liquid. Pound the meat to a fine purée. Add the mace, cayenne, 3 tablespoons of the clarified butter, salt and pepper to taste, and enough of the cooking liquid (about 3 table-spoons) to moisten the meat (the less liquid you add, the longer the meat will keep).

Pack the meat tightly into a buttered crock. Pour the rest of the clarified butter over it so that the meat is completely sealed (depending on the width of the crock, you may need a bit more butter—the layer should be at least ¼ inch thick). Set in a cool, dry place and keep for at least two weeks before using.

Makes 1½ cups

Anchovies

The pickling of anchovies was a brutal business. According to Mary Randolph's recipe for curing herrings, "the best method" is to "throw them alive into the brine; let them remain twenty-four hours. . . . The brine the herrings drink before they die, has a wonderful effect in preserving their juices: when one or two years old, they are equal to anchovies."

Even had we been sufficiently hard-hearted, we would not have been able to duplicate the process exactly, because it is no longer possible to get the necessary Salt-petre or Salprunella (which, despite Dr. Johnson's fulminations to the contrary, are *not* identical, one being a nitrate, the other a nitrite) for private pickling purposes.

We reproduce here Hannah Glasse's somewhat gentler recipe:

To make Anchovies

To a Peck of Sprats, two Pounds of common Salt, a quarter of a Pound of Bay-Salt, four Pounds of Salt-Petre, two Ounces of Salprunella, two penny-worth of Cochineal, pound all in a Mortar, put them in a Stone-pot, a Row of Sprats, and a Layer of your Compound, and so on to the Top alternately. Press them hard down, and cover them close, and let them stand six Months, and they will be fit for Use. Observe that your Sprats be very fresh, and don't wash nor wipe them, but just take them as they come out of the Water.

We didn't feel compelled to follow this too faithfully. We were fortunate in being able to obtain very fresh Sprats, but we did both wash and wipe them; in fact, in defiance of tradition, we even gutted them. We had about a quarter of the quantity Hannah calls for, so we scaled down the above recipe accordingly, and simply eliminated the unavailable. Despite the lack of nitrites, our anchovies were a becoming shade of red, thanks to the cochineal (our interpretation of a half-pennyworth came out to ½ teaspoon). We cannot yet report as to their long-term keeping qualities, but at last tasting, after six weeks in a cool dark cellar, they were chewy and compressed and very salty indeed: everything an anchovy ought to be.

(A small note here as to which fish is which: technically, the sprat is a member of the sardine/herring/pilchard family, but the word is also used generically to denote any small fish of similar ilk—including the anchovy. And for curing purposes they are all more or less interchangeable.)

Pickled Gherkins

The cooks of the late eighteenth century covered their pickles close by means of "a Bladder, and a Leather." Meg Dods elaborates: "Pickles are most safely prepared in stone-ware vessels; but they must, at all events, be kept in small glass or stone jars well stopped, and the corks or *bungs* must be wrapped round with bladder or leather, with an upper covering of the same, if they are to be long kept." The bladder in question was a piece of sheep or ox bladder, which, in combination with the stronger and less-porous leather, served to seal the jar and keep out intruders.

2 pounds very small pickling cucumbers	1 teaspoon whole allspice
1 cup plus 1 tablespoon sea salt	1 teaspoon mustard seed
Water	2 bay leaves
1 quart white vinegar	1 knob fresh ginger, about 1 inch long
½ nutmeg, cut in pieces	1 teaspoon peppercorns
1 teaspoon whole cloves	¼ teaspoon fennel
1 teaspoon mace	¼ teaspoon dill seed

Scrub the cucumbers. Dissolve 1 cup of the salt in 2 quarts water. Add the cucumbers and let them stand for 2 hours.

Remove the cucumbers from the salt water and pack them into a crock. Combine all the remaining ingredients with 1⅓ cups water.

Pour the resulting brine over the cucumbers. Weight the cucumbers to keep them submerged (if you do not have a bladder and a leather you can use a plastic bag partly filled with water). Seal the crock and store in a cool dark place for 2 weeks before using.

Makes 2 pounds

Dog's Body/Pease-Pudding

Fenton, the second lieutenant, maintained that it was great nonsense to say
' 'Im called dog's body. 'Tis pease-pudden really, but we say dog's body.
You—like—'im, dog's body?' to a man who could play such a hand at whist
and beat all comers at the chess-board. —The Surgeon's Mate, *195–6*

On deck Captain Aubrey, eating a piece of cold or at least luke-warm pease
pudding with one hand and holding on to the aftermost maintopgallant
standing backstay with the other, did indeed urge his ship on with con-
tractions of his belly-muscles and a continuous effort of his will.
—The Far Side of the World, *138*

Pease-pudding in any form may not, on the face of it, seem to be in-spired fare; but these are both solid, satisfying, and comforting messes to have under one's belt on the eve of a battle or in the teeth of a black squall.

(For information on preparing and cooking puddings, see "About Puddings," p. 273.)

1 pound dried split peas	1 teaspoon salt
¼ pound (1 stick) butter	Pepper
4 tablespoons flour	

Tie the peas loosely in a pudding-cloth. Place in a large pot with boiling water to cover. Simmer, covered, 1½ hours. As the peas cook, you may occasionally need to add more boiling water. It is also a good idea to lift the pudding-cloth now and then to keep it from sticking to the bottom of the pot.

Remove the pudding-cloth from the pot and place it in a strainer. When it is cool enough to handle, squeeze out as much liquid as possible.

Untie the cloth and scrape the peas into a bowl. Add the butter, flour, and salt, and pepper to taste. Mix well. Put the mixture back into the cloth and tie it as tightly as possible. Place the pudding in a fresh pot of boiling water and cook for 1 hour.

Remove the pudding-cloth from the pot, untie it, and carefully turn the pudding out into a serving dish.

Serves 8 as a side dish

Variation: For a less delicate, more seamanlike Dog's Body, use 6 ounces of salt pork, cut in ½-inch dice, instead of butter.

Treacle Pudding

The gunroom had meant to regale their Captain on fresh turtle to begin with and then a variety of other delights, but the early extinction of the galley fires, put out as soon as the men's salt beef had been boiled, had reduced them to a cold, or sometimes luke-warm, collation; however, it included soused pig's face, one of Jack's favourite dishes, and treacle pudding, which he always said ate better if it did not scald your gullet.

—The Reverse of the Medal, *106*

The original treacle, known as theriac or Venice treacle, was a dark and sticky medicinal compound dating back to the Middle Ages, made up of some seventy-odd drugs and other dubious substances, including opium and pounded viper's flesh. It was supposed to be an antidote to poisons and various malignant diseases.

In the seventeenth century (presumably because of its superficial resemblance to the earlier treacle) the name was given to another dark and sticky substance, the uncrystallized syrup that was a by-product of the refining of sugar. This treacle, known today as London black treacle, is what would have been used for Treacle Pudding or Treacle-Dowdy (p. 84) in Jack's time.

To confuse matters still further, the word has since migrated in two other spurious directions. The first, yet another dark and sticky substance, is molasses, the syrup drained from raw sugar. Some reference works define molasses and treacle as synonymous, but we must strenuously disagree. Treacle is distinctly darker, more viscous, more pungent, and much more assertive than molasses.

Ranging yet farther afield is the present-day practice of referring to golden syrup as treacle. We are baffled. Granted that golden syrup is also a by-product of the refining process for sugar—and that it is sticky—it has nothing else in common with treacle, being pale where the other is dark, and cloyingly sweet where the other is harsh.

(For information on preparing and cooking puddings, see "About Puddings," p. 273.)

½ pound soft fresh bread crumbs	1 egg
1 cup flour	1 inch-long knob fresh ginger, peeled and grated
¼ pound suet, finely grated	Juice and grated zest of 1 lemon
2 tablespoons treacle	
3 tablespoons sugar	½ cup milk

In a large bowl, combine all ingredients thoroughly.

Scrape the batter into a greased 6-cup pudding-basin. Tie a well-floured cloth over the pudding. Place the pudding in a pot of boiling water, cover, and steam for 2½ hours.

Unmold and serve hot, accompanied by Lemon Sauce (p. 265).

Serves 12

Cold Duff

See Plum-Duff (p. 105)

Thin-Sliced, Raw Salt Beef

There was no point in even trying to make ourselves believe that what we were doing bore any resemblance to the raw salt-horse in question, but as a purely symbolic gesture we thin-sliced and ate some of our modern corned beef raw. If you like raw beef (we are evenly divided on the issue), it's not bad at all.

Cold Mutton

See Leg of Mutton (p. 191)

Adagio
from the Sonata, Op. 13

Johann Nepomuk Hummel
(1778-1837)

CHAPTER SIX

Jack Ashore

Presently Captain Aubrey and Dr Maturin were asked to dinner at Mapes; they were pronounced excellent young men, most agreeable company, perfectly well-bred, and a great addition to the neighbourhood. It was clear to Sophia, however, that poor Dr Maturin needed feeding properly: 'he was quite pale and silent,' she said. But even the tenderest heart, the most given to pity, could not have said the same for Jack. . . . He had eaten everything set before him with grateful voracity, and even Mrs Williams felt something like an affectionate leaning towards him.

'Well,' she said, as their hoof-beats died away in the night, 'I believe that was as successful a dinner-party as I have ever given. Captain Aubrey managed a second partridge—but then they were so very tender. And the floating island looked particularly well in the silver bowl: there will be enough for tomorrow. And the rest of the pork will be delicious, hashed. How well they ate, to be sure: I do not suppose they often have a dinner like that. I wonder at the admiral, saying that Captain Aubrey was not quite the thing. I think he is very much the thing. Sophie, my love, pray tell John to put the port the gentlemen left into a small bottle at once, before he locks up: it is bad for the decanter to leave port-wine in it.'

'Yes, Mama.'

—Post Captain, 33–4

Even Lucky Jack Aubrey cannot spend all of his time at sea. Many of his most memorable meals are eaten on land. The houses, inns, palaces and hovels that he and Stephen visit (or inhabit) may have their own eccentricities, but at least their kitchens are not subject to the restrictions and privations peculiar to shipboard life.

The "set" dinner of the eighteenth century, served *à la française,* was a complex performance in itself. It began with soup and fish—that is, several different kinds of soups and fish, which were placed on the table, in symmetrical arrangements interspersed with ornaments, pyramids of fruit, *entrées* and *entremets,* before the guests were seated. Once the soup was eaten it was replaced by various "removes," ranging from small made-dishes and cakes to whole joints and fowls, all comprising the first course.

The first course was then removed, as was the cloth, under which was a fresh cloth—and now the meal began in earnest. The second course echoed the first in variety and complexity, but the dishes were larger and more ostentatious, roast meats and towering pies, accompanied by salads, vegetables, creams, sweets and jellies. (Meat dishes were sweet as often as they were savory; in fact, sweet and savory foods were served side by side until well into the nineteenth century.)

The final course was dessert, which consisted of more sweets, fruits, cheeses, and sometimes for good measure a few more little meat dishes. Then followed nuts, more fruit, small sweets such as comfits, and port.

Nobody was expected to eat *everything* at one of these dinners; but Jack must have been in his element.

Dinners at the Crown in Port Mahon

Roast Pollo   Solomongundy

THE FIRST DINNER

Ragoo'd Mutton   Alamode Beef   Soused Hog's Face

Stewed Boar   Kickshaws

Roast Pollo

'Mercy! Mercy! Oh, there you are, my dear. What can you bring me to eat, manger, mangiare? Pollo? Cold roast pollo? And a bottle of wine, vino—two bottles of vino . . .'

'Yes, Teniente,' said Mercedes, her eyes rolling in the candlelight and her teeth flashing white.

'Not teniente,' cried Jack, crushing the breath out of her plump, supple body. 'Capitan! Capitano, ha, ha, ha!'   —Master and Commander, *14*

Jack eats this "pollo" cold, but it is wonderful hot, served with its own pan drippings. The recipes of the period call for frequent basting with a great deal of butter; we found it superfluous, perhaps because today's roasting chickens are so much fatter and juicier than their eighteenth-century counterparts.

(For information on spit-roasting, see "About Roasting," p. 282.)

1 large roasting chicken, about
    7 pounds
   Salt and pepper

Stuffing:
¼ pound suet, finely grated
½ pound stale French bread,
    coarsely crumbled (about
    3 cups)
2 ounces ham, coarsely
    chopped

3 chicken livers, finely chopped
   Zest of ¼ lemon, coarsely
    chopped
2 eggs
1 tablespoon chopped fresh
    sage
1 teaspoon chopped fresh
    parsley
½ teaspoon fresh thyme leaves
1 teaspoon salt
¼ teaspoon pepper

Clean the chicken and rub it inside and out with salt and pepper.

Thoroughly combine the remaining ingredients. Fill the cavity and crop of the chicken with the stuffing and sew up or skewer the openings. Truss the chicken securely. Center it on the spit, and set it to roast in front of a clear fire for about 2½ hours.

Serves 6

Solomongundy

As they drew nearer to the town Jack fell silent. 'We will have a pint of sherry at Joselito's for old times' sake,' he said to himself, 'order a handsome dinner at the Crown—a beefsteak pudding, a solomon gundy, and those triangular almond cakes to finish with—and then walk about, looking at the places we used to know, until it is ready.' —The Ionian Mission, *197*

"Solomongundy" is a corruption of "salmagundy," which in turn almost certainly comes from the French *salmigondis,* a stew of leftover meats. There is some suggestion that it may have been named after a lady-in-waiting of Marie de Medicis in the early seventeenth century, but we are inclined to accept the etymology given by Larousse: *sel* (salt) and the Old French *condir* (to season—as in "condiment"). This is all the more plausible, as most sources suggest that *salmigondis* itself comes from *salmis,* a ragoût of half-roasted game. In any case, early in the eighteenth century the dish crossed the Channel and became what Charles Carter in 1730 referred to as "Sallad Mogundy"—

strongly resembling what we now know as Chef's Salad. (To our great glee we discovered that "salad" also comes from the same root as "salt"—as does "sauce," but that's another story.)

Appropriately enough, given its varied contents and origins, Solomongundy also has another, figurative meaning: miscellany . . . hodgepodge . . . olla podrida . . . lobscouse.

By the way, the *Oxford Dictionary of Nursery Rhymes* reports that it was in 1842—on a Monday, naturally—that "Solomon Grundy" was born.

Hannah Glasse gives no fewer than four recipes for "Salamongundy" (in each of which she spells the name differently), and several of them call for Station or Stertian Flowers, i.e., nasturtium blossoms, a spicy and attractive garnish.

1 head romaine or other leaf lettuce, cut in thin strips	2 tablespoons chopped fresh parsley
8 hard-boiled eggs	½ pound snap peas or French beans, blanched
1 pound boneless breast of chicken, cooked, cut in thin strips	10 anchovies (p. 135) or 2 ounces (1 can) flat anchovy fillets
1 pound smoked ham, cut in thin strips	6 tablespoons olive oil
2 pickling cucumbers, peeled and thinly sliced	1 tablespoon vinegar
3 ribs celery, thinly sliced	1 tablespoon lemon juice
3 shallots, peeled and thinly sliced	½ teaspoon dry mustard
2 tablespoons nonpareil capers	Salt and pepper
	Station flowers

Line a large serving dish with the shreds of lettuce. Chop the egg yolks and egg whites separately. Arrange the meats, vegetables, anchovies, yolks, whites, and herbs in pleasing and fanciful groupings.

Combine the oil, vinegar, lemon juice, mustard, and salt and pepper to taste, and mix vigorously. Pour this dressing over the Solomongundy. Garnish with the station flowers.

Serves 6–8

THE FIRST DINNER

'Allow me to press you to a trifle of this ragoo'd mutton, sir,' said Jack.
'Well, if you insist,' said Stephen Maturin. 'It is so very good.'
'It is one of the things the Crown does well,' said Jack. 'Though it is
hardly decent in me to say so. Yet I had ordered duck pie, alamode beef and
soused hog's face as well, apart from the kickshaws. No doubt the fellow
misunderstood. Heaven knows what is in that dish by you, but it is cer-
tainly not hog's face. I said, visage de porco, *many times over. . . . I am*
ashamed of having nothing better to offer you.' —Master and Commander, *34*

Ragoo'd Mutton

But since we have learned from effeminate France
To eat their ragoos as well as to dance,
We are fed up with nothing but vain complaisance.
                    —R. Leveridge, "The Roast Beef of Old England"

We were dismayed to discover that we could not get mutton—in
fact, some of our sources told us it was illegal in the United States. We
are still not entirely convinced that we couldn't have obtained it
through fair means or foul; but since much of the lamb available here
is old enough to be borderline mutton anyway, we feel we achieved a
reasonable compromise.

Odd though it may seem, it is perfectly proper to use canned oysters if you cannot easily get fresh ones—we consider them the equivalent of the bottled or pickled oysters that were popular in the
eighteenth and nineteenth centuries.

Stock:

1 ounce bacon

¼ cup cider vinegar

1 pound mutton bones

1 medium onion, peeled and quartered

1 medium carrot, peeled and cut in large pieces

½ teaspoon black peppercorns

½ teaspoon white peppercorns

3 whole cloves

Pinch of mace

1 ounce stale French or Italian bread, toasted very dark

Few sprigs of fresh parsley

Few sprigs of fresh thyme

Few sprigs of fresh savory

1½ quarts water

Ragoo:

2–3 pounds boneless mutton lamb, preferably leg or shoulder, cut in egg-sized pieces

Flour for dredging

Fat (lard, oil, dripping, slush, etc.) for browning and frying

3 medium onions, peeled and cut in 1-inch pieces

2 medium white turnips, peeled and cut in 1-inch pieces

2 large carrots, peeled and cut in 2-inch pieces

1 rib celery, cut in 1-inch pieces

1 cup red wine

6 ounces mushrooms, quartered

4 tablespoons Mushroom Ketchup (p. 269)

Salt and pepper

1 anchovy fillet, finely minced

2 tablespoons chopped fresh parsley

1 recipe (about 3 dozen) Forcemeat Balls (p. 267)

1½ dozen oysters, shucked, or ½ pint canned oysters

Steep the bacon in the vinegar for 30 minutes. Reserving the vinegar, place the bacon and all the other stock ingredients in a pot. Cover the pot, bring to a boil, uncover, and simmer until the stock is reduced by half (about 1 hour). Strain.

Dredge the meat in the flour. In a large stewpot, heat 2 tablespoons of fat and brown the meat, a few pieces at a time, on all sides, adding more fat as necessary.

Remove the meat, and in the same pot brown the onions, turnips, carrots and celery, adding more fat if necessary. Deglaze the pot with the wine.

Return the meat to the pot and add the stock, mushrooms, Mushroom Ketchup, reserved vinegar, and salt and pepper to taste. Cover and bring to a boil. Simmer until the meat is tender (about 1 hour for lamb, a little longer for mutton).

When the meat is nearly ready, add the anchovy and the parsley. Let the Ragoo continue to simmer gently.

Heat 2 tablespoons of the fat in a skillet. Fry the Forcemeat Balls until they are nicely browned on all sides. Set aside and keep warm. Dredge the oysters in flour and fry them quickly, adding more fat if needed.

To serve, ladle the Ragoo into bowls and garnish with the Forcemeat Balls and oysters.

Serves 6

Alamode Beef

3	pounds shoulder of beef	¾ cup water
¼	pound bacon	12 small onions, peeled and
½	teaspoon mace	scored with a deep "X" at
½	teaspoon ground nutmeg	the root end
½	teaspoon ground cloves	½ pound mushrooms, quar-
½	teaspoon ground thyme	tered
½	teaspoon pepper	Few sprigs of fresh savory
½	cup cider vinegar	Few sprigs of fresh thyme
½	cup flour	1 bay leaf
	Salt and pepper	1 tablespoon butter
1	cup red wine	2 tablespoons finely chopped
1	tablespoon brandy	fresh parsley

Cut the beef into 6 equal pieces.

Cut half the bacon into thin strips about 3 inches long. Mix together mace, nutmeg, cloves, ground thyme, and ½ teaspoon pepper. Dip each bacon strip into the vinegar, then roll it in the spice mixture. (Reserve any remaining vinegar for the sauce.) With a larding needle, lard each piece of beef with several of the prepared strips of bacon, placing them about 1 inch apart.

In a large stewpot, sauté the remaining bacon until the fat is rendered. Remove and set aside.

Season the flour with salt and pepper and dredge the beef. (Reserve any remaining flour for thickening.) Brown the beef in the hot bacon fat.

Pour in the wine, brandy, water, and reserved vinegar, and deglaze the pot. Add the onions, mushrooms, savory, fresh thyme, and bay leaf. Return the bacon to the pot (by this stage we have usually eaten some of the bacon, but we try to save most of it for the sauce). Add salt and pepper to taste.

Cover and bring to a boil. Simmer about 2 hours, or until the beef is very tender.

Remove the beef and the vegetables and keep them warm. Discard the bay leaf.

Work the butter and the reserved flour into a paste. Stir the paste into the sauce with a whisk, add the parsley, and let the sauce simmer for a few minutes to thicken. Slice the beef, arrange it on a platter with the vegetables around it, pour the sauce over it, and so send it away to table.

Serves 6

Soused Hog's Face

'It's all one, sir,' said Killick. 'Miss told me to say the pig weighs twenty-seven and a half pound the quarter, and I am to set the hams to the tub the very minute I come aboard—the souse she put aside in thicky jar, knowing you liked 'un. The white puddings is for the Doctor's breakfast.'

'Very good, Killick, very good indeed,' said Jack. 'Stow 'em away.'

'To think a man's heart could break over a soused hog's face,' he reflected.

—Post Captain, *261–2*

The recipes of the period give the casual impression that once the pig's head has been cooked up it is a simple matter to slip out the skull, somehow leaving the shape of the face intact. Would it were so.

1 pig's head, about 10 pounds,
  cleaned but not skinned
2 pounds (6 cups) white cornmeal
3 cups white wine
3 cups white vinegar
1 cup water

2 bay leaves
1 tablespoon salt
12 peppercorns
1 knob fresh ginger, about 1
  inch long, sliced
1 nutmeg, cut in half

Place the head in a large bucket with half the cornmeal and cold water to cover. Soak 2 hours or longer.

Remove the head from the water, rinse well, and place in a large pot with the remaining cornmeal and water to cover. Bring to a boil, covered, and simmer 3 hours. Remove from the pot. When it is just cool enough to handle, pick all meat from the bones. Reserve the tongue and ears.

Wring out a cloth in warm water. Put all the meat into the cloth and tie up as tightly as possible. Chill until firm.

Combine the wine, vinegar, 1 cup water, and the spices. Untie the cloth and pack the meat into a crock. Add the tongue and ears. Pour the wine mixture over the meat. Weight the meat to keep it submerged (a plastic bag partly filled with water works nicely). Seal the crock and store in a cool dark place for up to 2 weeks before serving.

Serves 6

Stewed Boar

'I have not eaten so well for many a day ... upon my word,' said Stephen Maturin. . . . 'This excellent dish by me, for instance (and I see that they did their best to follow your orders), is jabalí *in Spanish, whereas in Catalan it is* senglar.*'*

'Is it swine's flesh?'

'Wild boar. . . .'

'It is capital eating, to be sure; but I should never have guessed it was swine's flesh. What are these well-tasting soft dark things?'

'There you pose me. They are bolets *in Catalan: but what they are called in English I cannot tell. They probably have no name—no country name, I mean, though the naturalist will always recognize them in the bo-letus edulis of Linnaeus.'*   —Master and Commander, *34–5*

Wild boar is indeed capital eating, as we were delighted to discover. This recipe is based on a traditional Catalan stew. And the well-tasting soft dark things, as it turns out, are commonly known today as cèpes or porcini.

½ pound slab bacon, cut in 1-inch cubes

5 pounds shoulder of boar

1 medium onion, peeled and cut in ½-inch pieces

½ pound fresh mushrooms, quartered

½ cup red wine vinegar

½ cup red wine

2 large plum tomatoes, peeled and diced

½ ounce dried wild mushrooms, soaked in 1 cup hot water

9 juniper berries

1 bay leaf

½ teaspoon peppercorns
Salt

1 pound navy beans, soaked 12 hours in cold water to cover

In a large stewpot, cook the bacon until it is brown and the fat has been rendered. Remove the bacon and set aside.

Over medium heat, brown the boar on all sides in the bacon fat. Remove and set aside.

In the same pot, brown the onion and the fresh mushrooms. Deglaze the pot with the vinegar and the wine. Return the bacon and boar to the pot. Add the tomatoes and the wild mushrooms with their soaking liquid. Add the juniper berries, bay leaf, peppercorns, and salt to taste.

Bring to a boil, reduce heat, cover, and simmer gently for 1 hour. Add the beans and continue to cook until the beans are tender, about 2 hours. Remove the bay leaf.

Serves 10–12

Kickshaws

Having lumped several other dishes under the category of "Kickshaw" (see Kickshaws, p. 37), the idea of producing "some thing" more struck us as redundant. Instead, we offer these two opposing views of the subject, separated by a little over a century.

To make Kickshaws

Make Puff-paste, roll it thin, and if you have any Moulds, work it upon them, make them up with preserved Pippins. You may fill some with Gooseberries, some with Rasberries, or what you please; then close them up, or either bake or fry them; throw grated Sugar over them, and serve them up.

—Hannah Glasse, *The Art of Cookery Made Plain and Easy* (1747)

To make any quelquechose:

Take eggs, and half the quantities of white to yolks. Beat them. Add some cream, currants, cinnamon, cloves, mace, salt, a little ground ginger, spinach, endive and marigold flowers—coarsely chopped. Add well-chopped Pigg's Pettitoes; stir well. Melt butter in a frying pan and cook this mixture well on one side, turn and brown on the other and serve. This can be done with other mixtures of herbs and meats in the eggs . . . flesh, small Birds, sweet Roots, Oysters, Mussels, Cockles, Giblets, Lemons, Oranges, or any Fruits, Pulse or any Sallet herbs whatsoever.

—Gervase Markham, *The English Hous-wife* (1615)

Malta

Polenta   Marchpane

Polenta

They had reached the sitting-room and the little round table upon which Mrs Fielding's supper was laid out: three triangles of cold polenta, a hard-boiled egg, and a jug of lemonade. 'Will you believe it, my dear,' he said, sitting down opposite her and instantly seizing upon one of the triangles, 'that best coat of mine cost eleven guineas. . . .' She poured him a glass of lemonade and watched a little wistfully as he reached out for the egg.

—Treason's Harbour, *234*

Polenta is what you make of it. In its most basic form it is simply cornmeal mush, comfort food, not exciting in itself, but a good bland accompaniment for spicier dishes. Cold and unadorned, it is not particularly appetizing, which makes Mrs. Fielding's meagre supper all the more pathetic.

Mrs. Fielding's resources presumably did not run to butter or cheese, but from a purely gastronomic standpoint we consider them (as well as frying or grilling) a great improvement.

4 cups water
1 teaspoon salt
1 cup coarsely ground Italian
     cornmeal
4 tablespoons butter (optional)

4 tablespoons freshly grated
     Parmesan cheese (op-
     tional)
   Olive oil for frying or
     grilling (optional)

In a heavy saucepan, bring the water to a boil. Add the salt. Gradually add the cornmeal, stirring constantly with a wooden spoon to prevent lumps. Continue cooking over low heat, still stirring constantly, about 20 minutes. The mixture should be smooth and very thick. Remove from heat.

(If you are using butter and cheese, add them now and stir until they are completely melted.)

Rinse a large shallow dish (such as a 9-inch pie plate) with cold water. Pour the hot Polenta into the wet dish (the water will prevent the polenta from sticking) and spread it evenly. It should be about ½ inch thick.

Chill until firm. Cut into triangles.

To fry or grill, dry the triangles on a rack for 20–30 minutes, brush lightly with olive oil on both sides, and fry or grill over high heat until brown and crisp.

Serves 6–8

Marchpane

'Here is a box of Portugal marchpane for you, Killick,' said Stephen.
'Well, I take it kindly that you remembered, sir,' said Killick, who was passionately fond of marchpane.   —The Thirteen-Gun Salute, *71*

Stephen said nothing either for a while, but then observed, 'Pudding. Sure, it starts with pudding or marchpane; then it is the toss of a coin which fails first, your hair or your teeth, your eyes or your ears; then comes impotence, for age gelds a man without hope or reprieve, saving him a mort of anguish.'   —The Truelove, *115*

Marchpane, now more commonly called marzipan, has a long and convoluted history. According to Karen Hess (whose exhaustive research on the subject appears in her wonderful *Martha Washington's Booke of Cookery*), the earliest known recipe appears in a fourteenth-century Catalan manuscript, though other documented references in several cultures date back to the twelfth century. The actual origins and etymology, however, seem to be lost in the mists of Arab antiquity.

Eighteenth-century Marchpane called for a great deal of rose water, which was supposed to counteract the oiliness of the almonds. We have found that the only thing it counteracts is the almond flavor of the confection, which, unlike today's more assertive marzipan, contains no bitter almond extract. We do like our Marchpane to taste of almonds, and we have moderated our use of rose water accordingly.

You may want to try some of these eighteenth-century food dyes: cochineal, beet juice, or cranberry juice for red; spinach, watercress or parsley juices for green; a combination of saffron and turmeric steeped in a little hot water for yellow; burnt sugar for brown. Except for the cochineal, which is startlingly vibrant, the colors are pale and delicate compared to modern commercial food colorings; and they add some interesting subtle overtones to the flavor of the Marchpane.

1 pound blanched almonds	Few drops rose water (op-
2 cups superfine sugar	tional)
2 egg whites	Food coloring (optional—
	see above)

Preheat oven to 150°.

Pound or grind the almonds as fine as you can. (If they become oily, add a little rose water.) Mix in the sugar and the egg whites.

Knead the mixture until it is smooth.

To make flat Marchpane cakes:
Roll the paste out until it is about ¼ inch thick. Cut it into squares or diamonds with a sharp knife, or into shapes with cookie cutters.

To make Marchpane fruits:
Pinch off walnut-size lumps of dough and shape them as best you can (the paste is not very easy to work with—but it *can* be done). Roll out a small piece of the dough until it is ⅛ inch thick, and cut it into leaf shapes with a sharp knife. Press the leaves gently into place on the fruits.

Using a small paint brush and whatever colors you prefer, paint the fruits and leaves to your liking.

Place the Marchpane cakes or fruits on a lightly greased cookie sheet and bake for 40 minutes to 1 hour. Dry them on racks.

Makes 50–75 small cakes

Dinner with Captain Christy-Pallière

Gigot en Croûte   Trifle

'Dinner,' said Captain Christy-Pallière. . . . 'I shall start with a glass of Banyuls and some anchovies, a handful of olives, black *olives; then I believe I may look at Hébert's fish soup, and follow it with a simple langouste in court-bouillon. Possibly his gigot en croûte: the lamb is exquisite now that the thyme is in flower. Then no more than cheese, strawberries, and some trifle with our coffee—a saucer of my English jam, for example. None of your architectural meals, Penhoët; my liver will not stand it in this heat. . . .'*

'Two roast-beefs to see you, sir,' said an orderly. . . .

'Who are they?'

'The first is Aubrey, Jacques. He claims to be a captain in their navy,' said the orderly, narrowing his eyes and scanning the official slip in his hand. 'Born 1 April 1066, at Bedlam, London. Father's profession, monk: mother's, nun. Mother's maiden name, Borgia, Lucrèce. The other pilgrim is Maturin, Etienne—'

'Quick, quick,' cried Captain Christy-Pallière. 'My breeches. . . . Penhoët, we must have a real dinner today—this is the English prisoner I was telling you about. Excellent seaman, charming company. You will not mind speaking English, of course. How do I look?'

'So pimping as possible,' said Captain Penhoët in that language. 'Camber the torso, and you will impose yourself of their attention.'

—Post Captain, *90–1*

Gigot en Croûte

In *Food in England,* Dorothy Hartley speaks feelingly of the importance of seasoning meat "with the flavour of the food the animal ate," and the example she chooses, appropriately enough, is that of sheep that have grazed on the spicy flowers of wild thyme. She uses the charming word "tracklements," a term she claims to have coined herself, to express this piece of folk wisdom. The principle is no less valid for a French dish than for an English one, and we put it into practice with felicitous results.

If you are boning the lamb yourself, you will find it easier to work with the shank half.

(For information on spit-roasting, see "About Roasting," p. 282.)

Half leg of lamb, 5–6 pounds

Forcemeat:
2 teaspoons butter
½ pound mushrooms, coarsely chopped
1 egg
¼ pound veal, finely minced
¼ pound suet, finely grated
¼ cup bread crumbs

1 tablespoon brandy
1 tablespoon chopped fresh rosemary
2 tablespoons fresh thyme leaves
Salt and pepper

1 tablespoon butter, melted
1 recipe (1 pound) Puff Paste (p. 270)
½ teaspoon water

Prepare a bright clear fire (or preheat oven to 425°).

Bone and trim the lamb (you may want to reserve the bones for Barley-Broth, p. 239, or to make stock for a sauce). Sew or skewer the edges of the meat together to form a pocket for the forcemeat.

To prepare the forcemeat:
Melt the 2 teaspoons butter and sauté the mushrooms over high heat until they give up their liquid. Beat the egg and set half of it aside for glazing the pastry. Combine the remaining half of the egg with the mushrooms and the rest of the forcemeat ingredients.

Fill the pocket of the lamb with the forcemeat, and sew or skewer the opening. Center the meat on the spit (or place it on a rack in a roasting pan). Brush the meat with the melted butter and set it to roast close to a bright, clear fire (or place it in the oven). Roast it about 1 hour, or until it reaches an inside temperature of 120°.

Remove the roast from the fire (or oven), place it on a platter, remove the spit, and let the meat cool for 30 minutes.

Set the oven to 450°.

On a lightly floured board, roll out the Puff Paste until it is about ¼ inch thick.

Carefully remove the skewers and/or stitches from the meat. Lay the sheet of Puff Paste over the meat. Tuck the pastry around the meat, covering the top and sides but leaving the underside exposed. Trim the excess pastry as you go.

Mix the reserved egg with the ½ teaspoon water.

Cut decorative shapes from the pastry scraps and arrange them on the crust, cementing them in place with the egg wash. Brush a thin layer of the remaining egg wash over the entire crust.

Place the lamb on a rack in a roasting pan, and bake it about 20 minutes. Turn the oven down to 400° and continue baking for 10–15 minutes. The meat will be rare when it reaches an inside temperature of 135°.

Remove the pan from the oven. Let the lamb rest for 15 minutes, without removing it from the rack or the pan (this will prevent the crust from becoming soggy as the juices accumulate). Transfer to a warmed platter and serve.

Note: The Gigot can be served either with its own pan juices, deglazed with a spoonful or so of stock, or with Wine Sauce (p. 264), omitting the Mushroom Ketchup and adding the pan juices.

Serves 4–6

Trifle

We had better confess immediately that this recipe really has no business here. It appears as the result of an error on our part—a mistake of the most obvious and embarrassing kind. Not once in the Aubrey/Maturin novels does anyone actually eat—or even mention—Trifle. In our own defense we offer Captain Christy-Pallière's predilection for "the English pudding" and his suggestion of "some trifle with our coffee"—it's a mistake that anyone in our suet-fuddled condition could have made. Furthermore, Trifle is perfectly legitimate for the period, and just the sort of thing that Jack would have loved. Besides, we didn't discover our egregious error of interpretation until after we had made the Trifle . . . and by that time we were in love with it and didn't want to give it up.

½ pound Naples (p. 83) or
  Savoy (p. 271) biscuits,
  split
½ cup plus 1 tablespoon
  medium-dry sherry
2 teaspoons grated lemon zest
2 tablespoons plus 1 teaspoon
  slivered almonds

1 cup raspberry jam, slightly
  warmed
½ pint fresh strawberries
1 recipe (1½ cups) Custard
  Sauce (p. 264)
  Juice of ½ lemon
3 tablespoons sugar
1 cup heavy cream

Lay the biscuits, cut side up, in the bottom of a 6-cup glass dish, forming an even layer about 1 inch deep. Drizzle the ½ cup of sherry over the biscuits. Sprinkle 1 teaspoon lemon zest, then the 2 tablespoons slivered almonds, over the moistened biscuits.

Pour in the jam and spread it evenly. Reserve half of the strawberries for garnish. Cut the remaining berries in half and distribute them over the jam. Pour in the Custard Sauce. Chill at least an hour.

Combine the lemon juice, the remaining zest, and the remaining sherry in a large bowl. Add the sugar and stir to dissolve. Pour in the cream and whip it to soft peaks. Spread the whipped cream over the Trifle.

If the Trifle is not to be served immediately, it may be chilled for an hour or two.

Just before serving, garnish with the reserved strawberries and slivered almonds, and Comfits, tiny Shrewsbury Cakes, fresh or candied violets, or what you fancy.

Serves 8

Pontet-Canet in the Connecticut ...

Squirrels in Madeira

Pontet-Canet ... broke in. . . . 'I myself was in the Connecticut, in the back grounds of the state, hunting savage turkeys with a veritable American farmer. . . .'

. . . 'Pray, sir, did you find your turkeys?'

'Yes, yes!' cried Pontet-Canet. 'And some grey squirrels. I was the one that shot them all, ha, ha, ha! I was the best fusil of the party; and, I allow myself to say without forfantery, the best cook.'

'How did you dress them?'

'Sir?'

'How did you cook them?'

'The squirrels in madeira; the turkey roast. And all round the table was heard "Very good! Exceedingly good! Oh, dear sir, what a glorious bit!"'

—The Fortune of War, *132*

Squirrels in Madeira

4 grey squirrels, skinned and dressed	4 shallots, peeled and coarsely chopped
Flour for dredging	1 cup Madeira
Salt and pepper	2 cups stock (or reconstituted Portable Soup, p. 240)
5–6 tablespoons butter	
½ pound mushrooms, quartered	1 tablespoon chopped fresh parsley

Cut the squirrels into serving pieces. Season flour with salt and pepper. Dredge the squirrel pieces in the flour and set aside.

Heat 3 tablespoons of the butter in a large, heavy pan over medium heat. Add the mushrooms and shallots and sauté, stirring occasionally, until the mushrooms are slightly brown. Remove and set aside.

In the same pan, brown the squirrel pieces on all sides, a few pieces at a time, adding more butter as needed. Set them aside.

Deglaze the pan with the Madeira. Return the squirrels, shallots, and mushrooms to the pan. Add the stock, and salt and pepper to taste. Bring to a boil. Cover, reduce heat, and simmer 1 hour. Add the parsley and simmer 10 minutes more, or until squirrels are tender.

Serves 8

... and at Toulon

Côôôôq au Vin   Rrâââble de Lièvre

'Do you believe to bully me?' cried Pontet-Canet. 'You damned rogue. By God, it will not be so . . . I'll overboard you like a dead cat . . . if I find you too heavy, I'll cling to you with hands, legs, nails, everything; my life is nothing to send such a dog to hell. . . .'

. . . Stephen remembered where he had seen him before: it was at a little inn high above Toulon, much frequented by the greedier part of the French navy. A French officer, Captain Christie-Pallière, had taken Jack and Stephen to dinner there, during the peace of Amiens, and this man, passing by their table, had spoken to Christie-Pallière. Stephen remembered his Dijon accent: he was about to eat a 'côôôôq au vin' and the rest of his party a 'rrâââble de lièvre'; and he had taken particular notice of Jack, who was speaking English. —The Fortune of War, *136–7*

Côôôôq au Vin

1 chicken, 6 or 7 pounds	4 shallots, peeled and chopped
4 tablespoons butter	¼ cup brandy
½ pound bacon, cut in ½-inch pieces	1 cup rich brown stock (or reconstituted Portable Soup, p. 240)
Flour for dredging	
Salt and pepper	3 cups red wine
12 small white onions, peeled and scored with a deep "X" at the root end	Few sprigs of fresh parsley
	Few celery leaves
½ teaspoon sugar	Few sprigs of fresh hyssop
¾ pound mushrooms	Few sprigs of fresh savory
	1 small bay leaf

Cut chicken into serving pieces. In a large heavy stewpot, melt 3 tablespoons of the butter over medium heat. Add the bacon and cook until brown and crisp. Remove and reserve the bacon.

Season the flour with salt and pepper. Dredge the chicken in the flour and brown it on all sides in the bacon fat. Remove and set aside.

While the chicken is browning, melt the remaining tablespoon of butter in a small frying pan over fairly high heat. Add the onions and brown them slightly on all sides. Sprinkle the sugar into the pan and cook until the sugar dissolves, shaking the pan frequently to coat the onions evenly.

Sauté the mushrooms in the bacon fat. Remove and set aside.

Sauté the shallots in the bacon fat until they soften. Return the chicken to the pot. Add the mushrooms and onions.

Warm the brandy slightly in a small saucepan or a heavy ladle. Flame the brandy and pour it evenly over the chicken. After the flames have died down, add the stock and the wine. Tie the herbs into a piece of cheesecloth, and put them into the pot with salt and pepper to taste. Cover and bring to a gentle boil, reduce heat and simmer 1½ hours. Remove and discard the bundle of herbs before serving.

Serves 8

Rrâââble de Lièvre

2 hare saddles, about ¾ pound each
Salt and pepper
½ cup oil (vegetable, corn, etc.)
¼ cup wine vinegar
4 large carrots, peeled and coarsely chopped
2 medium onions, peeled and coarsely chopped

4 large shallots, peeled and coarsely chopped
2 bay leaves
Large handful of fresh parsley, coarsely chopped
Large handful of fresh thyme, coarsely chopped
½ cup heavy cream
1–2 teaspoons lemon juice

Place the saddles in a nonreactive heatproof dish. Rub them with salt and pepper, then with the oil and vinegar. Add the combined vegetables and herbs, arranging them so that the meat is completely surrounded. Cover and let marinate in a cool place for at least 2 hours, turning the meat once.

Preheat oven to 425°.

Rearrange the saddles in the dish, wiping them off and placing them on top of the bed of vegetables. Bake 30 minutes.

Remove from oven, and take out and reserve the vegetables, draining any juices back into the dish. Pour the cream over the saddles and return them to the oven for 10 minutes, basting frequently with the pan juices.

Purée the vegetables and pour them into a heated serving dish. Place the saddles on the bed of vegetables. Finish the sauce by stirring the lemon juice into the pan juices, then pour it over the saddles.

Serves 4

Note: For further insight into Pontet-Canet, see p. 126.

Dinner with the Bey

A Roasted Lamb with a Pudding of Bright
Yellow Rice in Its Belly

Vine-Leaves

A Roasted Lamb with a Pudding of Bright Yellow Rice in Its Belly

'We had no plates or knives or forks (though we each had a tortoiseshell spoon) and dinner was not served quite in our way either, there being no removes, but dishes following one another separately, to the number of thirty-six, not counting the sweetmeats. Each came in to the sound of kettledrums, brought by black men who put them down on a monstrous fine gold salver nestling in an embroidered cushion in the middle of the table: then we all reached out and took lumps with our fingers, unless it was very soft, when we used our spoons. One of the dishes was a roasted lamb with a pudding of bright yellow rice in its belly, and the Bey seized it by the legs, tearing it very neatly to pieces for us.' —The Ionian Mission, 296

The giver of this feast is the Bey of Mesenteron, on the Turkish-occupied Ionian coast—so we have based our pudding of bright yellow rice on traditional Turkish recipes. We confess to having taken some liberties in approximating the Bey's kitchen arrangements. Since we made this dish during the summer, and since our fireplace is not large, we felt it would be reasonable to roast our beast before an open fire on the beach. Not having a spit large enough for a lamb this size, we jury-rigged a five-foot length of reinforced steel bar on supports stuck in the sand, which served the purpose nicely.

(For information on spit-roasting, see "About Roasting," p. 282.)

1 lamb, about 20 pounds, skinned, decapitated, and eviscerated
½ teaspoon saffron
¼ cup hot water
4 tablespoons olive oil
1 pound lean ground lamb
2 large onions, peeled and coarsely chopped
4 cups long-grain rice

3 quarts chicken or lamb stock, or reconstituted Portable Soup (p. 240)
1 cup shelled pistachio nuts
2 tablespoons coriander, coarsely ground
1 tablespoon turmeric, plus extra for rubbing
1 teaspoon ground cinnamon
½ teaspoon rose water
Salt and pepper
3 eggs

Wash the lamb and wipe it dry, inside and out.

Set the saffron to steep in the hot water.

Heat 2 tablespoons of the olive oil in a large, heavy pot. Brown the ground lamb over high heat. Remove, drain, and set aside.

Lower the heat slightly and sauté the onions (adding more olive oil as necessary) until they are limp. Add the rice, stir, and cook over low heat until translucent.

Add 2 cups of the stock to the rice, stir, and cook until the stock is almost completely absorbed. Continue adding stock in this manner, 2 cups at a time, until about half the stock has been used.

Stir in the saffron mixture and the pistachios, coriander, turmeric, cinnamon, and rose water.

Continue adding stock as above until all the stock has been used.

Remove from heat and allow to cool slightly. Stir in the ground lamb, and season to taste with salt and pepper. Beat the eggs and stir them thoroughly into the rice mixture.

Rub the inside of the lamb with salt and pepper. Spoon the rice mixture into the belly. Sew up the cavity with strong cotton string.

Center and secure the lamb on the spit. Rub it all over with turmeric, and set it to roast before a clear fire. It will be medium rare after about 3½ hours, or when it reaches an inside temperature of 140°.

Serves 20

Vine-Leaves

This is loosely based on a seventeenth-century Greek recipe.

48 vine leaves
 1 medium onion, peeled and finely chopped
 1 tablespoon olive oil
 1 pound lamb, ground
 1 pound suet (mutton suet if possible), finely grated
 2 cups cooked rice
 2 eggs, lightly beaten
 Pinch of saffron
 1 teaspoon turmeric
 ½ teaspoon ground cloves
 1 teaspoon ground coriander
 1 teaspoon salt
 ½ teaspoon pepper
 1 tablespoon chopped fresh parsley
 1 quart rich brown stock (or reconstituted Portable Soup, p. 240)
 Juice of 1 lemon

Cut the stems off the vine leaves. Bring a large pot of water to the boil. Blanch the leaves for a few seconds, or until they are limp. Plunge them into cold water, then drain them.

Sauté the onion in the olive oil until limp and golden.

Combine the onions with the lamb, suet, rice, eggs, spices, and parsley. Divide the mixture into 48 equal portions, and shape into small logs.

Place a log on the back of a vine leaf. Wrap it into a tight little package and squeeze gently. Lay the package, seam-side down, in a wide pan. Repeat with the remaining logs and leaves, packing them snugly into the pan.

Pour the stock and the lemon juice over the leaves. Bring to a boil, reduce heat, and simmer gently for 30 minutes.

Gently lift out the leaf bundles, place on a platter, and keep warm. Skim the fat from the stock and continue cooking until its volume is reduced by half. Pour over the vine leaves and serve.

Serves 8

Stephen in Bombay

Bidpai Chhatta   A Whole Leaf of Pondoo

Bidpai Chhatta

Diana clapped her hands. . . .
  'Have you eaten yet, Maturin?'
  'I have not,' he said. . . .
  They sat on a divan, with the tables grouped in front of them. She explained the dishes with great volubility and a fair amount of open greed. 'You will not mind eating in the Indian way? I love it.' She was in tearing high spirits, laughing and talking away at a splendid rate, as though she had been long deprived of company. . . . 'Ha, he has given us bidpai chhatta; how I loved it as a child—still do. Let me help you. . . .' She sat cross-legged on a cushion in front of him, dipping into a dozen bowls, dishes, plates, and feeding him with balls that exploded in a pink glow inside his stomach, others that cooled and dulcified his palate.
  —H.M.S. Surprise, *219–22*

Bidpai Chhatta is an odd sort of hybrid among Indian breads, made from more or less the same dough as poori or chapati; it is deep-fried like a poori and puffs up in much the same way, but since it is rolled out much thinner it is exceptionally light and crisp, not unlike a poppadum.

The name appears to be drawn from Bidpai, sometimes called the Aesop of India, and the Pan*chata*ntra, his cycle of Sanskrit fables.

⅔ cup whole wheat or chapati
    flour, sifted
⅓ cup unbleached flour, sifted

½ teaspoon salt
⅓ cup water (approximately)
Sufficient oil for deep frying

Combine the flours and the salt. Work in the water with your fingers, a little at a time, gradually adding enough to form a fairly stiff dough (the amount of water necessary will vary according to the humidity and the hardness of your flour).

Knead on a well-floured surface until smooth (about 5 minutes). Let rest about 30 minutes in a bowl covered with a damp cloth.

In a heavy saucepan or deep-fryer (we like a wok because it is wide enough and requires less oil), heat the oil to about 370°, or until it will brown a ½-inch cube of bread in 20 seconds.

Divide the dough into 8 equal portions. Roll each piece into a ball and flatten it with your hand. On a floured surface, and with a floured rolling pin, roll out each piece into as thin a disk as possible—it will be about 6 inches in diameter.

Gently slide one of the disks of dough into the oil. It will begin to puff almost immediately—as soon as it does, carefully turn it over. Turn it twice more as it cooks; it will be done when it is golden brown on both sides. Lift it out, letting the excess oil drip back into the pan, and set it to drain on a dish lined with absorbent paper.

Makes 8

A Whole Leaf of Pondoo

A warm hand slipped into his, and looking down Stephen saw Dil smiling up at him. '. . . I have a whole leaf of pondoo: come and eat it before it spills. . . . Lean thy head forward,' she said, unfolding the leaf and setting the turgid mess between them. . . . 'Dost not see thy shirt all slobbered, oh for shame. Where wast thou brought up? What mother bore thee? Forward.' Despairing of making him eat like a human being, she stood up, licked his shirt clean, and then, folding her brown jointless legs under her she squatted close in front of him. 'Open thy mouth.' With an expert hand she moulded the pondoo into little balls and fed him. 'Close thy mouth, Stephen. Swallow. Open. There, maharaj. Another. There, my garden of nightingales. Open. Close.' The sweet, gritty unctuous mass flowed into him, and all the time Dil's voice rose and fell. 'Thou canst not eat much better than a bear.' —H.M.S. Surprise, *209–10*

This is a variation on a traditional dish of the fisher-folk of Gujarat, a little to the north of Bombay. It is actually not so much sweet as savory and pungent, though the coriander does give it a slightly sweet aroma. The addition of a little ground cinnamon would also tend to enhance this effect—but we like it better without.

1 cup green lentils or other *dhal*	1 bay leaf
6–7 tablespoons oil or ghee	½ teaspoon dried chili peppers, coarsely crumbled
1 cup millet	1½ teaspoons ground cumin
1½ teaspoons cumin seed	1½ teaspoons ground coriander
1½ teaspoons mustard seed	½ teaspoon ground turmeric
1 teaspoon coriander seed	½ teaspoon freshly ground black pepper
1 large onion, peeled and chopped	Juice of 1 lemon
1 knob fresh ginger, about 1½ inches long, peeled and grated	2½ cups water
	1½ teaspoons salt
	4 large arum leaves

Put the lentils in a bowl and pour in boiling water to cover. Let them soak for 30 minutes. Drain and put in a pot with cold water to cover. Bring to a boil, covered, and simmer 10 minutes. Drain.

In a large heavy skillet with a lid, heat 2–3 tablespoons of oil. Add the millet. Cook over medium heat until golden (about 5 minutes). Remove and reserve.

Heat the remaining oil in the same pan. Add the cumin, mustard, and coriander seeds, and cook over high heat for about 2 minutes—you will need to cover the pan when the seeds begin to pop. When the spitting subsides, reduce the heat to medium and add the onion, ginger, bay leaf, and dried chili peppers. Cook until the onion is soft and slightly golden.

Add the remaining spices and stir. Return the millet to the pan. Add the lentils, lemon juice, water, and salt. Bring to a boil. Reduce heat, cover, and cook at the barest simmer until tender (about 45 minutes). Remove the bay leaf. Cool slightly. Serve on arum leaves and eat with the fingers.

Serves 4

Queenie's Rout

Rout-Cakes   Voluptuous Little Pies

from Post Captain, 159ff.

From the standpoint of the hostess (and her staff), one of the great advantages of giving a rout is that it requires comparatively little in the way of food preparation. The Constantia wine, rout-cakes and "voluptuous little pies" served at Queenie's might make up the entire menu for such a fashionable evening party, or might at most be supplemented by fruit, comfits, and other such kickshaws.

Rout-Cakes

6 eggs
½ pound (2 sticks) butter
1 cup sugar
  Zest of 1 lemon, grated
½ teaspoon almond extract

3 cups flour
½ recipe Icing (p. 272)
¼ cup raw sugar for garnish
  (optional)

Preheat oven to 350°.

Separate 2 of the eggs and reserve the whites (save one to glaze and decorate the cakes—the other can be used to make the Icing). Cream the butter and sugar together. Add the 4 whole eggs, 2 yolks, lemon zest and almond extract, and mix thoroughly. Stir in the flour.

Scrape the batter into a greased 10-inch baking dish (the batter should be about 1 inch deep). Bake 30 minutes.

Let the cake cool slightly, remove it from the pan, and set it on a rack until it has cooled completely.

Set the oven to 200°.

Spread the Icing smoothly over the top of the cake. Cut the cake into squares, diamonds, or triangles. Brush the sides of each piece with egg white and press them lightly into the raw sugar. Place the cakes on a cookie sheet and dry them in the oven for 10 minutes.

Makes about 4 dozen 1½-inch cakes

Variation: Decorate some of the cakes with bits of pink Icing piped on top.

Voluptuous Little Pies

Today's cooks would be more likely to form the pastry for these into small free-standing patty shells—which would certainly work just as well—but this way of using puff paste is typical of the period. The size and shape of the shell is arbitrary, in any case; it's the filling that's voluptuous.

½ pound Puff Paste (p. 270)	2 drops rose water
Bread for blind baking	2 tablespoons sugar
½ cup heavy cream	½ cup almonds, coarsely ground
2 teaspoons grated lemon zest	6 tablespoons apricot jam (more or less as needed)
2 teaspoons lemon juice	2 teaspoons Almond Comfits (p. 39)
2 tablespoons Madeira or medium-dry sherry	

Preheat oven to 400°.

Lightly butter 6 small (about 3-inch) tart pans. Roll the Puff Paste out on a floured board, with a floured rolling pin, until it is about 3/16 inch thick. With a fluted cookie cutter (or the rim of a glass) cut 6 rounds large enough to line the pans. Place each pastry circle in a tart pan and prick the bottoms with a fork. Place a piece of bread, cut to fit, in each tart shell—this will keep the pastry from rising too much.

Bake 15–20 minutes, or until delicately brown. Remove from oven, discard the bread, and allow to cool completely. Gently pry the pastry shells free of the pans.

In a chilled bowl, combine the cream, lemon zest and juice, Madeira, rose water, and sugar. Whip to stiff peaks. Fold in the ground almonds.

Spread a thick layer of apricot jam in each shell, then spoon in the cream mixture. Garnish with Almond Comfits.

Makes 6 pies

Ashgrove, Mapes, and Barham Down

Jugged Hare   Pigeon Pie   Seed-Cake
Gooseberry Fool   Quaking Pudding

Jugged Hare

*He had laid out the mildewed sheets of his private correspondence. . . .
Stephen almost certainly deciphered a hare, a present from Captain
Polixfen, eaten jugged on Saturday or Sunday or both.*

—The Mauritius Command, *202–3*

For the jug in question, use any vessel that can be thoroughly sealed
and that will keep steam in and water out when set to cook in a hot-
water bath.

Hare is a tough, comparatively dry meat, so it benefits greatly from
this kind of slow, moist cooking.

1 hare, about 3 pounds, cut into serving pieces	Small handful of fresh parsley
3 slices bacon, cut in thin strips	Small handful of fresh savory
1 medium onion, peeled and stuck with 4 cloves	Small handful of fresh thyme
Small handful of fresh hyssop	¼ teaspoon mace
	Salt and pepper

Lard the hare with the bacon strips. Place the hare in a jug with all
the other ingredients and seal tightly. Put the jug in a larger pot, and
pour cold water into the pot to within an inch of the top of the jug.

Bring to a boil, reduce heat, and simmer, covered, 3 hours, replenishing with boiling water as necessary.

Serves 4

Pigeon Pie

Stephen Maturin had dined with the ladies of Mapes, Mrs Williams, Sophia, Cecilia and Frances—traces of brown windsor soup, codfish, pigeon pie, and baked custard could be seen on his neck-cloth, his snuff-coloured waistcoat and his drab breeches, for he was an untidy eater and he had lost his napkin before the first remove, in spite of Sophia's efforts at preserving it. —H.M.S. Surprise, *12–13*

With the possible exception of large unwieldy creatures like geese and turkeys, the birds in these pies were quite often left on the bone, especially if they were small and delicate. We used wild Scottish wood pigeons, which were appropriately gamy and very tender, barring the occasional pellet of shot.

(For information about preparing raised pies, see "About Raised Pies," p. 279.)

1 recipe (4½ pounds) Hot Water Paste (p. 269)
6 wood pigeons, about ½ pound each
6 ounces flap mushrooms Butter for sautéing
½ teaspoon mace
½ teaspoon ground nutmeg
½ teaspoon ground cloves
½ teaspoon pepper

¾ pound bacon
1 pound boneless chicken breast, finely minced
½ cup coarse bread crumbs
2 eggs Zest of ½ lemon, grated Salt and pepper
½ cup rich brown stock (or re-constituted Portable Soup, p. 240)

Put one-quarter of the Hot Water Paste in a bowl, cover with a damp cloth, and set aside in a warm place.

Form the remaining dough into a ball and place on a well-greased pan. Working quickly while the dough is warm, begin to raise your coffin, continuing in stages until it is about 12 inches across and 3 ½ inches high. Chill the coffin for at least an hour, or until it is firmly set.

Clean the pigeons, cutting off the feet and removing any shot that may remain.

Cut the flaps in quarters, reserving the stems. In a large pan, sauté the flap pieces in 2 tablespoons butter until they are soft. Remove and set aside.

Using the same pan, melt 2 tablespoons butter (more if necessary) and brown the birds on all sides over high heat, sprinkling them as they cook with the mace, nutmeg, cloves and ½ teaspoon pepper.

Chop the stems of the mushrooms and ¼ pound of the bacon as fine as possible. Make a forcemeat by combining them with the chicken, bread crumbs, 1 egg, lemon zest, and salt and pepper to taste. Stuff each pigeon with forcemeat, reserving about half the forcemeat to line the coffin. Wrap the birds individually in the remaining bacon.

Line the coffin with the remaining forcemeat. Place the birds in the coffin. Tuck the sautéed mushroom flaps in among them.

Preheat oven to 450°.

Beat the remaining egg with 1 teaspoon of water. Set aside.

On a floured board, roll out the remaining pastry until it is about ³/₁₆ inch thick. Cut a circle slightly larger than the diameter of the coffin. Cut a ½-inch hole in the center of the circle. Place the top crust over the pie. Moisten the edges of the two crusts with the egg wash and seal them tightly together by crimping with your fingers.

Cut decorative shapes (leaves, anchors, knots) from the pastry scraps and arrange them on the top crust, cementing them in place with the egg wash. Brush a thin layer of the remaining egg wash over the top of the pie.

Heat the stock until it is barely simmering. Using a small funnel, carefully pour as much stock as you can through the hole in the crust. Place the pie in the oven *immediately* (if you wait, the hot stock will begin to melt the coffin).

Bake 15 minutes at 450°, turn the oven down to 350°, and bake 45–50 minutes.

Serves 10–12

Seed-Cake

Jack pulled the bell, and through the various ship-noises, all muted in this calm, he heard the quick pittering of his steward. 'Killick,' he said, 'bring me a couple of bottles of that Madeira with the yellow seal, and some of Lewis' biscuits. I can't get him to make a decent seed-cake,' he explained to Stephen.
—Master and Commander, *363*

This cake sometimes included dried and candied fruits such as citron and lemon peel; we have omitted them because we do not care for them, and have added the somewhat less common cardamom and coriander. There is precedent for this—recipes for Seed-Cake vary greatly from one source to another. The chief common features are the rich and almost invariably yeast-based dough, and of course the caraway seeds—though Mrs. Glasse does say "you may leave out the Seed if you chuse it, and I think it rather better without it; but that you must do as you like."

6 cups flour
1 cup sugar
1 ounce compressed (or 1½ teaspoons active dry) yeast
2 cups warm milk
3 eggs
3 tablespoons caraway seeds
1 tablespoon cardamom seeds (optional)
1 tablespoon coriander seeds (optional)

½ pound (2 sticks) butter, melted
2 tablespoons brandy
8 drops rose water
1 teaspoon ground cinnamon
1 teaspoon ground allspice
1 teaspoon grated nutmeg
Pinch of saffron
⅛ teaspoon turmeric
Caraway Comfits (p. 39) for garnish

Combine the flour and sugar in a large bowl. Make a well in the center and put in the yeast. Pour in 1 cup of the warm milk. Cover the bowl with a damp cloth, and set it in a warm place until it is bubbly (about 15 minutes).

Add all the remaining ingredients except the Comfits, mix well, cover again with the cloth, and set in a warm place to rise until doubled in bulk (about 1 hour).

Preheat the oven to 400°.

Stir the batter down with a wooden spoon. Pour it into a well-greased springform pan and bake until a toothpick inserted in the center comes out clean (about 40 minutes). Sprinkle immediately with Comfits (the heat of the cake will melt the sugar just enough to make the Comfits stick). Cool on a rack.

Serves 20–30

Gooseberry Fool

'I am contemplating on the means,' said Stephen; but the pale, reserved ferocity of his expression faded entirely with the entry of Nelly with the pudding and Padeen with Brigid. She sat there on her high-cushioned chair and as Stephen helped her to gooseberry fool she turned her face to him. He thought he saw a distinct look of acceptance, but he dared not speak directly. It was only when the meal was nearly over that he said, in Irish, 'Padeen, let you bring the little mare in twelve minutes,' and the words brought a quick turn of the small fair head, ordinarily immobile, absorbed in an inner world.   —The Commodore, 63*

Depending on whom you believe, fool either originated as custard and evolved into cream; or the reverse; or both. Hannah Glasse gives a recipe for Gooseberry Cream which contains eggs but no cream; she also has one for Gooseberry Fool which she says can be made *either* with eggs and milk *or* with cream and no eggs. Having made uncounted custards and custard sauces in the course of our research, we found ourselves strongly attracted by the prospect of a cream-based fool.

Further controversies involve the etymology (it may or may not be related to Trifle) and the question of whether the cooked fruit should be strained (one source says that straining is permissible but unimportant, while another maintains that it is the major identifying characteristic of the dish). We, as usual in such situations, have followed our own preference.

Almost any fruit can be used for a fool (the apricots left over from our Ratafia Biscuit experiment made a particularly delicious one). If you do use gooseberries, the end result will resemble a pale green cloud, even if, unlike Hannah Glasse, you do not enhance the color with "spinage" juice.

4 cups gooseberries (or other fruit)	1 cup sugar (or to taste—gooseberries are especially tart)
Water	2 cups heavy cream

Trim the tips and tails from the gooseberries with small sharp scissors. Put the gooseberries in a heavy saucepan with ¼ cup water. Cook over low heat, stirring frequently (and adding a little more water if necessary to keep the fruit from burning), until fruit is very tender (30–40 minutes).

Put the gooseberries through a fine sieve. Add the sugar and stir to dissolve. Let the purée cool to room temperature.

Lightly whip the cream (it should thicken and softly hold a shape, but not be stiff enough to form peaks). Gently fold in the gooseberry purée.

Serve chilled, in goblets or cut-glass dishes.

Serves 8

Quaking Pudding

Mrs Warren brought in the pudding, flustered and upset by all this activity. She tied the child's bib rather sharply, squaring her in her chair, clapped the pudding down (common quaking pudding) and said to Clarissa 'The post-boys say they are to water their horses and walk them up and down for an hour, no more. Am I to give them something to eat?'

'Bread, cheese, and a pint of beer for each,' said Clarissa. 'My dear Brigid, you are not to play with your food. What will your father think?'

Brigid had indeed been beating her pudding to make it quake in earnest, but she stopped at once and hung her head. After a while she whispered in Irish 'Would you like a little piece?'

'A very little piece, if you please,' said Stephen. —The Commodore, *133–4*

This pudding was a revelation to us. The preparation of the cloth, with its mess of butter and flour, was so daunting that we could not imagine anything remotely appetizing coming out of it; pouring the exceedingly liquid batter into it was an act of faith. We needn't have worried. Quaking pudding has a light, custardy texture, a delicate flavor, and a homely, comforting presence—and it does indeed quake.

(For information on preparing and cooking puddings, see "About Puddings," p. 273.)

6 egg yolks	¼ teaspoon salt
3 egg whites	Pinch of ground nutmeg
1 pint heavy cream	Pinch of mace
¼ cup sugar	3 drops rose water
3 tablespoons medium-dry sherry	3 cups coarse bread crumbs
	Butter
¼ teaspoon ground cinnamon	Flour
¼ teaspoon ground ginger	

Beat the egg yolks and whites together. Add the cream, sugar, sherry, spices, and rose water, and stir until smooth. Add the bread crumbs and stir until blended.

Bring a large pot of water to a boil.

Generously butter and flour a large circle in the middle of one side of a pudding-cloth. Place the cloth, buttered side up, in a bowl. Pour the pudding batter into the cloth and tie securely, leaving the bag loose enough to allow for expansion.

Immerse the pudding at once in the rapidly boiling water, cover, and cook 30–45 minutes.

To serve, untie the cloth and quickly turn the pudding out into a deep serving dish. Serve with Sherry Sauce (p. 266).

Serves 8–10

English Inns and Taverns

Hare Soup   Warden Pie
A Nice Loin of Weal

THE GEORGE, PORTSMOUTH

Halibut with Anchovy Sauce   Leg of Mutton
Venison Pasty   Mrs. Pullings's Pie

Hare Soup

Dolby begged Diana and her party to stay to dinner—there would be a famous hare soup, and blackcock from Somerset.   —The Yellow Admiral, 81

The outstanding features of Hare Soup are its rich taste and texture. Hannah Glasse, in one of her hare recipes, says "let it do softly till it is as thick as Cream," and the description is apt—the soup has a creamy quality that belies its composition.

1 hare, about 6 pounds	Small handful of fresh basil
Flour for dredging	Small handful of fresh hys-
Butter or oil for browning	sop
1 quart rich brown stock (or	1 bay leaf
reconstituted Portable	4 whole cloves
Soup, p. 240)	4 small onions, peeled
Small handful of fresh pars-	½ teaspoon mace
ley	Salt and pepper
Small handful of fresh thyme	2 cups water
Small handful of fresh mar-	2 medium potatoes
joram	¼ cup red wine

Cut the hare in pieces and dredge them with flour. In a large stewpot, heat 2 tablespoons butter or oil (we use both, in equal proportions), and brown a few pieces at a time (adding more fat as necessary). Set the pieces aside. Deglaze the pot with the stock.

Return the hare to the pot. Make a bouquet garni of the parsley, thyme, marjoram, basil, hyssop and bay leaf tied together in a piece of cheesecloth, and add it to the soup. Stick a clove in each onion, and add them to the soup. Add the mace, and salt and pepper to taste. Cover, bring to a boil, reduce heat, and simmer 2 hours.

Discard the bouquet garni and strain the soup, reserving the hare and onions. Return the soup to the pot and add the water. Peel and quarter the potatoes, add them to the soup, bring to a boil, and cook until the potatoes are soft (about 10 minutes). Remove the potatoes and keep the soup warm over the lowest possible fire.

Pull the meat off the bones. Choosing the nicest-looking bits, cut about half the meat into bite-size pieces. Pound the remaining meat, onions, and potatoes to a fine purée. Add the purée to the soup and blend thoroughly. Stir in the red wine. Bring the soup to a gentle simmer. Add the pieces of meat and continue to cook until they are heated through.

Serves 6–8

Warden Pie

The cloth was drawn and the wine appeared together with warden pie, treacle tart and every kind of cheese known in the three kingdoms.

—The Yellow Admiral, *241*

The Warden is a cooking pear whose documented use dates back to medieval times. It is known for its firm texture and its admirable keeping qualities—the name is probably taken from the French *garder,* "to keep." It was brought to America in 1775, but we are not at all sure it still exists; we have been unable to substantiate rumors of a Warden tree, living under the name of Pickering, in an eponymous garden in Salem, Massachusetts. (We were briefly excited by the discovery of the Worden Seckel Pear; a false scent, alas.)

Of the various pears we tried, the red Anjou was by far the best: it holds its shape well and makes a wonderfully rich, sweet pie.

This is the only raised pie we have made that actually requires a mold—the pastry can be raised successfully into a fine free-standing coffin, but it is not sturdy enough to withstand heat on its own; it collapses within minutes of being put into the oven, as we discovered to our great chagrin. If you do not have a coffin-mold, a springform pan or even a deep dish will do (though the latter will affect the texture of the crust).

Incidentally, our recipe, loosely based on that of Gervase Markham, is probably not materially different from what Perdita served to the sheep-shearers in *The Winter's Tale*, except for the saffron: even by the seventeenth century, the dyeing of warden pies had long since gone out of fashion.

(For information about preparing raised pies, see "About Raised Pies," p. 279.)

3 cups white wine	*Pastry:*
½ cup white vinegar	4 cups flour
2 cups sugar, plus extra for garnish	½ teaspoon salt
	1½ tablespoons sugar
1 knob of ginger, about 1 inch long, bruised	6 ounces cold butter
	2 eggs, lightly beaten
9 large cooking pears (Warden, Anjou, etc.)	⅔ cup water
	9 cinnamon sticks
	27 whole cloves
	1 egg, separated
	½ teaspoon water
	½ cup heavy cream

In a large, nonreactive pot, stir together the wine, vinegar, sugar and ginger. Bring to a boil, reduce heat, and simmer 5 minutes.

Meanwhile, peel and core the pears. Cut off a thin slice at each end so that the pears will stand upright and be of uniform height.

Set the pears upright in the poaching liquid. Cover and simmer 1 hour.

While the pears are cooking, prepare the pastry. Sift the flour, salt and sugar together. Cut the butter into small bits and work it quickly into the flour with your fingers. Stirring with a fork, gradually add the eggs and the water. Turn out onto a floured board and knead until smooth, adding more flour as necessary. Put in a bowl, cover with a damp cloth, and let rest in a warm place until wanted.

Remove the pears from the liquid and let cool. Continue to cook the liquid until it is thick and syrupy, about 20 minutes. Remove the ginger knob. (Eat it—it is delicious.)

Preheat oven to 450°.

Put three-quarters of the pastry into an 8-cup raised-pie mold, and raise it into a coffin. Place the pears, still upright, in the coffin. Stick 3 cloves in the top of each pear, and put a cinnamon stick (trimmed to fit if necessary) in each cavity.

On a lightly floured board, roll out the remaining pastry until it is about 3/16 inch thick. Cut it to fit and slightly overlap (by about 3/4 inch) the top of the pie. Cut a small hole in the center. Cut decorative shapes from the pastry scraps. Lightly beat the egg white with the 1/2 teaspoon water, brush a thin layer over the top crust, and gently press the decorations into place. (Reserve the egg white wash—you will need it again.) Lay the top crust lightly over the pie—do not pinch or secure the edges.

Bake 10 minutes at 450°, then reduce heat to 375° and bake an additional 30 minutes.

While the pie is baking, combine the cream and the egg yolk in a small, heavy saucepan and cook gently, stirring frequently, until the mixture thickens (about 5 minutes).

Remove the pie from the oven and carefully lift off and set aside the top crust. Pour the pear syrup into the pie (and into the pear cavities), filling it to within an inch of the top. Pour the custard on top of the syrup.

Brush the top crust with the remaining egg white wash and sprinkle generously with sugar. Pick up the top crust very carefully, shake off the excess sugar, and gingerly replace it on the pie. Put the pie back in the oven for about 5 minutes, just long enough to crystallize the sugar.

Take the pie out of the oven and allow to cool about 30 minutes before removing the mold.

Serve warm.

Note: Many of the period recipes for this sort of pie instruct the cook to cut the top crust, after it is baked, "in little three-corner Pieces, and stick about the Pye." We suspect this serving suggestion covered a multitude of sins. If you do it intentionally the pastry is almost bound to crumble, but it is a good fall-back position if your top crust has met with an accident on the way on or off the pie. It is also a good argument for arranging the pears attractively, since there is always a chance they may be exposed to unexpected scrutiny.

Serves 8–10

A Nice Loin of Weal

'Killick,' said Jack, 'God damn your eyes. Cut along to the kitchen and desire Mrs Broad to step up. Mrs Broad, what have you for dinner? I am amazing sharp-set.'

'No beef or mutton, Mr Killick says,' said Mrs Broad, but I have a nice loin of weal, and a nice piece of wenison as plump as you could wish; a tender young doe, sir.' —Post Captain, 400

This dish, served at the Grapes in the Liberties of the Savoy, may appear a little elegant and Frenchified for Mrs. Broad, but by eighteenth-century standards it is really quite straightforward: no coxcombs, truffles, forcemeat balls, or other outlandish fripperies. And, all modesty aside, we cannot recommend it too highly.

If possible, have your butcher loosen (but not remove) the chine or backbone—this will make carving easier.

(For information on spit-roasting, see "About Roasting," p. 282.)

6-pound loin of veal, at room temperature
Suet for barding (optional)
2 pounds veal bones
2 medium onions, peeled and cut in half
1 rib celery, cut in large pieces
1 carrot, peeled and cut in large pieces
Few sprigs of fresh savory
Few sprigs of fresh thyme
Few sprigs of fresh parsley
1 bay leaf
Salt and pepper
3 tablespoons butter
2 tablespoons flour
½ cup heavy cream
Juice of ½ lemon
12 mushrooms, coarsely chopped
8 shallots, peeled and coarsely chopped

Bard the veal either with thin slices of its own outside fat or, if it is very lean, with thin slices of suet. Tie it securely using butcher's twine or stout string. Place the meat on the spit, making sure the spit goes behind the ribs rather than through the fillet. Set it to roast in front of a clear fire.

Place the veal bones, onions, celery, carrot, herbs, and salt and pepper to taste in a saucepan with water to cover. Cover and bring to a boil. Reduce heat and simmer 1 hour. Uncover and cook over medium heat until stock is reduced to about 2 cups. Strain and set aside.

Melt 2 tablespoons butter in a saucepan and add the flour, stirring frequently until the flour is thoroughly cooked but not brown. Stirring constantly, gradually add the reserved veal stock, the cream and the lemon juice. When the sauce is smooth and thick, remove it from the heat.

Sauté the mushrooms and shallots in the remaining tablespoon of butter until they are soft and lightly browned.

When the veal has cooked about 2 hours, remove it from the fire and place it, spit and all, on a platter. Cut or untie the strings. Discard the barding fat. With a sharp knife, carefully scoop out the fillet, leaving a "wall" about ½ inch thick at each end of the loin.

Finely chop the fillet, and combine it with the mushrooms and shallots. Mix in enough of the sauce to bind the stuffing. Spoon the stuffing into the cavity and retie the loin. If necessary, sew or skewer the ends to keep the stuffing from oozing out.

Return the meat to the fire and roast another hour or until it reaches an inside temperature of 150°. Put it on a platter, remove the spit, cover the meat lightly to keep it warm, and let it rest for about 15 minutes before serving. Reheat the remaining sauce and serve as an accompaniment to the roast.

Serves 6–8

THE GEORGE, PORTSMOUTH

'Indeed, you look quite destroyed. Drink this up, and we will go straight to the dining-room. I have ordered a halibut with anchovy sauce, mutton, and a venison pasty—simple island fare.'

The worn lines eased out of Jack Aubrey's face, a rosy glow replaced the unhealthy grey; he seemed to fill his uniform again. 'How much better a man feels when he is mixed with halibut and leg of mutton and roebuck,'
he said. —Post Captain, *204*

Halibut with Anchovy Sauce

Halibut, a large flat fish with a lovely delicate flavor, seems to have gone out of fashion, more's the pity. Even when it is sold today, it is usually cut into steaks suitable for grilling, a method of cookery that we feel does not set it off to its best advantage. In our opinion you cannot do better by your halibut than to poach it.

Salt   2 pounds fresh leaf spinach
1 large piece of halibut, about
     5 pounds

In a large pot, bring to a boil enough water to cover the fish. Salt to taste. Add the fish, and when the water begins to bubble again, turn the heat down to a bare simmer. Cook 10 minutes for every inch of thickness.

Wash the spinach and remove any tough stems. Put it in a pot over medium heat (the water that clings to the leaves will be sufficient to keep it from burning) and cook, stirring often, until just wilted. Arrange the spinach on a platter.

Remove the fish from the poaching liquid, place it on the bed of spinach, and carefully take off the skin.

Serve immediately, accompanied by hot Anchovy Sauce (recipe follows).

Serves 10–12

Anchovy Sauce

 2 shallots, peeled and chopped
    Small handful of fresh thyme
    Small handful of fresh pars-
      ley
    Few leaves of fresh lemon
      balm (optional)
10 anchovy fillets, rinsed and
      patted dry
 ¼ teaspoon pepper
 2 cups red wine
 ½ cup cider vinegar

 2 tablespoons Mushroom
      Ketchup (p. 269)
 ¼ teaspoon dry mustard
 2 whole cloves
 1 small whole nutmeg
 ¼ teaspoon mace
 2 pieces (about 1 inch square)
      Portable Soup (p. 240)
 ¼ pound (1 stick) plus 1 table-
      spoon butter
 1 tablespoon flour

Place all the ingredients except the butter and the flour in a saucepan. Bring to a gentle boil and cook until the anchovies dissolve (20–30 minutes). Cover, reduce heat, and simmer 10–12 minutes.

Rub the sauce through a fine strainer. Return it to the heat, add the ¼ pound butter, and cook, stirring occasionally, until the butter melts. In a small dish, work the 1 tablespoon butter into the flour to make a smooth paste, and stir it into the sauce. Continue to cook, stirring constantly, about 2 minutes, or until the sauce thickens. Serve immediately.

Makes 1½ cups

Leg of Mutton

Nobody seems to boil large joints of meat (or large fowls such as turkey) any more, but it was a perfectly typical treatment in Jack's time. We see no reason why it should not come back into favor.

1 small leg of lamb or mutton, about 8 pounds
2 large yellow turnips, about 1½ pounds each, peeled and quartered

4 large carrots, peeled and cut into 2-inch pieces
Salt and pepper
2 tablespoons butter

In a large pot, bring to a boil enough water to cover the meat and vegetables. Add salt (roughly 1 teaspoon per quart of water) and pepper to taste. Put in the meat and the vegetables. Bring slowly to a boil, skimming occasionally. Reduce heat, cover, and simmer very gently for 2 hours.

Remove the turnips, drain them, and mash them with the butter, adding salt and pepper to taste (or hack them with Balmagowry—see Bashed Neeps, p. 70). Put the mashed turnips on a warm platter, place the joint thereupon, surround it with the carrots, and serve it forth accompanied by Caper Sauce (recipe follows).

Serves 6–8

Caper Sauce

4 tablespoons nonpareil capers

½ pound (2 sticks) butter
1 tablespoon caper liquid

Chop 2 tablespoons of the capers as fine as possible. Melt the butter in a small saucepan. Put in the chopped and whole capers, add the liquid, and stir vigorously.

Makes about 1½ cups

Venison Pasty

Jack held the point of his carver over a dimple in the venison pasty and said, 'Allow me to cut you a little of this pasty, ma'am. It is one of the few things I can carve. When we have a joint, I usually call upon my friend Dr Maturin, whom I hope to introduce to you this afternoon. He is such a hand at carving.' —Post Captain, *437*

What is a pasty? (And why isn't it a pie?) We know there is meat. We know there is pastry. Beyond that, the authorities are at odds:

It's a large piece of meat wrapped in a shapeless sheet of pastry, the defining factor being that it is baked without benefit of dish. Yet many eighteenth-century recipes begin by lining a dish with pastry. . . .

Very well, then, it's meat baked in a raised crust or a pastry-lined dish, the defining factor being that it is surrounded by pastry. Yet some eighteenth-century recipes call for a deep dish and a top crust only. . . .

It has also been suggested that the distinction between a pasty and a pie is that the former has only one main ingredient, whereas the latter contains a mixture of divers elements. Yet to this rule, as to the others, there are many exceptions.

(Then there is the ground-meat turnover known as a Cornish Pasty, but that is a peculiarly regional form, and as such has no place in the debate.)

What is a pasty and why isn't it a pie? We don't really know.

5 pounds boneless shoulder of venison, cut into 2-inch pieces
Salt and pepper
1 medium onion, peeled and coarsely chopped
2 tablespoons butter
Large handful of fresh sage, coarsely chopped
Small handful of fresh thyme, coarsely chopped

Small handful of fresh savory, coarsely chopped
4 recipes (2 pounds) Short Pastry (p. 271), sugar omitted
1 egg, beaten with 1 teaspoon water
½ pound bacon
⅓ cup red wine
¼ cup red wine vinegar
4 1-inch squares Portable Soup (p. 240)

Trim the venison of all gristle and rub with a generous amount of salt and pepper. Reserve the trimmings and any meat juices.

Sauté the onion in the butter until it is soft and slightly golden. Combine with the meat and herbs.

Preheat oven to 400°.

Set aside one-quarter of the pastry. Roll out the remaining pastry on a floured board, with a floured rolling pin, until it is about ³⁄₁₆ inch thick. Line a greased dish (we use an 8-cup soufflé dish) with the sheet of pastry, cutting and crimping as necessary to make it fit.

Roll out the reserved pastry into a circle about 1½ inches larger than the top diameter of the dish. Cut a ½-inch hole in the center.

Cut decorative shapes (leaves, anchors, knots) from the pastry scraps and arrange them on the top crust, cementing them in place with the egg wash.

Fill the pastry-lined dish with the meat mixture. Place strips of bacon over the meat so that it is completely covered.

Lay the top crust lightly over the dish, and brush a thin layer of the remaining egg wash over it.

Bake for 10 minutes, then reduce heat to 300° and bake 1½ hours.

While the pasty is in the oven, put the meat trimmings, juices, wine, vinegar, and Portable Soup in a small pot, bring to a boil, and simmer gently for 20 minutes. Strain and reserve the liquid, discarding the meat scraps.

Remove the pasty from the oven and carefully lift off the top crust. Pour the stock into the pasty, replace the crust, and return the pasty to the oven for 20 minutes.

Serves 8–10

Mrs. Pullings's Pie

The elder Mr Pullings was a farmer in a small way on the skirts of the New Forest, and he had brought a couple of sucking-pigs, a great deal of the King's game, and a pie that was obliged to be accommodated with a table of its own. . . .

'*Truffles!*' *cried Stephen, deep in the monumental pie, Mrs Pullings's particular dish, her masterpiece (young hen pheasants, boned, stuffed tight with truffles, in a jelly of their own life's blood, Madeira and calves' foot). 'Truffles! My dear madam, where did you find these princely truffles?'— holding one up on his fork.*

'*The stuffing, sir? We call 'em yearth-grobbets; and Pullings has a little old spayed sow turns 'em up by the score along the edge of the forest.*'

—Post Captain, *211–12*

Baby pheasants can be bought either "bone-out" or "bone-in;" we strongly recommend the former, as boning small birds is a dreadfully tedious process. Even a "bone-out" pheasant, however, will still have leg and wing bones, which must be removed. If you have a wonderful butcher who is willing to do this part of the job for you, be sure to ask for the bones for the stock-pot.

We used summer truffles, which are available from April to June, for several reasons. Unlike the true black winter truffles, they would have been in season at the time of Pullings's feast; they are milder than black truffles, so they don't overwhelm the delicate flavor of the young pheasants; and they are (relatively) affordable—we can't all live at the edge of the New Forest.

This splendid pie is served cold, so the blood (which would normally be considered a thickening agent) does not really add anything to it—fortunately, as pheasant blood is not exactly easy to find. We are not, in fact, at liberty to reveal how we came by the blood that we used; if you are unable to obtain any, we can assure you that leaving it out will not ruin the dish.

(It is only fair to warn you, by the way, that the Calf's Foot Jelly alone takes a full day to make.)

(For information about preparing raised pies, see "About Raised Pies," p. 279.)

1 recipe (4½ pounds) Hot
    Water Paste (p. 269)
8 baby hen pheasants, about ¾
    pound each, boned (bones
    reserved)
2 small onions, peeled
2 carrots, peeled and cut in half
1 rib celery with leaves
    Salt and pepper
9 large summer truffles (about
    ¾ pound)
1 pound boneless chicken
    breast, finely minced
¼ pound suet, finely grated
½ cup bread crumbs
1 egg white
¼ cup milk
1 tablespoon chopped fresh
    thyme
3 tablespoons chopped fresh
    parsley

3 tablespoons chopped fresh
    savory
½ pound morels
1 tablespoon butter
½ pound bacon, cut in ½-inch
    pieces
4 large shallots, peeled and
    coarsely chopped
2 tablespoons chopped fresh
    chives
2 tablespoons chopped fresh
    chervil
2 tablespoons chopped fresh
    hyssop
½ cup Calf's Foot Jelly
    p. 268)
½ cup Madeira
3 tablespoons brandy
1 egg beaten with 1 teaspoon
    water
3 tablespoons pheasant blood
    (optional)

Put one-quarter of the Hot Water Paste in a bowl, cover with a damp cloth, and set aside in a warm place.

Form the remaining dough into a ball and place on a well-greased pan. Working quickly while the dough is warm, begin to raise your coffin, continuing in stages until it is about 10 inches across and 3½ inches high. Chill the coffin for at least an hour, or until it is firmly set.

Place the pheasant bones in a pot with the onions, carrots, celery, salt and pepper to taste, and water to cover. Bring to a boil, reduce heat, and simmer, covered, 2 hours.

Chop one of the truffles as fine as possible. Make a forcemeat by combining it with the chicken, suet, bread crumbs, egg white, milk, thyme, and 1 tablespoon each of the parsley and savory.

Trim the tips of the morel stems and cut the morels in half. Peel or scrape the black skin off the remaining truffles. Chop and reserve the peelings.

Melt the butter in a large frying pan, add the bacon and cook over medium heat until soft. Add the shallots and the remaining herbs, and stir to coat. Add the morels and sauté, stirring frequently, until slightly softened.

Pushing the morel mixture to the sides of the pan, put in 2 or 3 of the pheasants, skin side down. Cook them briefly (not more than 2 minutes), just enough to firm the flesh. Remove and set aside, and repeat with the remaining pheasants.

Strain and skim the stock, then cook it over high heat, uncovered, until it is reduced to about 1½ cups. Add the Calf's Foot Jelly, Madeira, brandy, 4 tablespoons of the truffle peelings, and salt to taste. Stir the stock well and let it continue to reduce over medium heat while you assemble the pie.

Line the coffin with a thin layer of forcemeat. Place a pheasant skin-side down on a plate or board (you may prefer, as we do, to hold it in your hand). Put a truffle in the middle, then a generous spoonful of the morel mixture. Fold the pheasant into a tight little package and place it, seam-side down, in the coffin. Repeat with the remaining pheasants.

After all the pheasants are snugly packed in the pie, distribute the remaining morel mixture into the interstices among them. Spread another layer of forcemeat over the pheasants.

Preheat oven to 450°.

On a floured board, roll out the remaining pastry until it is about 3/16 inch thick. Cut a circle slightly larger than the diameter of the coffin. Cut a ½-inch hole in the center of the circle. Place the top crust over the pie. Moisten the edges of the two crusts with the egg wash and seal them tightly together by crimping with your fingers.

Cut decorative shapes (leaves, anchors, knots) from the pastry scraps and arrange them on the top crust, cementing them in place with the egg wash. Brush a thin layer of the remaining egg wash over the top of the pie.

Reduce the heat under the stock until it is barely simmering. Add the blood, gently swirl the pan to combine (do not stir or the mixture will curdle), and continue to simmer about 3 minutes.

Using a small funnel, carefully pour as much stock as you can through the hole in the crust. Place the pie in the oven *immediately* (if you wait, the hot stock will begin to melt the coffin).

Bake 15 minutes at 450°, turn the oven down to 350°, and bake 45–50 minutes.

Serves 10–12

Rule, Britannia

by Dr. Arne

CHAPTER SEVEN

In Durance
Vile

Men so exposed to the caprices of the elements might be expected to develop a philosophical attitude, and before this Stephen had seen his shipmates accept the unkinder strokes of fate with a fine equanimity; but even so he was surprised to see how quickly they recovered their spirits on this occasion and put a good face on adversity. It is true that since their ship had not been taken they had not been pillaged; what little they had been able to save they still possessed, and this softened the blow, since they were able to round out the sparse French rations with better food and wine than ever the Ariel had afforded them. On the other hand, once they found they were not to be robbed or starved they complained bitterly about the quality of the tea; and on Jack's first visit to the men it was represented to him that this here French bread, full of holes, could not nourish a man: if a man ate holes he must necessarily blow himself out with air like a bladder, it stood to reason. They did not much care for the oatmeal either, probably harvested green and parched in the ear: nor the soup. —The Surgeon's Mate, *312*

One does not expect much of prison fare, and all too often one is justified. There are, however, noble exceptions. Among the great pleasures of this project, for instance, was the recreation of the dishes eaten by Jack, Stephen and Jagiello during their enforced sojourn in France. Through the generosity of Duhamel, the good graces of the

Young Person, and the more mercenary services of that amiable slut Madame Lehideux, they dine sumptuously during their imprisonment.

Jack and Stephen are also well-treated and well-fed—if not quite as spectacularly so—when they are held in Boston after the battle between *Constitution* and *Java*.

Some of their other prison experiences are less gastronomically satisfying. . . .

Boston

Bisque de Homard   Clam Chowder
Spoon-Bread

Bisque de Homard

The series teems with lobsters: they are obviously a favorite food. This soup ("... a most uncommonly good dish made principally of pounded lobsters, with their carefully shelled claws aswim in the rosy mass ..." [*The Commodore*, 91]) appears four or five times, in various parts of the world.

In the matter of killing the lobsters, the method we used is the traditional one for a bisque, but we realize that it may be rather disconcerting, since the pieces continue to wiggle long after the lobsters themselves are well and truly dead. If you are uncomfortable with this procedure you may prefer to plunge them very briefly in boiling water (this will not only kill them instantly but also suppress any reflex movements) before beginning to dismember them.

4 live lobsters, about 1½ pounds each	1 bay leaf
11 tablespoons butter	⅜ cup brandy
1 small onion, peeled and diced	½ cup dry white wine
1 carrot, peeled and diced	5–6 cups fish stock or court-bouillon
Small handful of fresh parsley	2 tablespoons dry sherry
Small handful of fresh thyme	4 cups milk
	¾ cup flour
	¼ cup heavy cream

Kill the lobsters by severing the spinal cord with a sharp knife (inserted at the back where the tail and body meet). Remove the claws and legs. Separate the tails from the bodies.

In a large stewpot, melt 3 tablespoons of the butter. Add the onion and carrot and sauté until the onion is transparent. Add the parsley, thyme, and bay leaf.

Add the lobster and cook over medium heat, turning the pieces frequently, until the shells are deep red on all sides. Warm the brandy, set it aflame, and pour it over the lobster. After the flames have died down, add the wine and 1 cup of the stock. Cover, bring to a boil, reduce heat, and simmer 20–25 minutes.

Remove the lobsters and let them cool. Remove the vegetables from the cooking liquid; reserve both the vegetables and the liquid.

Pick the meat from the shells. Crush the shells and set aside. Dice the meat finely, reserving a few big rosy pieces for garnish. Sprinkle the meat with the sherry and set aside.

Pour the milk and 4 cups of the remaining stock into the pot and bring it to a boil. Meanwhile, melt 6 tablespoons of the butter in a small saucepan. Add the flour, stir well, and cook over low heat until the flour is completely absorbed. Reduce the heat under the soup. Add the roux to the soup and stir until slightly thickened. Add the crushed shells and the cooked vegetables, along with the reserved cooking liquid. Simmer, covered, 1½ hours.

Strain the soup through a very fine mesh and return it to the pot. Thin if necessary with the remaining stock. Add the cream, the remaining brandy and butter, and the lobster meat. Cook until the butter is melted and the lobster heated through. Serve with a loaf of crusty French bread (a True French Short Bastard, for instance) and a salad.

Serves 6 as a main course, 12 as a remove

Clam Chowder

Jack eats clam chowder "voraciously" when he is convalescing in Boston after the battle between *Constitution* and *Java* (*The Fortune of*

War, 149). We are on home ground here, as we dig our own clams and chowder is something of a staple for us—one which we too eat voraciously. As well we might, since according to Patrick O'Brian it is "a dish that is served in Heaven, every Friday" (*Patrick O'Brian Newsletter*, March 1994).

Modern "chowders" are often thick, rich and creamy—more in the nature of bisque, really—but the original chowder was a poor fisherman's dish, with a thin broth tasting very strongly of its principal ingredient.

(Quantities given are appropriate for a large beach party or clambake, on Friday or any other night—scale down or up as needed to feed a single mess or a full ship's company.)

12 dozen very large hard-shell clams, well scrubbed	6 tablespoons flour
1½ pounds salt pork, cut in ¼-inch cubes	1 teaspoon fresh thyme leaves
5 pounds (about 15 medium) potatoes	Salt and pepper
	1 gallon milk
3 pounds (about 9 medium) onions, peeled and coarsely chopped	¼ pound (1 stick) butter, cut in 4 pieces

Put 1 dozen of the clams (or as many as will fit) in a large pot with ¼ cup water. Cover and cook over fairly high heat until the clams pop open. Remove and set them aside, draining the liquid into the pot as you do so. Continue until all the remaining clams are open—you will not need to add more water. Discard any clams that refuse to open.

Scrape all the clams out of their shells, reserving their liquid, and chop them coarsely. Add the clam liquid to the cooking broth. Strain and reserve the clam broth (you should have about 3 quarts).

Put the salt pork into an enormous heavy cauldron and cook over medium heat until the fat is rendered and the cubes are crisp and brown. Remove the pork bits and set aside.

Scrub the potatoes and cut them into ½-inch dice (we prefer not to peel them, but that is as you wish).

Sauté the onions in the pork fat until they are limp and golden. Add the potatoes and sprinkle them with the flour. Add the clam broth (if there is not enough broth to cover the potatoes, supplement it with water). Cover, bring to a boil, then turn down heat and simmer gently until the potatoes are almost tender (about 10 minutes). Add the clams, thyme, and salt and pepper to taste.

Cook gently until the clams and potatoes are done (about 10 minutes).

Scald the milk, pour it into the pot, and slowly bring the chowder to a bare simmer. Add the butter and continue to simmer until the butter melts. Just before serving, add the cubes of salt pork.

Serves 40

Spoon-Bread

Mrs Wogan had come back, followed by a slatternly black woman and two small black boys with the tea-tray and its grubby appurtenances.

'I do hope it will be to your liking,' said Mrs Wogan, looking anxiously into the pot. 'Sally is better at mint-juleps than tea.'

At one time Stephen had been marooned on a bare rock in the south Atlantic, and his only drink was the warm rainwater that remained in the guano-filled hollows: it had been more disagreeable than Mrs Wogan's tea, but only very slightly so. The taste of his bitter cup stayed with him the rest of the day, although he had endeavoured to qualify it by eating lumps of an amorphous grey substance, said to be spoon-bread, a Southern delicacy.

—The Fortune of War, *163–4*

One can only hope that Sally's mint-juleps were also better than her Spoon-Bread; which, when properly prepared, should be neither grey nor amorphous.

2 cups water	2 tablespoons butter
½ teaspoon salt	2 eggs
1 cup cornmeal	1 cup milk

Preheat oven to 425°.

Butter a 6-cup ovenproof dish (a soufflé dish works very well).

In a heavy saucepan, bring the water to a boil. Add the salt. Gradually add the cornmeal, stirring rapidly with a wooden spoon to prevent lumps. Cook over a low fire, still stirring, for about 2 minutes. Remove from heat, add butter, and stir until butter is absorbed.

Beat the eggs and milk together. Add to the cornmeal mixture and stir thoroughly.

Pour the batter into the buttered dish and bake for 45 minutes, or until the top is brown and a toothpick inserted in the middle comes out clean.

Serve the Spoon-Bread from the dish in which it is cooked.

Serves 6–8

Variation: We sometimes like to add ½ cup of grated cheddar cheese before baking, though it is really very satisfying without.

France

BREST

Gratin of Lobster　　　Black Pudding　　　Flummery

ON THE ROAD TO PARIS

Sweetbreads in Malmsey

Little Balls of Tripe a Man Might Eat For Ever

Boned Larks in a Pie　　　Freshwater Crayfish, Lightly Seized

PARIS—THE TEMPLE

Civet de Lapin　　　Poule au Pot

The period during which Jack, Stephen and Jagiello are prisoners of the French is one of the great culinary sequences in the novels. It was a particular pleasure to follow them from Brest to Paris, recreating several of the dishes they ate (and two that they didn't) along the way.

BREST

'A young person for Monsieur Jagiello,' said the guard, with a grin. He stood away from the door, and there was the young person, holding a cloth-covered basket, blushing and hanging her pretty head. The others walked away to the window and talked in what they meant to be a detached, natural way; but few could help stealing glances at the maiden, and none could fail to hear Jagiello cry, 'But my dear, dear Mademoiselle, I asked for black pudding and apples, no more. And here is foie gras, a gratin of lobster, a partridge, three kinds of cheese, two kinds of wine, a strawberry tart . . .'

'I made it myself,' said the young person.

'I am sure it is wonderfully good: but it is much more than I can ever afford.'

'You must keep up your strength. You can pay for it later—or in some other way—or however you like.'

'But how?' asked Jagiello, in honest amazement. *'By a note of hand, do you mean?'*

'Pray step into the passage,' said she, pinker still.—The Surgeon's Mate, *315*

Gratin of Lobster

Jagiello must have been very attractive indeed, if the young person felt compelled to make this elegant and elaborate dish for him.

Court-Bouillon:
- 1 gallon dry white wine
- 1 gallon water
- 2 large onions, peeled and quartered
- 4 carrots, peeled and cut in large pieces
- 2 ribs celery, with leaves, cut in large pieces
- 1 teaspoon peppercorns
- 8 whole cloves
- 2 tablespoons salt
- Large handful of fresh parsley
- Large handful of fresh tarragon
- Large handful of fresh thyme

- 6 live lobsters, about 1½ pounds each
- 1 pound mushrooms, cleaned and cut in ½-inch dice
- 8 tablespoons butter
- 7 tablespoons flour
- ½ cup heavy cream
- 4 tablespoons dry sherry
- 1 cup grated Swiss (Emmenthaler or Gruyère) cheese
- 1 cup grated Parmesan cheese

Put the ingredients for the court-bouillon in a large stockpot, cover, and bring to a boil. Reduce the heat and simmer 20 minutes.

Bring the court-bouillon back to a rapid boil and plunge the lobsters in, head-first. Cover and bring to a boil again, then reduce heat and simmer 10 minutes. Remove the lobsters and set them to cool face-down on a flat surface, placing a weight on each one to keep the tail from curling.

Strain the court-bouillon, return it to the pot, and cook, uncovered, over high heat, for 30 minutes.

Sauté the mushrooms in 2 tablespoons of butter until they give up their juices. Set aside.

Melt the remaining butter in a heavy saucepan, stir in the flour, and cook over low heat, stirring frequently, until the flour is thoroughly cooked but not brown. Gradually add 4 cups of the hot court-bouillon, whisking all the while to prevent lumps.

Bring the sauce to a gentle boil and cook for 2 minutes. Remove from heat and stir in the cream and sherry. Reserving 3 tablespoons of each, add the cheeses to the sauce and combine thoroughly. Set aside.

Remove claws from lobsters. Remove and reserve legs. Cut the under-shell away from the tail, being careful not to sever the tail from the body. Pull out the tail meat and remove the intestinal vein. Cut the meat into ¼-inch slices and set aside.

Pull out the thorax, head, and sac. Pick out the meat (and the roe and tomalley, if you like them) and discard the rest (except the claws, legs, and body shells). Pick out the meat from the claws, keeping the shells intact if possible. Finely dice the claw and thorax meat.

Preheat oven to 425°.

Rinse the body shells and pat dry. Place them in a large baking dish, propping each one against the shells from its claws to keep it from spilling when you fill it.

Put the claw and thorax meat in a bowl with the mushrooms and 1¼ cups of the sauce. Mix well.

Pour a little sauce into each shell. Arrange the slices of tail meat in the tail section. Stuff the chest cavity with the meat and mushroom mixture. Pour the remaining sauce over the lobsters. Sprinkle with the re-served cheeses.

Bake until hot, browned and bubbly, about 20 minutes. Garnish amusingly with the legs.

Serves 6

Black Pudding

This is what Jagiello actually requested, and what the young person would presumably have brought him had he been less prepossessing.

25 feet of large (hog)
    sausage casings
2 cups steel-cut oats
4 cups water
2 cups fresh pork blood
½ pound leaf lard, minced or
    cut in small dice
Small handful of fresh sa-
    vory, chopped

Small handful of fresh
    thyme, chopped
Small handful of fresh mar-
    joram, chopped
Small handful of fresh pars-
    ley, chopped
Pinch of ground cloves
Pinch of mace
2 teaspoons salt

Soak the casings in cold water for at least 2 hours.

Gradually stir the oats into the 4 cups of water. Set over medium heat and bring to a boil. Reduce heat and simmer 15 minutes, stirring constantly. Remove from heat.

When the oats have cooled, combine them with the remaining ingredients. Stuff the casings fairly full, tying off individual sausages either with a twist in the casing or with a small piece of string.

Bring a large pot of water to a boil. Remove from heat, add a small amount of cold water (not more than about ½ cup) to stop the boiling, and put in the sausages. After 5 minutes, prick the sausages with a needle and return the pot to the heat. Bring to a boil and simmer 30 minutes, pricking the sausages again as they rise to the surface.

Take the sausages out of the pot and hang them in a cool, dry place for a day or two.

To serve, soak the sausages in hot water for 15 minutes, then fry them over medium heat until they are browned on all sides.

Makes about 2 dozen 4-inch sausages

Flummery

And now their dinner was spread: it came from the best establishment in the town, recommended by the Admiral, whereas Jagiello had chosen the cheapest cookshop; yet it made a poor show compared with his—only a couple of bass, two pairs of fowls, a saddle of mutton, half a dozen side-dishes, and a floating island.

'The mutton was tolerable,' said Jack . . . 'though it lacked red-currant jelly. But the French may say what they please—they have no notion of pudding, grande nation or not. This is not even a flummery: it is mere show and froth.'   —The Surgeon's Mate, *316–7*

We do have a recipe for French Floating Island elsewhere (see Archipel Flottant, p. 80), so we have taken a slight liberty here: in defiance of Jack's remark, this "mere show and froth" *is* a flummery—a French one, of course.

2 cups heavy cream	¼ teaspoon almond extract
½ stick cinnamon	2 tablespoons sugar
Zest of ½ lemon, in large, identifiable pieces	1¾ cups unflavored Calf's Foot Jelly (see variation,
Pinch of saffron	p. 268)
4 drops rose water	

Put the cream, cinnamon, lemon zest, and saffron into a heavy saucepan. Bring to a bare simmer, and cook over infinitesimal heat for 15 minutes, stirring constantly. Remove from heat, and cool to room temperature.

Locate and discard the cinnamon and lemon zest. Add the rose water, almond extract, and sugar.

In another heavy saucepan, melt the Calf's Foot Jelly over low heat. When it is completely dissolved, pour it into the cream mixture. Stir briskly to combine.

Rinse a 4-cup mold with cold water and shake out the excess. Pour in the flummery. Refrigerate until set (about 3 hours).

To unmold: Dip the mold briefly (not more than a few seconds) into very warm water, then quickly reverse onto a serving dish. Wait.

Serves 8

ON THE ROAD TO PARIS

Duhamel seemed . . . above human weakness except at meal times. . . . They dined and supped at the best inns in the towns they travelled through, a galloper being sent ahead to reserve a private room, to order particular dishes that varied town by town, and to desire that stated wines should be ready to accompany them. Duhamel did not eat at the same table, nor did he depart from his impenetrable reserve, but he did send over particularly successful dishes—lamb's sweetbreads in malmsey, little balls of tripe a man might eat for ever, boned larks in a pie—and presently they took to relying wholly on his judgment, although his judgment ran to an extraordinary number of courses, which he ate up entirely, wiping his plate with a piece of bread, a look of quiet satisfaction on his face.

—The Surgeon's Mate, *319–20*

Sweetbreads in Malmsey

To our great regret, we were unable to obtain lamb sweetbreads, which are smaller and even more delicate than those of veal. (On the other hand, we are passionately fond of veal sweetbreads.)

We were amply compensated for our disappointment by the discovery of a bottle of Malmsey where we least expected to find it: gathering dust on the shelf of our village liquor store.

All in all, a most felicitous combination.

3 pairs (about 3 pounds) veal
   sweetbreads
2 quarts water
4 tablespoons lemon juice
1 teaspoon salt
   Ice water
½ pound mushrooms, cut in
   small pieces
3 tablespoons chopped shallots
6 tablespoons butter

6 tablespoons brandy
1 cup Malmsey or Madeira
½ cup very rich brown stock
   (or reconstituted Portable
   Soup, p. 240)
3 tablespoons nonpareil capers
3 tablespoons heavy cream
1 tablespoon flour
½ pound Puff Paste (p. 270)

In a glass bowl, soak the sweetbreads for 1 hour in acidulated water (made by combining 1 quart water, 2 tablespoons lemon juice, and ½ teaspoon salt).

Drain the sweetbreads and put them in a nonreactive pot with the remaining water, lemon juice, and salt. Bring slowly to a gentle simmer, being careful not to let the water boil, and cook for 15 minutes.

Preheat oven to 450°.

Remove the sweetbreads from the pot and immediately plunge them into ice water. Carefully remove the membranes and tubes (blood vessels) and any extraneous connective tissue. Cut the sweetbreads into ½-inch dice.

Sauté the mushrooms and shallots in 3 tablespoons butter until they are soft. Set aside.

In the same pan, lightly brown the diced sweetbreads in 1½ tablespoons butter. Return the mushrooms and shallots to the pan. Warm the brandy in a small saucepan, pour it over the sweetbreads, and set it alight. After the flames subside, add the Malmsey, the stock, the capers and the cream. Cook over low heat until the sauce begins to simmer.

In a small bowl, work the flour into the remaining butter to form a smooth paste, and stir it into the sweetbread mixture. Continue to cook, stirring gently, for 2–3 minutes, or until the sauce is smooth and thick. Remove from heat, cover, and keep warm while you prepare the pastry.

Set out 6 1-cup ramekins. On a lightly floured board, roll out the Puff Paste until it is about ¼ inch thick. Cut 6 circular pieces the same size as the ramekins. Cut little decorative shapes out of the Puff Paste scraps, and place one or more on each circle as you please, brushing the undersides lightly with water and pressing down gently to cement them in place.

Spoon the sweetbread mixture into the ramekins (it will nearly fill them). Place one Puff-Paste circle on each ramekin. Put the ramekins on a baking sheet (in case the sauce bubbles over) and bake for 10 minutes.

Serve immediately, preferably accompanied by fresh young asparagus.

Serves 6

Little Balls of Tripe a Man Might Eat For Ever

1 pound honeycomb tripe, cleaned and parboiled
2 ounces suet, finely grated
1 cup bread crumbs
Zest of ½ lemon, grated
½ small onion, peeled and finely chopped
1 egg
1 tablespoon chopped fresh parsley
Small handful of fresh thyme
Small handful of fresh savory

½ teaspoon mace
½ teaspoon ground nutmeg
1 teaspoon salt
¼ teaspoon pepper
Flour for dredging
Oil or butter for frying

Sauce:
½ teaspoon dry mustard mixed with ½ teaspoon water
1 tablespoon melted butter
Pinch of cayenne

Put the tripe in a heavy nonreactive pot with salt water to cover. Bring it to a boil and simmer gently, covered, for 4 hours, changing the water halfway through the cooking process.

Drain the tripe, let it cool, and pat it dry. Mince it finely and combine it with the suet, bread crumbs, lemon zest, onion, egg, herbs and spices. Refrigerate the mixture at least an hour.

Roll the tripe mixture into 1-inch balls and dredge them in flour. Heat the oil or butter in a large frying pan, and fry the tripe balls to a nice brown.

Just before serving, whisk the mustard, butter, and cayenne together to make a dipping sauce.

Makes about 40

Boned Larks in a Pie

Our lark pie is actually as larkless as our Steak and Kidney Pudding, and for the same reason. In the case of the pudding it was both possible and authentic to omit the larks altogether; for this dish we did not have that option. The smallest birds we could obtain were quail, and we can report that we certainly wouldn't want to have to bone anything smaller.

(For information about preparing raised pies, see "About Raised Pies," p. 279.)

1 recipe (4½ pounds) Hot Water Paste (p. 269)

12 quail

1 medium onion, peeled

1 carrot, peeled and cut in 2-inch pieces

1 rib celery with leaves, cut in 2-inch pieces

Salt and pepper

3 tablespoons butter

¼ pound bacon, coarsely chopped

2 scallions, white and green parts, chopped

2 large shallots, peeled and chopped

Small handful of fresh savory, chopped

2 tablespoons chopped fresh parsley

½ ounce dried wild mushrooms such as cèpes, soaked in hot water, drained, and cut in ½-inch pieces

¼ pound fresh mushrooms, quartered

1 ounce truffles, sliced (optional)

1 recipe (1 pound) Godiveau (p. 267)

1 egg beaten with 1 teaspoon water

Put one-quarter of the Hot Water Paste in a bowl, cover with a damp cloth, and set aside in a warm place.

Form the remaining dough into a ball and place on a well-greased pan. Working quickly while the dough is warm, begin to raise your coffin, continuing in stages until it is about 10 inches across and 3½ inches high. Chill the coffin for at least an hour, or until it is firmly set.

Bone the quail. Place the bones in a pot with the onion, carrot, celery, salt and pepper to taste, and water to cover. Bring to a boil, reduce heat, and simmer, covered, 2 hours.

Melt the butter in a large frying pan, add the bacon and cook over medium heat until soft. Add the scallions, shallots and herbs, and stir to coat. Add the mushrooms and sauté, stirring frequently, until they give up their juices. Add the truffles and stir.

Pushing the mushroom mixture to the sides of the pan, put in 2 or 3 of the quail, skin side down. Cook them briefly (about a minute on each side), just enough to firm the flesh. Remove and set aside, and repeat with the remaining quail.

Line the coffin with a thin layer of Godiveau. Take a quail in your hand, skin side down. Put a small lump of Godiveau and a small spoonful of the mushroom mixture in the middle of the bird, fold it into a tight little package, and place it, seam side down, in the coffin. Repeat with the remaining quail.

After all the quail are snugly tucked into the pie, distribute the remaining mushroom mixture amongst them. Roll the remaining Godiveau into small balls and place them here and there in the pie.

Preheat oven to 450°.

On a floured board, roll out the reserved Hot Water Paste until it is about 3/16 inch thick. Cut a circle slightly larger than the diameter of the coffin. Cut a ½-inch hole in the center of the circle. Place this top crust lightly over the pie—do not crimp the edges together.

Cut decorative shapes (leaves, anchors, knots) from the pastry scraps and arrange them on the top crust, cementing them in place with the egg wash. Brush a thin layer of the remaining egg wash over the top of the pie.

Bake 15 minutes at 450°, turn the oven down to 350°, and bake 25 minutes.

While the pie is baking, strain and skim the stock. Return it to a low fire and let it continue to reduce.

Remove the pie from the oven. Carefully lift off the top crust and set it aside. Pour about ½ cup of the hot stock (or as much as possible) into the pie. Holding your breath, delicately replace the top crust.

Return the pie to the oven and bake for another 10 minutes.

Remove the top crust at the table just before serving.

Serves 12

Variation: If you are able to get larks, substitute them for the quail. You will need 36 of them, and they should be packed into the pie in 3 layers: 12 larks, a thin layer of Godiveau, another 12 larks, and so on.

Then at Alençon Duhamel's judgment failed him. As he walked into the kitchen of the inn his keen eye perceived a tub of freshwater crayfish, and although they had not fasted long enough to purge themselves of the filth upon which they had been regaling he ordered them to be boiled at once. 'Very lightly boiled—just seized, you understand—it would be a crime to spoil their flavour, such fine fat beasts.'

Stephen's reflections had left him with little appetite; but Jagiello, who did not feel the need to reflect, ate several score, and Jack, muttering 'that no Frenchman should outdo him' kept pace. In his already weakened, upset condition he became so quickly ill, so obviously and transparently disordered in the middle of an empty road that at last Duhamel suggested that Dr Maturin should do something for him, should prescribe physic, or take some appropriate measures. Stephen had been waiting for this with mounting impatience: 'Very well,' he said, writing on his knee. 'If you will have the goodness to tell one of the soldiers to take this to an apothecary, I believe we may travel on in something more nearly resembling comfort.'

—The Surgeon's Mate, *320–1*

Freshwater Crayfish, Lightly Seized

Either our crayfish had already fasted sufficiently to purge themselves, or they had been purged in some other manner by the time they reached us—in any case, we are happy to say that we suffered no ill effects whatsoever. They were fine fat beasts, and we enjoyed them mightily on more than one occasion.

3	pounds fresh live crayfish	6	whole scallions, cleaned and trimmed

Court-bouillon:
    Large handful of fresh thyme
    Large handful of fresh savory
    Large handful of fresh parsley
6 whole cloves
1½ teaspoons peppercorns
2 quarts dry white wine
2 quarts water

6 whole scallions, cleaned and
    trimmed
2 small onions, peeled and
    quartered
3 carrots, peeled and cut in
    large pieces
2 cloves garlic
2 tablespoons butter
1 tablespoon salt

Rinse the crayfish thoroughly to remove any traces of mud. (If you are still concerned about the possibility of "filth," you may also want to let them soak in a tub of salted water for an hour or so.)

Tie the thyme, savory, parsley, cloves, and peppercorns into a piece of cheesecloth. Put this and the rest of the court-bouillon ingredients into a large stockpot. Bring to a boil, reduce the heat, and simmer, covered, for 30 minutes or more. Strain the liquid and return it to the pot.

Bring the court-bouillon once again to a rolling boil and put in the crayfish (this will kill them instantly). After the liquid returns to a boil, reduce the heat slightly and cook the crayfish for 5 minutes. Remove them immediately with a large slotted spoon, and serve them in soup plates, either hot or cold, accompanied by a sauce such as Mayonnaise (p. 262). The court-bouillon may be discarded or strained and kept for future use.

Serves 6 as a first course

PARIS—THE TEMPLE

'There is no difficulty,' said the guard. 'I know a little place not a hundred yards from here: Madame veuve Lehideux, cooked dishes at all hours, choice wines. . . . I do not say it is the Emperor's table; I will not deceive you, gentlemen. It is only an honest cuisine bourgeoise, but such a civet de lapin!'—kissing his thick fingers—'such a truly velvet poule au pot! And the great point is, you get your dishes hot. I always say, food must be hot. It is only a small

place, but it is not a stone's throw from here: it is in the rue des Neuf Fiancées,
without a word of lie; so the food can be brought in hot, if you understand me.'
     'Then let us send to Madame Lehideux,' said Stephen.

—The Surgeon's Mate, *331–2*

Civet de Lapin

A classic civet (from the French *cive*, "chive") is a ragoût of rabbit or
other small game, thickened at the last with the blood of the animal.
If (as frequently occurs in these benighted times) your rabbit is short
of blood, you can use some of the liver as a supplement or substitute.

2 rabbits, 3–4 pounds each	1 teaspoon dry mustard
⅔ cup rabbit blood (and/or the rabbit livers, cut in small pieces)	1 cup rich brown stock (or re-constituted Portable Soup, p. 240)
4 teaspoons cider vinegar	1 tablespoon chopped fresh parsley
4 ounces salt pork, cut into ½-inch cubes	Few sprigs of fresh thyme
16 small onions, peeled and scored with a deep "X" at the root end	Few sprigs of fresh savory
	Few sprigs of fresh hyssop
	Small handful of fresh chives
Flour for dredging	Small handful of fresh sage
Salt and pepper	
½ pound mushrooms, halved or quartered	1 bay leaf
	1 recipe (about 3 dozen) Forcemeat Balls (p. 267)
¼ cup brandy	
2 cups burgundy	Butter or oil for frying

Clean the rabbits. Put the blood, the livers (if you are using them) and
the vinegar in a bowl, cover, and set aside. Cut the rabbits into serving pieces.

In a large heavy stewpot, brown the salt pork over medium heat until
most of the fat has been rendered. Remove the pork cubes and set
them aside.

Brown the onions on all sides in the pork fat. Remove and set aside.

Season the flour with salt and pepper. Dredge the rabbit pieces in
flour and brown them, a few at a time, in the pork fat. Set them aside.

Sauté the mushrooms in the pork fat. Remove and set aside.

Deglaze the pot with the brandy. Add the burgundy and simmer for 5 minutes to cook off the alcohol. Make a smooth paste of the mustard and 1 tablespoon of the stock. Add the paste and the remaining stock to the liquid in the pot.

Return the rabbit, onions, mushrooms, and salt pork to the pot. Add the herbs. Bring gradually to a boil, cover, reduce the heat and simmer gently for 2 hours, stirring occasionally. Remove the bay leaf.

Put the blood and vinegar through a fine sieve (if you are also using the livers, you will need to mash them a bit to produce a purée). Add the mixture to the pot, stirring as little as possible (the blood should be evenly distributed, but it may tend to curdle if it is stirred too much). Simmer 10–15 minutes.

While the Civet is simmering, heat 2 tablespoons of the butter or oil in a skillet. Fry the Forcemeat Balls until they are nicely browned on all sides.

Serve in wide soup plates and garnish with the Forcemeat Balls.

Serves 8

Poule au Pot

"Truly velvet" it is.

1 large chicken, about 6 or 7 pounds
Salt and pepper
2 ribs celery, cut in 2-inch pieces, leaves reserved
3 large carrots, peeled and cut into 2-inch pieces
1 large onion, peeled
2 sprigs of fresh rosemary
3 large leeks
¼ pound bacon
10 or more small onions, peeled and scored with a deep "X" at the root end

½ pound large mushrooms, halved
3 large potatoes (about 1½ pounds altogether)
Few sprigs of fresh thyme
Few sprigs of fresh tarragon
Few sprigs of fresh parsley
1½ cups red wine
1 cup brown stock (or reconstituted Portable Soup, p. 240)

Rub the chicken inside and out with salt and pepper. Put the celery leaves, 2 or 3 carrot pieces, the large onion, and a sprig of rosemary in the cavity. Truss the chicken.

Trim the roots of the leeks and cut off the tops, leaving about an inch of green. Cut them in half lengthwise and wash them thoroughly under running water, pulling the leaves apart to make sure all grit is removed. Cut them into 2-inch pieces.

In a heavy stewpot or Dutch oven, cook the bacon until it is translucent. Remove and set aside. Brown the chicken on all sides in the bacon fat. Remove and set aside.

Brown the small onions, leeks, carrots, celery and mushrooms in the bacon fat over fairly high heat. Meanwhile, peel the potatoes and cut them into large chunks (about 1½ inches). When the vegetables are well browned, add the potatoes, a sprig of rosemary, the thyme, tarragon and parsley, and salt and pepper to taste. Stir all together for a few minutes.

Set the chicken, breast-side up, on the bed of vegetables. Lay the bacon strips over the chicken. Add the wine and the stock. Cover, bring to a boil, then reduce heat and simmer, covered, 30 minutes. Turn the chicken breast-side down, cover, and simmer another 30 minutes.

To serve, place the chicken in a deep platter, surrounded by the vegetables. Skim the fat from the sauce and pour the sauce over the chicken.

Serves 6

The widow Lehideux gave the utmost satisfaction; her meals quickly became part of their daily pattern, and their chief diversion. She was very willing to do her best and she sent little beautifully-written badly-spelt notes with suggestions according to the state of the market; and to these Stephen replied with comments on the last dish and recommendations, even receipts, for the next. 'It is only a woman's cookery, to be sure,' he said ... 'but ... how very good it is! She must be a knowing old soul, with great experience, no doubt in excellent service before the Revolution. Perhaps something of a slut: your amiable slut makes the best of cooks.'

—The Surgeon's Mate, *334–5*

SOUTH SEAS

Sour Breadfruit Pap

There is another prison sequence, in *The Far Side of the World*, wherein Jack and Stephen are given sour breadfruit pap. Having plenty of breadfruit, we made this, as in duty bound; the results were so unpleasant that we haven't the heart to describe them in much detail.

1 "fit" breadfruit	A great many large (banana
Water	or palm, for instance) leaves

Place the breadfruit in a large pot with boiling water to cover. Boil until tender, about 30 minutes. Remove from water and allow to cool.

Peel the breadfruit, cut it open, and remove the seeds. Put it in a bowl and mash it to a pulp. Knead the pulp with your hands, adding a little water, until the mixture resembles a smooth, thick paste.

Wrap the paste in leaves. Dig a hole in the sand a foot or so deep, and line it with leaves or grass. Put the wrapped paste bundle in the hole, cover with more leaves, weight it down with stones, and fill in the hole with sand. If you dig it up in a day or two you will find it, as Captain Cook said, "soft and disagreeably sweet." Wait a few more days for the second fermentation—when you dig it up it will still be soft and disagreeable, but no longer sweet. Captain Cook says this mess will keep for 10–12 months, during which time it can be rolled into balls, baked, and eaten "either hot or cold, and hath a sour and disagreeable taste."

We did not have the patience to wait the full 10 months; but we can certainly vouch for the taste.

Makes an awful lot of pap

The Dusty Miller

Dusty was his coat.
Dusty was his colour.
Dusty was the kiss
   That I gat frae the miller.

CHAPTER EIGHT

The
Millers'
Tale

The story of the Millers in Onion Sauce
(in *H.M.S. Surprise*, 104-46)
is so enthralling that we felt
it required a chapter of
its own.

T ell me, Mr Callow,' said Jack, partly out of a wish not to hear too much and partly to make his guest welcome, 'how is the midshipmen's mess coming along? I have not seen your ram this week or more.' The ancient creature palmed off upon the unsuspecting caterer as a hogget had been a familiar sight, stumping slowly about upon the deck.

'Pretty low, sir,' said Callow, withdrawing his hand from the breadbarge. 'We ate him in seventy north, and now we are down to the hen. But we give her all our bargemen, sir, and she may lay an egg.'

'You ain't down to millers, then?' said Pullings.

'Oh yes we are, sir,' cried the midshipman. 'Threepence, they have reached, which is a God-damned—a crying shame.'

'What are millers?' asked Stephen.

'Rats, saving your presence,' said Jack. 'Only we call 'em millers to make 'em eat better; and perhaps because they are dusty, too, from getting into the flour and peas.'   —H.M.S. Surprise, *105–6*

How does one write a recipe for rats in onion sauce? The Dear only knows.

What kind of rats? Where to get them? How to dress them? Should they be grilled? Stewed? Dredged in flour? Browned? And if so, in what kind of fat? The onion sauce: brown or white?

We didn't really expect any of our usual culinary sources to provide the information we needed; and we were right. So we turned to the text, and on close examination it yielded the answers we sought:

> *'My rats will not touch anything but the best biscuit, slightly moistened with melted butter. They are obese; their proud bellies drag the ground.'*
>
> *'Rats, Doctor?' cried Pullings. 'Why do you keep rats?'*
>
> *'I wish to see how they come along—to watch their motions,' said Stephen. He was in fact conducting an experiment, feeding them with madder to see how long it took to penetrate their bones, but he did not mention this.*

Based on these innocent remarks made during breakfast in Jack's improvised cabin, and on Stephen's later lament (". . . my valuable rats. . . . Rats I had brought up by hand, cosseted since Berry Head . . ."), we felt it was fair to assume that the rats in question were not ordinary ship's rats. With some relief we relinquished our notion of emulating the cheese-and-noose hunting methods of Jack's youth, and settled instead for half a dozen "globular, kitten-sized" laboratory rats.

(We had better admit at once that we did not go so far as to feed them with madder, since we really had no wish to duplicate Stephen's experiment on our own bones.)

Once we had killed them and laid them out ("neatly skinned, opened and cleaned, like tiny sheep"), the next question was how to butcher them. Easily resolved. In his confession Babbington refers to having crunched up the bones "like larks"—so we left our rats on the bone and simply cut them into quarters.

How does a hungry young gentleman (or a three-legged sea-cook such as Johnson, supposing him to have been involved) cook a truly prime miller? Here again Babbington's confession supplied the key: "the rats being already dead, and dressed with onion-sauce"—this to us suggested braising, which is appropriate both to the period and to the tenderness and delicate flavor of the meat (and also produces the base for the onion sauce). Since "stores were well enough" except for the condemned butter and cheese, we felt it was reasonable to assume that a little flour would be available for dredging. Likewise Portable Soup, though the water for diluting it was admittedly at a premium. On the other hand, we deliberately omitted such articles as wine, cream, Mushroom Ketchup, and herbs, on the assumption that the midshipmen would not have had access to them.

What fat to use? Ordinarily the obvious, perhaps the only, choice would have been slush, which was usually plentiful. But we felt something more exciting was called for, and we did not have far to seek. In studying the chronology of the episode it became clear that the millers *must* have been stolen, dressed and eaten on Sunday afternoon, on the day of the fateful breakfast during which Callow learned of their existence. Immediately after dinner, Stephen and Nicolls row across to St. Paul's Rocks; as soon as they are well away, Callow nips down to Stephen's storeroom and makes off with the millers ("unknown hands . . . wafted these prime millers into the larboard midshipmen's berth"). Within a few hours the squalls strike, and during the "incessant labours" of the ensuing week (while Stephen is marooned on St. Paul's Rocks and living on Boiled Shit, p. 231) the entire ship's company is far too busy keeping afloat to concern itself with miller cookery. So the feast can only have taken place in the interval between Sunday dinner and the first squall.

Having determined thus much, it was the work of a moment to return to the breakfast scene of that morning and discover—what? The "steady champ" of Callow's jaws as "he engulfed twenty-seven rashers." Bacon fat! Too precious a commodity for a midshipman, as a rule, but in this case well worth a bribe to the cook in the form of a grog ration or so.

Millers in Onion Sauce

We were somewhat taken aback to discover that miller is absolutely delicious, rather like very young and tender rabbit. At the risk of defying logic and authenticity, we suggest tiny green peas and little boiled red potatoes as a suitable accompaniment.

Expect about 50 percent "yield" from a miller. Ours weighed about 12 ounces each on the hoof.

6 prime millers, about 6
    ounces each after skinning
    and cleaning
    Flour for dredging
    Salt and pepper
4–5 tablespoons bacon
    fat from the Captain's
    breakfast

1 large onion, peeled
    and thinly sliced
1¼ cups stock
    (or reconstituted Portable
    Soup, p. 240)

Cut the millers into serving pieces. Season the flour with salt and pepper. Dredge the millers in the flour and set aside.

Heat 2 tablespoons of the bacon fat in a large, heavy pan over medium heat. Add the onion and sauté, stirring occasionally, until limp and golden. Remove the onion and set aside.

In the same pan, brown the millers on all sides, a few pieces at a time, adding more bacon fat as needed. Set the millers aside.

Deglaze the pan with the stock. Return the millers and onions to the pan, add salt and pepper to taste, and bring to a boil. Cover, reduce heat, and simmer 20 minutes.

Serves 6 hungry midshipmen

Meanwhile, back on the rock . . .

Boiled Shit

'Tell me, Stephen, what did you drink on that infernal rock?'
'Boiled shit.' Stephen was chaste in his speech, rarely an oath, never an
obscene word, never any bawdy: his reply astonished Jack, who looked
quickly at the tablecloth. Perhaps it was a learned term he had misunder-
stood. 'Boiled shit,' he said again. Jack smiled in a worldly fashion, but he
felt the blush rising. 'Yes. There was one single pool of rainwater left in a
hollow. The birds defecated in it, copiously. Not with set intent—the whole
rock is normally deep in their droppings—but enough to foul it to the pitch
of nausea. The next day was hotter, if possible, and with the reverberation
the liquid rose to an extraordinary temperature. I drank it, however, until
it ceased to be a liquid at all. . . .'   —H.M.S. Surprise, *138*

We live at the seashore, surrounded by every imaginable kind of wa-
terfowl, so we are admirably situated for testing this dish. The guano,
of course, was all too easily obtained—indeed, it was hard to avoid.
Our sandy beaches do not boast rocks, hollow or otherwise, but they
are littered with clam shells, which made a perfectly adequate substitute.

We made it, but we do not claim to have drunk it. There are
lengths to which we will not go.

1 ounce assorted seabird guano   ¼ cup rainwater

Gather the guano in a large clam shell. Gradually add the water, stirring constantly. Set in a hot sun until it boils. Do not drink unless absolutely desperate.

Serves 1

Page	Time	What's Happening	Meanwhile...
	Sunday		
104		Jack invites Stephen, Pullings, and Midshipman Callow to breakfast.	
105	4 bells in the forenoon watch	Breakfast. "Look, there is a whole pile of bacon under that cover." Callow eats 27 rashers.	
106		"What are millers?" Stephen describes his proud, obese rats.	
107		Stores were well enough, but the cheese and butter had to be condemned ... the water was dangerously short.	
108	5 bells in the forenoon watch	Beat to divisions.	
115		Rig church.	Sail sighted two points on the starboard bow. Callow daydreams about having two dinners.
116	8 bells in the forenoon watch	Make it noon.	"Sail" identified as St. Paul's Rocks.
120	4 bells in the afternoon watch	Gunroom dinner.	Swimming-bath rigged on the larboard side.
123		Gunroom dinner ends.	Breeze dies away entirely. Rocks two miles away, to starboard.
124		Stephen asks for a boat to go to the Rocks. Even though it's Sunday, Nicolls offers to row him over. They set off in the jolly-boat.	[Callow watches them out of sight and nips down to the Doctor's storeroom.]
128		Stephen can see the ship from the top of the island, her sails slack.	
130		The first squall hits the island.	
131		Squall over—Nicolls, boat and boxes gone.	*Surprise* hull-down to the east, mizen and maintop gone.
133	About a week later	Stephen rescued.	
138	Next day	"Boiled Shit"	
139		"The incessant labours of the last week"	
141		"My rats have vanished... my valuable rats... brought up by hand..."	
142		Babbington confesses.	

Babbington looked wretchedly from one to the other, licked his lips and said, 'I ate your rat, sir. I am very sorry, and I ask your pardon.'

'Did you so?' said Stephen mildly. 'Well, I hope you enjoyed it. . . .'

'He only ate it when it was dead,' said Jack.

'It would have been a strangely hasty, agitated meal, had he ate it before,' said Stephen. —H.M.S. Surprise, *143*

Cantata on the 16th Sunday after Trinity

"Gottes Zeit ist die allerbeste Zeit"

Tenor Aria: Psalm 90, V. 12

Johann Sebastian Bach, BWV 106

CHAPTER NINE

The
Sick-Bay

G entlemen,' said Stephen to his assistants in their splendid new
sick-berth, full of light and air, furnished with capacious dispen-
saries, port and starboard, 'I believe we may now cross off the antimo-
nials, jalap and camphire, the eight yards of Welsh linen bandage, and
the twelve yards of finer linen, which sets us up for the first month, barring the tourniquets, the mercury, and the small list of alexipharmics
that Beale is sending over tomorrow. So much for our official supplies.
But I have added a certain number of comforts—they are in the cases on
the left, together with a chest of portable soup infinitely superior to the
Victualling Board's second-hand carpenter's glue. . . .'

—The Commodore, 97–8

If cooking was an inexact science in Stephen's day, medicine was
even more so, often with horrifying results (though Stephen himself
was both unusually skilled and unusually lucky in this respect).
Which we can't pretend to top it the medical expert, so for the most
part we will confine ourselves to discussing the actual foods served in
the sick-bay.

Virtually every period cookbook we studied contained a section on
invalid cookery, which was considered an important branch of the
household art. Some of these sections include herbal brews, purges,
Hysteric Waters, Snail Waters, and other medicinal compounds that
are truly terrifying (we have reproduced in this chapter one of Eliza

Smith's milder examples, Hiera Picra); even the more restrained among them invariably give recipes for the indispensable staples of the sickroom: Portable Soup, Barley-Water, Arrowroot Gruel, Posset, etc.

Diet was only one of several factors in the complicated process of "rectifying the humours," or adjusting the balance among the vital elements of health: cold and heat, moisture and dryness, acidity and alkalinity, phlegm and choler. Invalid cookery was based on the general principle that most diseases required either a "lowering" or a "strengthening" diet. The former included mild and meatless foods such as the various waters and gruels, which were thought to be efficacious in bringing down a fever or calming excitable nerves; the latter, usually based on proteins, milk or cream, and alcohol, was supposed to invigorate the blood and fortify the constitution.

Barley-Water

'Some lady of your acquaintance has been too liberal with her favours, too universally kind.'

'Oh, Lord,' cried Jack, to whom this had never happened before.

'Never mind,' said Stephen, touched by Jack's horror. 'We shall soon have you on your feet again: taken early, there is no great problem. It will do you no harm to keep close, drink nothing but demulcent barley-water and eat gruel, thin gruel. . . .'   —Master and Commander, *349*

'Killick! Killick, there.'

'Which I'm a-coming, ain't I?'—this from a certain distance; and as the cabin door opened, 'This is the best I can do, sir. Lemon barley-water made of rice, and loo-warm, at that; but at least the lemon is shaddocks, which is close on.'   —The Thirteen-Gun Salute, *250*

⅓ cup pearl barley   1 tablespoon lemon or lime
1 quart water   juice
1 tablespoon sugar

Put the barley and water in a saucepan over fairly high heat. Boil, skimming frequently, until the liquid is reduced by half (about 15 minutes). Put through a fine strainer, discard the barley (or re-use it in Barley-Broth, below) and add the sugar and the lemon or lime juice to the resulting liquid. Serve chilled.

Makes 1 pint

Variation: To reproduce the version Killick serves Jack in *The Thirteen-Gun Salute,* substitute rice for the barley and shaddock (grapefruit) juice for the lemon or lime juice—and serve loo-warm.

Barley-Broth

[Stephen] had rarely felt a more general irritation nor less certainty of being able to control it, and he plied his spoon as though salvation lay at the bottom of his soup-plate. In a way it did: the barley-broth, glutinous and lenitive, helped to bring his inner man more nearly in harmony with his outward appearance—so much for free-will—and by the time they reached the first remove little effort was needed for a proper complaisance.
—Desolation Island, *97*

In the eighteenth century, there were as many widely divergent approaches to making Barley (or Scotch) Broth as there were cooks. Some of them used beef or fowl instead of lamb or mutton; some used so little barley as to make the name a gross exaggeration; some added unlikely combinations of bread, butter, sugar, eggs, mashed vegetables, leeks, vinegar, nasturtiums, and marigolds. In some cases the meat was served separately with mustard or caper-sauce.

Barley-Broth could be strained, skimmed and diluted, and served as part of a lowering diet; more typically, as in this version, it was a hearty component of a strengthening diet. And it is certainly glutinous and lenitive.

2 pounds very meaty lamb or mutton bones	1 cup pearl barley
	½ cup dried split peas
1 large carrot, peeled and cut in 2-inch pieces	2 quarts water
	1 tablespoon chopped fresh parsley
1 rib celery, cut in 2-inch pieces	
1 large onion, peeled and quartered	Salt and pepper
	1 medium white turnip, peeled and cut in 1-inch pieces

Put everything except the turnip in a large heavy stewpot over medium heat. Bring slowly to a boil, skimming off any scum that forms on the surface. Once the scum has stopped rising (after about 5 minutes), reduce the heat, cover, and simmer 1 hour. Add the turnip (and, if necessary, more water), cover, and simmer another hour.

Skim whatever fat has accumulated on the surface. You may discard the bones or not, as you choose—the meat, however, should remain in the soup.

Serves 8

Portable Soup

'Oh,' she said, and absently she took three spoonfuls of the soup. 'Lord above,' she said, 'what is this?'

'Soup. Portable soup. Pray take a little more, it will rectify the humours.'

'I thought it was luke-warm glue. But it goes down quite well, if you don't breathe.'   —The Fortune of War, *318*

Portable Soup (also known as Pocket Soop or Veal Glew) is the ancestor of the modern bouillon cube (hence its frequent use in the sickroom) and a close cousin of the *Glace de Viande* used in French cooking: a stock based on meat bones with a few vegetables and herbs, first browned, then simmered a *long* time, then strained, skimmed, and cooked again for a *long* time, until it reaches a very high degree of concentration and a correspondingly low volume. Once it cools and congeals, the final product of 10 gallons of stock is a small brown rubbery slab about 6 inches by 12 inches by ½ inch, with an intense meaty taste. (It is a wonderful flavoring agent for sauces and gravies, but it is not particularly good on its own—and must have been considerably worse two hundred years ago, after many months or even years of imperfect preservation.)

How long is a *long* time? William Gelleroy says to boil the soup until "the meat has lost its virtue"; Hannah Glasse, from whom he copied his recipe, says until "the Meat is good for nothing." (Of course, the loss of virtue in a piece of meat is a highly subjective matter; we ourselves have never yet succeeded in boiling *all* the virtue out of any meat.) Mrs. Beeton says the first boiling should be "12 hours, or more, if the meat be not done to rags," and suggests 8 hours, stirring all the while, for the second.

Most eighteenth-century cooks included a further cooking stage, in which the soup was placed in a *bain-marie* arrangement until it was "thick and ropy." We have eliminated this step because we found that our soup became quite ropy enough without it.

30 pounds very meaty bones (any combination of beef, pork, and veal—shin, neck, etc.)

2 pig's feet or 1 pound ham (optional)

6 large onions, peeled and cut in half

6 large carrots, peeled and cut in half

6 ribs celery with leaves, cut in pieces

Large handful of fresh parsley

Large handful of fresh thyme

Large handful of fresh hyssop

Large handful of fresh marjoram

1 tablespoon mace

12 whole cloves

3 tablespoons peppercorns

Salt

In a large stewpot (several stewpots, actually), brown the bones on all sides, a few at a time, in their own fat.

Return all the bones to the pot(s) and add the vegetables, herbs, and spices, and water to cover. Bring slowly to a boil, skimming off any scum that forms on the surface. Cover, but not too tightly—leave a little room for steam to escape. Reduce heat and simmer at least 6 hours.

Strain and skim the stock, discarding the bones. (At this point you must determine for yourself whether or not the meat still has any virtue; if not, discard it too.) Put the stock in the widest pot or pan you can find. Bring to a gentle boil over medium heat. Cook, uncovered, skimming occasionally, until the liquid is reduced to about one-eighth its original volume (this will take at least another 6 hours).

Pour the reduced stock into a shallow pan and refrigerate until firmly set. Run a knife around the edges and take the soup out of the pan (you will find that you can pick it up as if it were a thick piece of translucent leather). Cut it into 1-inch cubes and freeze in an airtight container.

Depending on the concentration required, the dilution ratio will be approximately 4 cubes Portable Soup to 1 cup hot water.

Note: To be truly portable and authentic, this "soop" should be dried rather than frozen; and the cooks of the period spent many days turning slabs of jellied soup on fresh pieces of flannel "until the Glew be quite Hard." We have tried this, and can report that it is apparently a seasonal operation; attempting it at the seaside during the height of summer is apt to produce nothing but a mass of furry—and not very portable—lumps.

Makes about 3 pounds of "portable" soup cubes

Arrowroot Gruel, Reasonably Slab

'Listen, Jack,' said Stephen in the same low voice, 'Diana says that sea-captains can marry people. Is it true?'

Jack nodded, but no more, for Broke was at hand, politely asking for news of Mrs Villiers. Stephen said that the most distressing symptoms were over, that a tonic draught, such as coffee of triple or even quadruple strength, followed by a small bowl of arrowroot gruel, reasonably slab, would set her up by the afternoon. 'And then, sir,' he added, 'you would oblige me infinitely by marrying us, if you have the leisure.'

—The Fortune of War, *299*

If this preparation was expected to alleviate seasickness, we must question in all honesty whether the cure was not worse than the disease. The more "slab" (thick) it became, the less appetizing we found it.

2 teaspoons arrowroot	1 tablespoon medium-dry
2 tablespoons cold water	sherry
1 cup boiling water	1 teaspoon lemon juice
1 tablespoon sugar	Pinch of salt
3 tablespoons port	Ground cinnamon (optional)

In a small saucepan, combine the arrowroot with the cold water and stir to dissolve. Gradually add the boiling water, stirring constantly. Bring to a boil and cook gently for 2 minutes, stirring frequently. Add the sugar, port, sherry, lemon juice, and salt. Sprinkle with cinnamon and anything else you can think of. It will still be horrid.

Serves 1 very helpless invalid

Inspissated Juice (Rob)

They washed Martin with warm fresh water all over twice, then laid on sweet oil wherever it would do good. . . . From time to time he groaned or uttered a disconnected word; twice he opened his eyes, raised his head and stared about, uncomprehending; once he took a little water with inspissated lemon-juice in it; but generally speaking he was wholly inert, and the ha-bitual look of anxiety had left his face.   —The Wine-Dark Sea, *108–9*

Inspissated lime-juice, in kegs. Lemon rob, 15 kegs.
                                                       —The Letter of Marque, *244*

> Rob is something an uncouth word and haply formidable to the ig-norant countryman in these thieving times, and therefore in the first place I will explain the word. . . . Rob or Sapa is the juyces of a fruit, made thick by the heat either of the sun or the fire, that is capable of being kept safe from putrefaction.
> —Nicholas Culpeper, *Pharmacopoeia Londinensis* (1718)

This thickening was referred to as inspissation, and could be applied to any fruit, vegetable, or herb that produced juice. At various points in the Aubrey/Maturin series use is made of the inspissated juices of aconite, henbane, figs (the "cathartic" that keeps Fanshawe confined to the quarter-gallery in *The Yellow Admiral*), and lettuce.

> *'And as for the agitation, might not we add the inspissated juice of let-tuce to our present measures? The pulse is light, quick, and irregular; and there is an uncommon degree of nervous excitement and irascibility, in spite of the apparent stoicism.'*
> —The Fortune of War, *137*

The milky juice of lettuce stalks (lettuce, or *Lactuca*, takes its name from the Latin *lac*, "milk") was used medicinally in both dried ("Lac-tucarium") and inspissated forms. It was considered mildly narcotic, and was used "as a very mild hypnotic in the *wakefulness* caused by writing or other mental work late into the night."

Timing is everything. By the time we learned this, our lettuce had not only flowered and gone to seed, but had begun to dry out. We squeezed out a few pathetic white drops and did our best to inspissate them—but the results were too meagre to record. With the withered stalks mocking us from the compost heap, we turned our attention to the inspissation of lemon and lime juices.

Incidentally, the antiscorbutic value of lemon or lime Rob is negligible: one by-product of the long cooking process is that most of the vitamin C is lost. But as Culpeper says, "for whatever it is used now it matters not," and 2 teaspoons of Rob dissolved in 1 cup of boiling water makes a comfortable drink.

Juice of 12 lemons or limes   ¾ cup sugar (or more, to
     (approximately 1½ cups)   taste)

Put the juice into a saucepan and stir in the sugar. Cook over low heat until the sugar is completely dissolved.

Cover and set aside in a cool place for 24 hours.

Pour the juice into the top of a double boiler. Cook briskly over boiling water (replenishing the water as necessary) for about 3 hours, or until the mixture is reduced to a thick syrup.

Makes 1 cup

Posset

'Will the invalid gentleman take a little posset before he goes?' asked the landlady of the Crown. 'It is a nasty raw day—Portsmouth is not Gibraltar—and he looks but palely.' . . .

'I will try, Mrs Moss; but he is as obstinate as a bee in a bull's foot.'

'Invalids, sir,' said Mrs Moss, shaking her head, 'is all the same. When I nursed Moss on his death-bed, he was that cross and fractious! No goose-pie, no mandragore, no posset, not if it was ever so.'

'Stephen,' he cried, with a meretricious affectation of gaiety, 'just toss this off, will you . . . ?'

'I will not,' said Stephen. 'It is another of your damned possets. Am I in childbed, for all love, that I should be plagued, smothered, destroyed with caudle?'   —H.M.S. Surprise, *74*

Possets and caudles were hot, bracing drinks, generally considered appropriate for invalids, nervous young women, and anyone coming in from the cold. A posset was thick and rich, made of milk or cream curdled with wine or ale; occasionally, as in the sack posset of Sir Fleetwood Fletcher (whoever he may be), it also contained eggs, which made it more like a heavy custard than a drink. A caudle, even more closely associated with the sickroom, was apt to be less rich (no milk or cream), spicier and more gruel-like.

A LYRICAL RECEIPT FOR SACK POSSET

From fam'd Barbadoes, on the western main,
Fetch sugar, ounces four; fetch sack from Spain
A pint; and from the Eastern Indian coast
Nutmeg, the glory of our northern toast;
O'er flaming coals let them together heat
Till the all-conquering sack dissolve the sweet;
O'er such another fire put eggs just then,
New-born from tread of cock and rump of hen;
Stir them with steady hand and conscience pricking,
To see th' untimely end of ten fine chickens:
From shining shelf take down the brazen skillet,
A quart of milk from gentle cow will fill it;
When boil'd and cold, put milk and sack to eggs,
Unite them firmly like the Triple League,
And on the fire let them together dwell
Till miss sing twice—you must not kiss and tell:
Each lad and lass take up a silver spoon,
And fall on fiercely like a starv'd dragoon.

—Sir Fleetwood Fletcher

It would be hard to improve on Sir Fleetwood's "receipt," as to either language or content, but this oatmeal sack posset is very rich and comforting, if a bit cloying.

3 tablespoons oatmeal
2 cups milk
¼ teaspoon mace
Pinch of salt

¼ cup medium-dry sherry
¼ cup ale
3 tablespoons sugar

Grind the oatmeal to a fine powder. Put it in a saucepan with the milk, mace, and salt. Stir to combine thoroughly and cook over low heat until the oatmeal no longer tastes raw (about 15 minutes). In another saucepan, bring the sherry, ale, and sugar to a boil. Pour into the oatmeal mixture, stir, cook 1 minute, and pour into a basin. Let it settle for a few minutes. Serve hot.

Serves 1

Drugs

'You have no notion of what a hypochondriac your seaman is: they love to be physicked. . . .'   —Master and Commander, *42*

Ever since Stephen Maturin had grown rich with their first prize he had constantly laid in great quantities of asafetida, castoreum and other substances, to make his medicines more revolting in taste, smell and texture than any others in the fleet; and he found it answered—his hardy patients knew with their entire beings that they were being physicked.

        —Master and Commander, *350*

Some of this physic took the harmless form of such placebos as bread-pills, which are exactly what their name implies. Some of it was more drastic, as witness the examples given here. (Note: we have *not* tried these, nor do we recommend doing so.)

Hiera Picra

This time there was in fact something wrong with Mr Fox. Stephen could not tell what it was, but he did not like either the look or the feel of his pa-tient's belly, and since Fox was somewhat plethoric he decided to bleed and purge him. 'I shall put you on a course of physic and a low diet for a week. . . .'

For the first few days Fox was in serious discomfort, sometimes in considerable pain, for the rhubarb, hiera picra and calomel worked power-fully. . . . —The Thirteen-Gun Salute, *165*

Hiera Picra, sometimes also known as "higra pigra" or "hickory pick-ory," was a bitter purgative whose principal ingredients were aloe and cinnamon.

Nicholas Culpeper's recipe for Hiera Picra Simple:

Take of cinnamon, Xylobalsam [balm of Gilead], or wood of aloes, the roots of Asarabacca [Hazelwort], Spicknard [Valerian], Ma-stick [pistachio tree resin], Saffron, of each 6 drams, aloes not washed, 12 ounces and a half, clarified honey 4 pounds and 3 ounces, mix them into an electuary according to art.

(A simpler and more modern version calls for 4 parts aloe to 1 part cinnamon, both finely powdered, mixed "intimately.")

This revolting concoction was further adulterated by being made into a tincture, which according to Eliza Smith's recommendation should then be followed by an equally revolting drink.

To make Tincture of Hiera-Picra

Take a drachm of hiera-picra, a drachm of cochineal, and two drachms of aniseeds, and put them into a bottle, with a pint of the best sack and a pint of brandy; shake them well together five or six days, then let it stand to settle twelve hours, so pour it off into an-other bottle clear from the dregs, and keep it for use; it is very good against the cholick or stomach-ach, and removes any thing that offends the stomach; take four spoonfuls of it fasting, and fast two hours after it; you must take it constantly three weeks or a month, and it is well to drink the following drink after it.

Take new laid eggs and break them, save the shells, and pull off the skin that is in the inside; dry the shells, and beat them to powder; sift them, and put six spoonfuls of this powder into a quart of the following waters: take of fennel-water, parsley-water, mint-water, and black cherry-water, of each half a pint; take a quarter of a pint at a time, shaking the glass when you pour it out, three times a day, at eleven in the morning, at three in the afternoon, and eight at night; and you should take it as long as you take the hiera-picra.

—The Compleat Housewife (1727)

Liquor Ammoniae Acetatis

Mr Lewis had dealt with the medical situation perfectly well in Stephen's absence, but there was a most unfortunate deficiency in the portable soup and port wine intended for invalids: they and two Winchester quarts of Liquor Ammoniae Acetatis had quite certainly been stolen by some criminal hand as yet unknown, misled by the liquor part of the label. 'Once he starts upon it we shall certainly know,' said Mr Lewis. . . .

—The Ionian Mission, *207–8*

Liquor Ammoniae Acetatis is Spirit of Mindererus, a solution of acetate of ammonia (distilled vinegar and sesquicarbonate of ammonia) used in infinitesimal doses (measured in drops) as a febrifuge. In the larger quantities that the thief would be likely to imbibe it would produce hepatic failure, with symptoms as follows: on the first day, extreme sallowness; on the second day, uncontrollable vomiting and diarrhea, accompanied by brown and hairy-looking blotches on the skin; on the third day, drastic discoloration of the eyes (a flaming brownish-pink); at the end of the third day, death.

Yes, they would certainly have known.

Slime-Draught

'Good morning, Doctor,' said Jack. 'How are your patients?'
'Good morning, sir,' said Stephen. 'Some are a little contradictory and fractious, but a comfortable slime-draught at noon will deal with that. The others do tolerably well, and are looking forward to their Sunday duff.' —The Far Side of the World, *302*

'Cheer up, Brampton; many a man has been far worse than you, and you are in very good hands.'
'The woman tempted me,' said Brampton; and after a short silence, 'I shall go to Hell.' He turned his head away, his body heaving with sobs.
With the Captain gone they reverted to their Latin and Martin said 'Do you think I can decently offer him comfort?'
'I cannot tell,' said Stephen. 'For the moment I should exhibit a slime-draught with two scruples of asafoetida.' —The Nutmeg of Consolation, *185*

'I . . . wished my dement on to them, with a slime-draught to make him easy.' —Post Captain, *257*

We have been haunted by the riddle of the Slime-Draught ever since we first encountered it in *Post Captain*. And haunted to some degree we will remain: we cannot claim to have found the definitive solution. We have, however, studied the matter at length and discussed it with our medical advisers; and can at least offer some informed speculation as to the possible nature and uses of this spectacular-sounding specific.

We can say with some conviction that the Slime-Draught is probably apocryphal—at least, there is no mention of it by that name in any pharmacopoeia we consulted (and we went back as far as 1769). If it existed at all, it was either a cant term for some popular remedy or compound, or the creation of a quack such as one Dr. Tufts, the inventor (circa 1675) of the Marthambles, the Strong Fives, the Moon-

Pall, and the Hockogrockle—a crop of equally apocryphal diseases, all of which he claimed to be able to cure by the application of his own mysterious nostrum.

Judging from the context, the Slime-Draught appears to have had calming or even soporific properties, and perhaps some physically soothing and laxative properties as well. It has been suggested (possibly because of the similarity between the names) that there may be some connection to slippery elm (a "typical" mucilaginous demulcent, "grateful in . . . irritative dysentery")—and that would certainly accord both with the sliminess and with the "comfortable" qualities:

> *'It is only that I don't sleep. Toss, turn . . . and I am stupid all the rest of the day. And damned ill-tempered, Stephen; I sway away on all top-ropes for a nothing, and then I am sorry afterwards. . . . you will give me one of your treble-shotted slime-draughts to get me to sleep.'*
> —Post Captain, *338*

It is probably safe to say that the typical Slime-Draught did not contain any really powerful narcotic, or Stephen would not have felt compelled, in Brampton's case, to supplement its effects with the nerve sedative asafoetida. But some tranquilizing component it must have had, as witness Jack's request. Our prime candidate for this function is some kind of lactucarium—perhaps Inspissated Juice of Lettuce (p. 243), which we already know Stephen favored for relieving agitation, irascibility, and nervous excitement. Incidentally, the other effects of lactucarium (they vary according to form and dosage) sometimes include diarrhea and/or a lessening of sensation, either of which would be consistent with the effects of our hypothetical Slime-Draught.

Among the other slimy and demulcent elements of the draught might be gelatine (in the form of Calf's Foot Jelly, p. 268), egg whites (admittedly a luxury at sea), gum tragacanth, and various starchy substances such as arrowroot and Barley-Water (p. 238).

Such a potion would be of little use against the Strong Fives, which in *H.M.S. Surprise* is likened to apoplexy, but it might well have served to alleviate the Marthambles (according to *The Mauritius*

Command, a highly contagious "griping of the guts")—or perhaps even the Hockogrockle (symptoms unknown).

'If you please, sir,' said Emily, 'Padeen says may Willis have his slime-draught now?'
'He may have it at the third stroke of the bell,' said Stephen.
—The Wine-Dark Sea, *38*

Dead Horse

Solo   Chorus

A poor old man came rid- ing by. And they

Solo

say so, and they hope so. A poor old man came

Chorus

rid- ing by. Oh, poor old horse!

They say, old man, your horse will die!
    And they say so, and they hope so,
They say, old man, your horse will die!
    Oh, poor old horse.

Then if he dies, I'll tan his hide.
    And they say so, and they hope so,
Then if he dies, I'll tan his hide.
    Oh, poor old horse.

Then if he lives, why he I'll ride,
    And they say so, and they hope so,
Then if he lives, why he I'll ride,
    Oh, poor old horse.

Spoken: Old horse, old horse, what brought you here?
             You've carted stone for many a year
             From Bantry Bay to Ballywhack
             Where you fell down and broke your back.
             Now after years of sad abuse
             They salt you down for sailors' use.
             They tan your hide and burn your bones,
             And send you off to Davy Jones.

CHAPTER TEN

All
Ahoo

O nce again Stephen was about to tell Jack of his intimate convictions . . . that they were aboard a vessel belonging to women who did not like men; . . . and to say that he dreaded the possibility of Jack's being gelded, knocked on the head, and eaten. But before he could do so . . . Jack said, 'Here comes the captain, I believe . . .' She was a broad, squat woman, much darker than most, with a long trunk and short legs; she had a handsome, high-nosed, but exceedingly cross and authoritarian face. . . . She was casually nibbling at something she held. . . .

'Perhaps we should adopt a respectful submissive attitude,' murmured Stephen; and as the captain came nearer he saw that what she was gnawing was a hand, a smoked or pickled hand. She looked at Jack and Stephen without any pleasure or interest and without making any reply to their bows or their 'Your most humble devoted servant, ma'am,' and 'Most honoured and happy to be aboard you, ma'am.'

—The Far Side of the World, *271–2*

The division between the two rounds is very rough mountain country with forest going far down each side. The southern lobe belongs to Puolani. Rightly speaking she is queen of the whole island, but some generations ago the chiefs in the north rebelled, and now Kalahua, who

has knocked all the other northern chiefs on the head, says he is the right-
ful king of all Moahu, Puolani having eaten pork, which is taboo to
women. Everyone says that is nonsense. She certainly eats the usual
pieces of enemy chiefs killed in battle, according to custom, but she is a
very pious woman, and would never touch pork.'   —The Truelove, *137*

We had fondly hoped to produce a pair of rather outlandish chapters, but sometimes the best-laid plans of cookbook authors go all ahoo.

The first, "Cast Away," was to have consisted of foods eaten by those shipwrecked or marooned—pot luck in Micronesia, on Desolation Island, and in other places nameless or unknown. Grilled babirussa; bird's-nest swallows; coconut milk; flying squid; gazelle; a canister of discreditable green tea; a contemptible box of litchis; pith of tree-ferns, roots, bark, pounded leaves, yam; raw fish; sago; sea-elephant liver; sea-lion; green sea turtle.

The second, "Taboo," would have covered foods forbidden, feared, or frowned upon—in some cultures, at any rate. Albatross; bargemen; maggots; camel-calf seethed with almonds, honey, and coriander; edible dogs; eagle; human stew à la Puolani; pickled seal; boiled shit; rats in onion-sauce; ring-tailed apes; salted honey-buzzards; salted penguins; sea-slugs; sheep's eyes; smoked and pickled human hands.

But it quickly became obvious that most of the ingredients required were beyond even our considerable foraging abilities. Dogs, for instance, are not unknown in our part of the world; neither are lawsuits and criminal prosecutions (besides, we're a bit sentimental about dogs). Hedged round as we are by rabid conservationists—rabid conservationists ourselves, for that matter—we had to rule out albatrosses and eagles. And even the most exotic of markets in New York, that most depraved of cities, does not stock food-grade human parts. (The green tea, the coconut milk and the litchis we certainly could find—but having once found them there was no more to be said on the subject.)

As for our two resounding successes, the rats and the boiled shit, we have dealt with those elsewhere . . . and nothing beside remains.

Alas for our seethed camel-calf.

Stephen noticed the unmistakable helix of a human ear in his bowl and said to Tapia 'Please tell the Queen that man's flesh is taboo to us.'

'But it is Kalahua and the French chief,' said Tapia.

'Even so,' said Stephen. . . . —The Truelove, *252*

Lumps of Pudding

Thomas d'Urfey,
Pills to Purge Melancholy

When   I   was   in   the   low   coun- try.   When

I   was   in   the   low   coun- try.   What   sli- ces of pud- ding and

pie- ces of bread. My   mo- ther   would give me when I   was in need.

My mother she killed a good fat hog
She made such puddings would choak a dog
And I shall ne'er forget till I dee
What lumps of pudding my mother gave me.

She hung them up upon a pin
The fat run out and the maggots crept in
If you won't believe me you may go and see
What lumps of pudding my mother gave me.

And every day my Mother would cry
Come stuff your belly girl until you die,
'Twould make you to laugh if you were to see
What lumps of pudding my mother gave me.

I no sooner at night was got into bed
But she with all kindness would come with speed
She gave me such parcels I thought I should dee
With eating of puddings my mother gave me.

At last I rambled abroad and then
I met in my frolick an honest Man
Quoth he. "My dear Philli I'll give unto thee
Such lumps of pudding you never did see."

Said I. "Honest man. I thank thee most kind."
And as he told me indeed I did find.
He gave me lumps which did so agree
One bit was worth all my mother gave me.

CHAPTER ELEVEN

In the Galley & the Hold:

Useful Receipts,
Notes, & Substitutions

These are victualling notes,' he said. 'Compiled according to a system of my own. You will see that they add up to a yearly consumption of one million eighty-five thousand two hundred and sixty-six pounds of fresh meat; one million one hundred and sixty-seven thousand nine hundred and ninety-five pounds of biscuit and one hundred and eighty-four thousand three hundred and fifty-eight pounds of soft tack; two hundred and seventeen thousand eight hundred and thirteen pounds of flour; one thousand and sixty-six bushels of wheat; one million two hundred and twenty-six thousand seven hundred and thirty-eight pints of wine, and two hundred and forty-four thousand nine hundred and four pints of spirits.' —The Fortune of War, *194*

Useful Receipts

Mayonnaise Brown Onion Sauce Wine Sauce

PUDDING SAUCES

Custard Sauce Hard Sauce Lemon Sauce Sherry Sauce

Forcemeat for Raised Pies Forcemeat Balls
Godiveau Calf's Foot Jelly Mushroom Ketchup
Hot Water Paste for Raised Pies Puff Paste
Short Pastry Savoy Biscuit Icing

Mayonnaise

The first part of the supper came in, cold things the Captain's cook had under his hand with the ship lying off a plentiful market: roast beef yielded up by the gunroom with barely a sigh, chickens, capons, ducks, ham, quantities of vegetables and a great bowl of mayonnaise, decanters of Peruvian wine, a jug of barley-water that Jack emptied without thinking of it.

—The Wine-Dark Sea, *194*

There appear to be two possible derivations for the term "mayonnaise." Marie Antonin Carème and some other French cooks of the early nineteenth century refer to it as Magnonnaise (from *manier,* to handle or to work) because of the way it is beaten; for obvious reasons we prefer the other theory: that it was invented by the cook to the Duc de Richelieu during the French occupation of Port Mahon in 1756 . . . *et voilà,* Sauce Mahonnaise.

This recipe is based on Carème's classic Magnonnaise, though the jellied stock makes it more like today's Mayonnaise Collée.

¾ teaspoon white or tarragon
  vinegar
1 egg yolk
½ cup olive oil
  Salt and pepper

1½ teaspoons heavy cream
2 tablespoons unflavored
  Calf's Foot Jelly (p. 268)
  or jellied white stock (optional)

Beat ¼ teaspoon of the vinegar into the egg yolk. Add the olive oil, drop by drop, whisking constantly, until about half the oil is absorbed. Continue adding the oil in a thin stream, still whisking. When all the oil is absorbed, beat in the remaining vinegar, salt and pepper to taste, the cream, and the jelly or stock (if you are using it).

Makes about ¾ cup

Brown Onion Sauce

1 large Spanish onion, peeled
  and cut in ¼-inch slices
  Pan drippings from a roast,
  or 2 tablespoons butter or
  other fat
¼ cup burgundy

¾ cup rich brown stock (or reconstituted Portable Soup,
  p. 240)
2 tablespoons Mushroom
  Ketchup (p. 269)
2 tablespoons flour

Sauté the onion slices in the fat (if from a roast, do this directly in the drip pan) over low heat until they are limp and slightly brown. Pour off all but 2 tablespoons of the fat. Deglaze the pan with the burgundy. Add the stock and the Mushroom Ketchup (and any juices that have accumulated on the meat platter). When the sauce is hot, sprinkle in the flour. Continue to cook, stirring, until the flour is absorbed and fully cooked and the sauce is smooth and thick.

Makes about 1½ cups

Wine Sauce

1 small onion, peeled and
   chopped
¼ pound mushrooms, thinly
   sliced
   Pan drippings from a roast,
   or 2 tablespoons butter or
   other fat
½ cup burgundy

1 cup rich brown stock (or reconstituted Portable Soup,
   p. 240)
1 teaspoon Mushroom
   Ketchup (p. 269)
1 teaspoon arrowroot
1 teaspoon water

Sauté the onion and mushrooms in the fat (if from a roast, do this directly in the drip pan) over low heat until they are limp. Pour off all but 2 tablespoons of the fat. Deglaze the pan with the burgundy. Add the stock and the Mushroom Ketchup (and any juices that have accumulated on the meat platter).

In a small bowl, mix the arrowroot and water to make a paste. Remove the sauce from the heat, add the arrowroot paste and stir until blended. Return to very low heat and stir constantly until the sauce is thick and glossy.

Makes 1 cup

PUDDING SAUCES

Custard Sauce

"In England there are 60 different religions and only one sauce." This remark, originally made in French, has been attributed variously to Voltaire and to the Neapolitan admiral Prince Francesco Caracciolo. If the latter, could it be the reason he was subsequently hanged from the mast of the frigate *Minerva* at Lord Nelson's order? Could it also be the reason the sauce is known in France as *Crème Anglaise?*

4 egg yolks
¼ cup sugar
   Pinch of salt
1¼ cups milk

¼ cup heavy cream
4 drops rose water
1½ tablespoons brandy

In the top of a double boiler, beat the egg yolks with the sugar and the salt. Add the milk and the cream and stir well. Set the pot over (not in) gently boiling water and cook, stirring constantly, until the custard is thick enough to coat the back of a spoon (about 10 minutes). Remove from heat and stir in the rose water and brandy.

Note: This sauce can be served hot or cold. It will thicken as it cools.

Makes about 1½ cups

Hard Sauce

½ cup butter
1 cup pounded (superfine)
    sugar

2 tablespoons sherry or
    brandy

Cream the butter until it is soft. Gradually work in the sugar. Add the sherry or brandy and beat until fluffy.

Makes about 1 cup

Lemon Sauce

4 tablespoons butter
4 tablespoons sugar
8 teaspoons lemon juice
4 teaspoons medium-dry sherry

¼ teaspoon salt
1 cup plus 2 teaspoons water
2 teaspoons arrowroot

Melt the butter in a small saucepan. Add the sugar, lemon juice, sherry, salt and 1 cup water, and stir until the sugar is dissolved. In a small cup or bowl, mix the arrowroot and the 2 teaspoons water to make a paste. Remove the butter mixture from the heat, add the arrowroot paste and stir until blended. Return the pot to very low heat and stir constantly until the sauce thickens.

Makes 1½ cups

Sherry Sauce

4 tablespoons butter
4 tablespoons sugar

½ cup medium-dry sherry
1 teaspoon lemon juice

Melt the butter in a small saucepan. Add the sugar, sherry, and lemon juice, and stir until the sugar is dissolved.

Makes 1½ cups

Forcemeat for Raised Pies

½ pound veal or chicken
½ pound fatty bacon
¼ pound mushrooms
1 medium onion, peeled
¼ cup bread crumbs
1½ teaspoons grated lemon zest
1 egg
1 teaspoon chopped fresh
   parsley

1 teaspoon chopped fresh
   thyme
1 teaspoon chopped fresh savory
½ teaspoon salt
¼ teaspoon pepper
   Pinch of cayenne

Mince the veal, bacon, mushrooms and onion as fine as possible. Mix thoroughly with all remaining ingredients.

Makes about 1¾ pounds

Forcemeat Balls

For Ragoos, Civets, etc.

¼ pound veal, finely minced
¼ pound suet, finely grated
1 small onion, peeled and finely chopped
½ cup bread crumbs
1 egg
½ teaspoon chopped fresh parsley
½ teaspoon chopped fresh thyme
½ teaspoon chopped fresh savory
½ teaspoon salt
¼ teaspoon pepper
Pinch of ground nutmeg
Pinch of cayenne

Mix all ingredients thoroughly. Wetting your hands first, roll the forcemeat into small balls (about ¾-inch diameter). Chill until needed. Forcemeat Balls are typically used as a garnish, and may be fried or boiled depending on the requirements of the dish.

Makes about 3 dozen

Godiveau

½ pound suet, finely grated
6 ounces veal, finely minced
2 scallions, green and white parts, finely chopped
1 shallot, peeled and finely chopped
1 tablespoon chopped fresh parsley
1 teaspoon chopped fresh savory
1 egg
½ teaspoon salt
¼ teaspoon pepper
1 knob fresh ginger, about ½ inch long, grated
¼ teaspoon ground nutmeg

Mix all ingredients thoroughly.

Makes 1 pound

Calf's Foot Jelly

3 calves' feet, cleaned and split   1 cup Madeira
1 gallon water   1 cup sugar
6 egg whites   Juice and zest of 3 lemons
6 eggshells   1 sprig rosemary (optional)
2 cups white wine

Rinse the calves' feet and place them in a pot with the water. Bring gradually to a boil, skimming off the scum that forms on the surface. Reduce heat and boil gently, uncovered, until the liquid is reduced by half (about 3 hours).

Strain the liquid. Cool until firmly set (about 1½ hours). Remove the fat, which will have solidified on the surface, and put the jelly in a large saucepan over medium heat.

Beat the egg whites until they form soft peaks. Crush the eggshells. When the jelly is completely dissolved, add the egg whites, shells, wine, Madeira, sugar, and lemon juice and zest. Bring to a boil, stirring briskly. When the egg whites rise to the surface, stop stirring, reduce heat and simmer 10 minutes. Remove from heat, add the rosemary if you are using it, and allow to settle for 15 minutes.

Put the jelly through a very fine mesh strainer, a jelly bag, or a cloth (a clean pudding-cloth, for instance) wrung out in hot water. You may need to strain it several times—as Mrs. Dods says, "till it be perfectly pellucid."

Pour the jelly into a large cut-glass bowl, or into individual goblets, and chill until firmly set.

Makes about 4 cups (8 servings)

Variation: To make an unflavored jelly for use in savory aspics and such, omit the Madeira, wine, sugar, rosemary, lemon zest, and half of the lemon juice.

Mushroom Ketchup

This ketchup is based on Hannah Glasse's "To make Ketchup to keep twenty Years" (from her chapter entitled "For Captains of Ships"), so it is not supposed to require refrigeration. We did discover that after a few weeks fur grows on it, but once you skim that off the Mushroom Ketchup is still perfectly usable.

1 pint strong stale beer	5 ounces large flap mushrooms
10 Anchovies (p. 135) or 1 can (2 ounces) flat anchovy fillets, rinsed	1 two-inch-long knob fresh ginger
4 large shallots, peeled and coarsely chopped	1 teaspoon pepper
	½ teaspoon mace
	10 whole cloves

Put all ingredients into a saucepan, bring to a boil, and simmer gently about 30 minutes, or until liquid is reduced by half. Strain and bottle.

Makes about 1 cup

Hot Water Paste for Raised Pies

2 cups water	9 cups flour
½ pound (2 sticks) butter	1 tablespoon salt
½ pound lard	

Warm the water, butter and lard together over moderate heat until the butter and lard are melted.

In a large bowl, combine the flour and salt, then add the hot liquid and mix thoroughly.

Turn the paste out onto a lightly floured board and knead until smooth and thoroughly blended (3–5 minutes).

Place the dough in a bowl, cover with a damp cloth, and let rest in a warm place for at least 30 minutes.

Makes about 4½ pounds of pastry, enough for one large raised pie

Puff Paste

The chief difference between today's puff paste and that of Jack Aubrey's day is that, whereas today cooks typically make the basic dough with just flour and water, then add the butter all at once, eighteenth-century cooks made a softer dough to begin with by putting in part of the butter at the first stage, then gradually adding the rest in the successive "folds." We have tried both ways, and both produce very good puff paste, but we find the older method easier, and therefore preferable.

It is not our intention to offer a full course in this complicated series of maneuvers. Instead, for those who already have some knowledge of puff paste, we offer general guidelines for the eighteenth-century approach. You may prefer to substitute your own favorite recipe—or you may want to avoid the issue altogether by buying frozen puff paste, which is readily available and nearly as good.

2 cups flour, plus extra for rolling	½ pound (2 sticks) butter
½ teaspoon salt	Ice water

Sift the flour and the salt. Cut one-third of the butter into small pieces and quickly work it into the flour with your fingers, until it forms crumbly bits of dough about the size of a pea. Sprinkle 1–2 tablespoons ice water over the dough and work it in. Continue adding ice water in this manner until the dough just holds together (it will probably take about ½ cup of water, but this will vary depending on temperature, humidity, the dryness of your flour, etc.). Wrap the dough in wax paper and chill until firm.

On a lightly floured board or marble slab, roll the pastry out into a rectangle about ¼ inch thick. Spread half the remaining butter on one half of the rectangle. Dust the butter lightly with flour. Fold the other half of the dough over the butter and seal the edges by pinching them gently together. As with conventional puff paste, roll and fold 2 or 3 times, then wrap and chill.

Repeat this process with the chilled dough and the remaining butter. Continue to roll, fold, and chill until the desired number of layers is achieved.

Note: This paste freezes well, and can be refrozen.

Makes about 1 pound

Short Pastry

1 cup flour	4 tablespoons cold butter
1 tablespoon sugar	1 egg white
Pinch of salt	1 teaspoon cold water

Sift the flour, sugar and salt together. Cut the butter into small bits and work it quickly into the flour with your fingers. Beat the egg white until it forms soft peaks, then mix it into the pastry. Add the water, a few drops at a time, until you can gather the pastry into a ball (you may not need the whole teaspoon). Wrap the dough in wax paper and chill until firm.

Note: It may seem odd to mix in the beaten egg whites rather than folding them, but since the pastry is going to be rolled and filled it doesn't much matter. In any case, this is how it was done in the early nineteenth century—and it works.

Makes ½ pound

Variation: For a savory dish (such as Venison Pasty, p. 192), omit the sugar.

Savoy Biscuit

Savoys are closely related to sponge cake, and for most purposes can be used interchangeably with what used to be called "French role"— a sort of brioche. As with the Short Pastry, eighteenth-century cooks, after going to all the trouble of beating the egg whites separately, stirred this batter *vigorously* instead of folding it together. We have done it both ways; not surprisingly, we have found that the mixing method produces a rather dense biscuit. Tossing tradition aside, we have for once chosen the more modern approach—with light and pleasing results.

3 eggs, separated	2 teaspoons lemon juice
¾ cup sugar	¼ teaspoon salt
2 teaspoons grated lemon zest	1½ cups flour

Preheat the oven to 350°.

Beat the egg yolks until they are smooth. Continue to beat, gradually adding the sugar. Add the lemon zest, lemon juice, and salt.

In a separate bowl, beat the egg whites until they form soft peaks. Fold them into the egg yolk mixture.

Sift the flour into the egg mixture and stir gently until smooth.

Spoon the batter into a well-greased madeleine pan (or a small muffin tin), filling the cups three-quarters full (do not overfill, as the biscuits will spread and rise).

Bake 12–15 minutes, or until just golden brown at the edges. Turn out immediately and cool on a rack.

Makes 2 dozen

Icing

2 egg whites	½ teaspoon cochineal (for decoration only)
2 teaspoons lemon juice	
2½ cups superfine sugar	1 teaspoon hot water (for decoration only)

Beat the egg whites until they form stiff peaks. Add the lemon juice, then gradually add 2 cups sugar, continuing to beat all the while. Reserve ½ cup of Icing for decoration.

Colored Icing for decoration:
Pound the cochineal to a fine powder and set it to steep in the hot water for 5 minutes. Strain the liquid into the reserved icing and add enough of the remaining ½ cup of sugar to make a stiff paste. Put in a pastry bag and pipe into decorative patterns.

Makes enough Icing for one Plum-Cake the size of a moderate cart-wheel, plus 2 dozen Rout-Cakes

About . . .

ABOUT PUDDINGS

"I can't tell you the attachment for pudding of the Irish, or indeed English, soul. And it's a thing I dreadfully miss in France—I live in France—and they haven't a notion of pudding."
—Patrick O'Brian, interviewed by Robert Hass, April 19, 1995

What is pudding? There can be no more important question.

Many people believe pudding began its life as the French *boudin*. The *Oxford English Dictionary* suggests several possible common roots for the two words, including one meaning "guts" and another meaning "to swell." And Larousse defines *boudiner* as "to stuff." Any of them could be right—in fact, all three make sense to us, especially together: stuff a gut and cook it, and it will swell.

Such are the shared ancestral characteristics of *boudin* (both *noir* and *blanc*), Black Pudding, White Pudding, Blood Pudding or *Blutwurst,* and what Robert Burns calls the "great chieftain of the pudding race," Haggis.

As far as we know, then, pudding started out on a parallel course with sausage, then veered off in a more farinaceous direction with the addition of grains or porridge, and finally shed its guts altogether in favor of basins and cloths. Take this evolution one step farther and you have dumplings—but that far we dare not go.

Pudding can be either savory or sweet, depending on context and content; though to confuse the issue even more, it should be noted that to the English, it is also a generic word for "dessert." As Mr. O'Brian says, "after the various solid things, the edible roots and the more or less edible beef—you say, what's for pudding? and then, it may be flummery, it may be apple pie—it's any of those delights. . . ."

Suet Pudding

Patrick O'Brian feelingly calls it "the true heroes' delight":

> *Captain Aubrey, feeling that he must do honour to the gunroom's feast, already tolerably damped, held out his plate; and now for the first time he realized with a pang that a third slice was going to be more of a labour than a delight: non sum qualis eram drifted up from those remote years when he was flogged into at least a remote, nodding acquaintance with Latin; the rest he could not recall. It might have had nothing to do with pudding at all, but the effect was the same.*
>
> *'Mr Martin,' he asked, 'what is the Latin for pudding, for a pudding of this kind?'*
>
> *'Heavens, sir, I cannot tell,' said Martin. 'What do you say, Doctor?'*
>
> *'Sebi confectio discolor,' said Stephen. 'Will I pour you a glass of wine, colleague?'*
> —The Truelove, 110

Despite Stephen's characterization (*sebi confectio discolor* means, literally, "varied suet confections"), it must be confessed that most of the suet puddings described in the novels, when you boil them down, are very much alike. Indeed, when we came to study the origins of Spotted Dog (or Spotted Dick), Plum Duff, and Figgy-Dowdy (not to mention Treacle-Dowdy, Pandowdy, etc.), we were delighted to discover that "dog," "dick," "duff," and "dowdy" all come from the same Old English word meaning . . . dough.

This is not to say that there is no variety in suet puddings. A suet pudding may be boiled, steamed, or baked; it may be tied loosely in a cloth or packed into a pudding-basin; it may be a solid, doughy mass or a thin pastry envelope filled with meat or fruit. It is an acquired taste, perhaps—and we have acquired it all too easily. Worse, we have adopted the traditional practice of slicing leftover pudding and frying it in butter, and we regret to inform you that it is very good indeed.

Suet

'Do you know, sir,' said Jack to Professor Graham, 'this is the first decent pudding I have had since I left home. By some mischance the suet was neglected to be shipped; and you will agree that a spotted dog or a drowned baby is a hollow mockery, a whited sepulchre, without it is made with suet. There is an art in puddings, to be sure; but what is art without suet?'
—The Ionian Mission, *83*

Suet, with or without art, is fresh beef (or mutton, but that would be specified) fat taken from the area around the loin or kidney. To prepare it for use in pudding, remove all bits of meat and connective tissue, and grate or chop it finely. It is much easier to work with when it is partially frozen.

Grating suet by hand is a truly dreadful job. At the risk of offending the Luddites among our readers, we have found that the grating blade of a food processor produces very good results. We must, however, caution you against putting suet through a meat grinder or processing it with the chopping blade of the food processor. Either of these practices will ruin the consistency of the pudding.

Basic Equipment

The Pudding-Basin

A pudding-basin is a ceramic bowl with a convenient rim expressly designed to hold a pudding-string in place. If you do not happen to have an English pudding-basin about you, almost any heatproof bowl or mold of appropriate size will serve the purpose. (A typical 6-cup basin, such as the one we use for most of our steamed puddings, measures about 7 inches in diameter across the top, 3 inches across the bottom, and 4 inches deep.)

The basin should always be greased with butter or suet, depending on the nature of the pudding.

The Pudding-Cloth

*"[The pudding is] wrapped in a piece of sailcloth . . . and immersed in a
cauldron of water, and boiled—oh, for at least a watch, sometimes six
hours. And then when it comes out it is well and truly boiled, and if the
sailcloth has been tight, it has a small, close texture, and that is spotted dog,
and if you've left it a little loose it has a glutinous surface and glistens, and
that is drowned baby."*

—Patrick O'Brian, interviewed by Charlton Heston, April 25, 1995

You can use any square kitchen towel or similar piece of smooth cotton cloth for this purpose, as long as it is large enough. Not being in
the habit of cooking for an entire crew, we generally use flour-sacking
towels, approximately 30 inches square, and the puddings we produce
are sufficient to feed an average mess (eight to twelve men).

The Pudding-String

Any good stout cotton string will do. We use a relatively thick
string, partly because of its strength, but primarily because when the
pudding comes out of the pot, hot and steaming and rather slippery,
it is easier to grasp and untie a thick string than a thin one. For the
same reason, we strongly recommend tying the string with a bow or
a slippery reef knot; it is crucial that the knot be secure, but it is almost equally important that it be easy to untie.

The Pot

After several months of back-breaking post-pudding scrubbing, it
finally occurred to us that we could save ourselves a great deal of effort by using a nonreactive pot; and so it proved. We love our cast alu-
minum pots for most purposes, but they do discolor dreadfully when
used for boiling or steaming puddings, especially suet puddings. We
have learned the error of our ways, and we now use stainless steel or
enamel.

The size and shape of the pot, naturally, will vary according to the
pudding. In the case of a long one such as Roly-Poly, we find a fish-
poacher answers admirably, and that the basket makes it easy to de-
cant the finished product. (Our fish-poacher is 18 inches long, and
happens to be just the right size for our recipes; if you are making
such a pudding for a crew of three hundred you will require a much
larger one.)

Preparation and Cooking

Depending on the manner of preparation, the consistency of pudding varies from dense and cakelike to slippery and "agreeably glutinous."

Some puddings can be made in more than one way: Spotted Dog and Christmas Pudding, for instance, can be either steamed or boiled; Roly-Poly can be either boiled or baked; and so on. On the other hand, some puddings are defined by shape and texture as much as by taste, and must by definition be cooked one way and one way only: Cabinet Pudding, for example, must be steamed in a basin or it loses all its decorative appeal; whereas Quaking Pudding will not quake unless it is boiled in a cloth.

To Steam a Pudding in a Basin

Wring out the cloth in hot water, lay it on a flat surface, and flour the center, making a circle slightly larger than the top circumference of the basin. Lay the cloth over the pudding, flour side down, and secure it in place with a string tied snugly under the rim of the basin. For most puddings, the cloth should be stretched tightly over the basin; for puddings containing bread it should usually be loose enough to allow for a little expansion. Tie two opposite corners of the cloth together in a square knot over the top of the basin, then repeat with the other two corners. You should be able to lift the pudding-basin by the knots in the cloth.

The water in the pot should come up to within an inch of the top of the basin. It must be boiling rapidly when you put the pudding in, and should continue to boil merrily throughout the cooking process. In some cases (especially that of Christmas Pudding, which boils anywhere from five hours to four days) you will probably need to replenish the water at least once. Be sure to use water that is already boiling, so as not to interrupt the cooking.

To Tie Up a Long Boiled Pudding

Wring out the cloth in hot water, lay it on a flat surface, and flour about half. Place the pudding on the floured half of the cloth (a rolled pudding like Roly-Poly should be assembled first, then carefully lifted into place). Tuck the floured edge of the cloth snugly around the pudding, and roll the pudding up in the cloth. Some puddings (such as Roly-Poly) should be rolled as tightly as possible; others (such as Drowned Baby) must be wrapped more loosely to give them room to expand. Tie a piece of string securely around the cloth at each end of the pudding. We also find, especially on a tightly wrapped pudding, that another piece of string tied around the middle helps it to hold its shape.

To Tie Up a Round Boiled Pudding

The treatment of the cloth varies according to the recipe, and ranges from nothing at all (as for Dog's Body) to the application of butter and flour (as for Quaking Pudding)—a nasty, messy process, but well worth it.

This done, and the pudding components in place, gather up the edges of the cloth, and tie a string securely around the neck of the "bag." A recipe that calls for a loosely tied cloth implies that the pudding will swell and require room for expansion; the cloth around it should therefore be slack, but the string itself must always be tight.

To Boil the Pudding

The pudding should be completely immersed in the boiling water (again, in some cases the water must be replenished as the pudding cooks). Some eighteenth-century cooks advocate leaving the pot uncovered, but they don't explain why; we prefer to cover it, to prevent the water from boiling away too quickly. To keep a heavy pudding (such as Pease-Pudding) from sticking to the bottom of the pot, either place a saucer underneath it in the pot, or move it around from time to time as it is boiling.

"Drowned baby, yes, rarely at home, rarely at home, because it requires an immense cauldron and an immense amount of boiling and patience. . . . Spotted dog, also known as spotted dick, it's much the same and is very like plum duff. These things are made—I've not made any of them, I will admit, but I've seen them made, and I've eaten them with immense appreciation, because they're very often served at school, where there are a lot of very very hungry boys to satisfy, and they're really good and solid I do assure you, they outdo potatoes any day in the week for solidity."
—Patrick O'Brian, interviewed by Charlton Heston, April 25, 1995

ABOUT RAISED PIES

SAVOURY pies, made of fresh materials, properly seasoned, and not overdone—their besetting fault—are very generally liked. They are economical, since a good pie may be made of a piece of meat that would neither stew, roast, nor boil, so as to make a handsome dish; and they are convenient at table, since they may be divided and subdivided to any length, with little trouble to the carver. Pies can be made of almost every thing, and they eat better cold than meat dressed in any other way. A solid pie is a larder in itself, and is as useful on the moors or at sea as in country situations, where families are liable to the incursions of voracious visitors.

—Mistress Margaret Dods, *Cook and Housewife's Manual* (1826)

A "raised" pie is one in which the pastry is shaped by hand into a free-standing crust—rather like making pottery. Originally, in fact, the crust was merely a sort of disposable equivalent of the clay pot, and its sole purpose was to enclose tough meat such as venison so that it would become tender by dint of slow, moist cooking. The most important characteristic of such a crust was its sturdiness; that it later evolved into something marginally edible was quite an unexpected development. Even as late as Mrs. Beeton (1861), a recipe for Common Crust for Raised Pies ends thus: "This paste does not taste so nicely as the preceding one, but is worked with greater facility, and answers just as well for raised pies, for the crust is seldom eaten."

In the seventeenth and eighteenth centuries, the crust for a raised pie was frequently referred to as the "coffin"; a typical recipe would direct you to "raise your coffin on what fashion you please." For the inexperienced cook this might mean the use of a metal or wooden mold, but experts raised their coffins by hand; and we have managed to follow their example. (The crucial elements for so doing are the consistency and temperature of the paste, which must be soft enough to mold yet firm enough to hold its shape.)

Once the coffin was raised and had hardened sufficiently, it was lined with a "mortar" of forcemeat, then filled. A top crust, rolled out and fancifully ornamented, was crimped into place and secured with egg wash, and the whole thing was baked in what Hannah Glasse calls "a Quick oven, but not too fierce an Oven." The vent-hole was then sealed with an ornate pastry plug. Thus crimped and sealed, a pie could keep for weeks, which made it a good way of preserving meat without having to dedicate a precious pot to the purpose.

To Raise a Coffin

The coffin for a raised pie is built from Hot Water Paste (p. 269).

Thoroughly grease the pan in which the pie will be baked. Anything with a large flat surface will do—a roasting pan or even a cookie sheet. We find a paella pan ideal for most pies, because it is big and round and substantial, has a pair of convenient handles, and is deep enough to guard against potential disasters, whether major (a collapsing crust) or minor (overflowing gravy).

Gradually shape the dough into a crude round or oval bowl, beginning by indenting the top with your thumbs and pulling the paste up and outward with your fingers. We have found that the process is best taken in stages: let the dough cool slightly, begin shaping it, let it cool a little more, continue to shape it, and so on. Smooth it between the palms of your hands as you are pulling it up—you will soon get a "feel" for the right consistency (one benefit of working this dough, especially in dry, cold weather, is that the oils feel wonderful on the skin). It is important to keep the dough in one piece; holes or folds, no matter how solidly patched, will compromise the structural integrity of the coffin.

The finished coffin should have a substantial floor (this is particularly important, since you will need to lift the whole pie out of the pan after it is baked) and smooth vertical walls, between ¼ and ½ inch thick. It must be allowed to harden completely before it is filled.

Making the Top Crust

Mrs. Dods says that "practice and observation are essential to the proper preparation of pie-crust," and she is right: it is a tricky business. The top crust must not be rolled too thin or crimped too violently, or it will give way as the pie expands. Yet it must be attached securely to the edges of the coffin; for it plays a vital part in holding the pie together, and even the strongest of coffins will tend to bow somewhat during baking. And the proof of the pie is in the baking: a well-constructed pie will not collapse or crack.

There is another traditional approach to making a raised pie, in which the top, instead of being crimped on, is trimmed to the size of the coffin and placed loosely on the pie. The idea here is to bake the pie "dry" in a slow oven until it is nearly done, then remove the "lid," add the stock or gravy, replace the lid, and continue baking for another half-hour or so. The chief advantage of this method is that the coffin walls are solidly baked before the liquid is added, so there is less likelihood of their being weakened enough to collapse. On the other hand, the filling will not be as tender; and the pie, not being sealed, will not keep as well.

Some extremely elegant and complicated pies were made in this way, in two or more stages; at each of which the lid was removed, ingredients were added or rearranged, the lid was replaced, and the baking resumed. Such pies, as a rule, were only for the very rich—not only because they required rare or expensive ingredients, but because only the rich had their own ovens and thus the necessary control over temperature and cooking times. Poorer people typically took their pies to a local bakeshop, and could consider themselves lucky to get them back properly cooked.

Baking the Pie

"Raised paste must have a quick oven," says Mrs. Dods. "The state of the oven should be particularly attended to. Almost every oven has a temperament of its own." Nevertheless, eighteenth-century ovens all worked more or less the same way: the baker would heat the oven by filling it with hot coals; once it was hot enough the coals would be swept out, the pie put in, and the oven door closed, not to be opened until the pie was done. Of course, no matter how tightly the door was closed, the oven gradually lost heat. We have tried to simulate this "falling oven" effect by baking our pies at a very high temperature (450°) for a short time, then reducing the heat considerably as they bake.

Mrs. Glasse remarks: "This is a fine Dish; you may put in as many fine Things as you please;" and "a Slice of this Pye, cut down a-cross, makes a pretty little Side-dish for Supper."

Indeed.

ABOUT ROASTING

> No printed rules can make a good roaster. Practice and vigilant attention alone can produce that *rara avis* of the kitchen.
> —Mistress Margaret Dods, *Cook and Housewife's Manual* (1826)

In Jack Aubrey's time, the distinction between roasting and baking was more clearly drawn than it is today: meats cooked on a spit before an open fire were roasted; meats cooked in an oven were baked. Thanks to an ingenious, if slightly eccentric, contrivance set up on the hearth, we were able to roast our meats very nearly as Hannah Glasse or Meg Dods might have done. "Printed rules" we had none, or very few: the recipes of the period are woefully indistinct, and give almost no indication of times and temperatures, merely stipulating that meat should be cooked before "a bright, clear fire," until "it is enough."

So we lit "bright, clear" fires, and we cooked our meat until it was "enough," and we met with the most extraordinary success. If you *can* rig a spit in front of an open fire, we urge you to do so; it is well worth the trouble, the uncertainty, and the mess.

> I . . . must desire the Cook to order her Fire according to what she is to dress; if any Thing very little or thin, then a pretty little brisk Fire, that it may be done quick and nice: if a very large Joint, then be sure a good Fire be laid to cake. Let it be clear at the Bottom; and when your Meat is Half done, move the Dripping-pan and Spit a little from the Fire, and stir up a good brisk Fire; for according to the Goodness of your Fire, your Meat will be done sooner or later.
> —Hannah Glasse, *The Art of Cookery made Plain and Easy* (1747)

As we gained confidence, we began to realize that, differences in equipment notwithstanding, Mrs. Glasse's advice still holds true. Many of today's cooks still begin by searing meat to seal in its juices, then reduce the heat (as she does by pulling it back from the fire) so that it continues to cook more slowly and evenly.

(If you use an oven for these recipes, preheat it to 450°, cook at that temperature for 10 minutes, and then reduce the heat to 350°, to approximate the effect of pulling the spit back from the fire. As for cooking time, of the many many sources we consulted, only one offered even a hint: Mrs. Dods grudgingly suggests about 15 minutes to the pound, which we found a fairly sound rule of thumb for most meats, whether roast or baked.)

Mrs. Dods says, "In roasting, the management of the fire is half the battle. . . . Let it be clear and glowing, and free of ashes and smoke in front." It is important to keep the fire not only bright and clear, but of an even temperature; it will need constant attention and frequent feeding.

The roasting apparatus of the period consisted of either a horizontal spit, supported at both ends on adjustable racks and turned either by hand or by intricate clockwork arrangements; or (somewhat later) a vertical jack, such as the ingenious "Chimney Screw-Jack for suspending joints to" designed by Alexis Soyer, which "will fit on any mantel-shelf; and . . . enables the joint to be shifted nearer or further from the fire, as occasion requires." Mr. Soyer's invention sounded intriguing, but the engineering was beyond us; so we fell back on the horizontal design as being easier to rig and more appropriate to the time.

A spit can be turned by hand, dog, or electricity. Given a choice, we strongly recommend the latter. An electric spit is not difficult to obtain, and, with the Universal All-Purpose Tool—pieces of a wire coat-hanger, cleverly bent—it can be suspended quite easily from any pair of supports (we use fireplace-tool stands, their bases weighted with bricks). Set up a screen (we use a free-standing fire screen lined with foil) to ward off drafts and reflect the heat back onto the meat.

Be sure to place a large drip pan under the roast. Aside from protecting the hearth and collecting the pan juices for a sauce, you may want to use the dripping to baste the meat. We are of two minds about this. All of our period sources are vehemently in favor of basting, often calling for a great deal of melted butter to supplement the fat from the meat. On the other hand, their birds and meats were almost certainly far tougher, drier, and leaner than ours. At any rate, we found that basting was quite unnecessary. The leanest meat we roasted was the buffalo, and even in that case we decided it was more practical to bard it with suet than to baste it.

It is crucial to balance the weight of the meat evenly on the spit:

as Mrs. Dods remarks, "If the joint is not accurately balanced, no horizontal spit will work well."

It will be obvious that we tread a shamelessly fine line between authenticity and practicality (as witness the electric spit). One further concession to modern times: a meat thermometer can greatly reduce the uncertainty of the adventure, and can help to "ensure a well-roasted joint, of that fine amber colour, crisp, and lightly frothed, which speaks a language that all men understand."

General Notes

Baking powder was not commercially available until 1855, which is why you will not find it in any of our recipes. The puddings in particular will therefore be a little heavier and more dense than any you may have encountered elsewhere—but they are also much closer to what Jack and Stephen would have eaten.

Cochineal (Carmine) is a red dye derived from the cochineal beetle that feeds on the prickly pear cactus (especially the type known as Kew Nopal, which was of particular interest to Sir Joseph Banks because of its potential as an antiscorbutic). It is not currently available as a foodstuff, but it can be bought, in the form of whole dried carcasses, from suppliers of natural textile dyes (or you can gather your own, as we have also done, in the California desert). It has a slightly acrid odor, almost unnoticeable in the small quantities we call for. So far as we have been able to determine it is not poisonous, certainly not in the amounts we have consumed. On the other hand, it is not critical to any of our recipes—you can either omit it or substitute a commercial chemical food coloring if you feel safer doing so.

Equipment: Many of these recipes entail some fairly arduous preparation, and we have been deliberately vague as to how some of this massive chopping, pounding and puréeing is to be achieved. Let it be brazenly stated, however, that in situations where we felt the result would not be affected, we did occasionally allow ourselves to stray from the strictly authentic use of marline-spikes or such implements as would have been available two hundred years ago. We leave you to settle these points with your conscience as we have settled them with ours.

Flaps is a charming and graphic eighteenth-century term for large mushrooms such as portobellos.

Herbs: For the most part, we grow our own, so all those mentioned in our recipes are fresh unless specified otherwise. If you are using dried herbs, the rule of thumb for substitution is 1 to 3, i.e., 1 teaspoon dried to 1 tablespoon fresh (chopped). You will curse us, no doubt, when trying to determine how much of a dried herb to use where we have called for a "small handful"—we can only urge you to trust your instincts as we do, and as the cooks of the eighteenth century certainly did.

The only comparatively unusual herb we call for several times is *hyssop*, which is traditionally used in preparing rabbit. Don't worry if you have to omit it; it is a nice touch, but it will not make or break the dish.

Measurements: The 20-ounce Imperial pint did not become the English standard until 1826; so when we (or our sources) refer to pints, we always mean 16 ounces.

Rose water is available at health food stores, drug stores and some of the more elegant or exotic markets. Though it has fallen into disuse as a flavoring in this century, it once occupied the position now held by vanilla, which in the late eighteenth century was exceedingly rare and costly.

Sultanas are seedless white raisins, and they too were rare and costly in the late eighteenth century—far too rare for use in such day-to-day puddings as Spotted Dog. Accordingly, we have restricted our use of them to "special occasions"—Christmas Pudding, Mincemeat, and so on.

Yeast: Eighteenth-century recipes called for ale yeast, a staple in households that frequently did their own brewing. In the early nineteenth century, as home brewing became less and less common, ale yeast was supplanted by various other types of home-brewed yeasts; it is now virtually unobtainable. Rather than try to create an imitation we have simply substituted modern baking yeast in our recipes. We do recommend compressed yeast, if you can find it, over the active dry variety.

One final note about the humble *bay leaf:* In classical times the crown of poets and heroes, bay laurel is now the most familiar flavoring in the stewpot. We find it odd that so many contemporary cookbooks fail to make a point of telling cooks to remove bay leaves from a finished dish before serving, and that even those that do fail to explain why it is important. Despite Jack's pronouncement to the contrary, the leaf itself is not actually poisonous; but whole bay leaves do not break down with cooking, and they can present a serious choking hazard to the unsuspecting diner.

> *'My orders require me to harry the enemy installations along the coast, as well as his shipping, of course. . . . How I hope we shall find something worthy of the* Lively! *I should be sorry to hand her over without at least a small sprig of laurel on her bows, or whatever is the proper place for laurels.'*
>
> *'Does laurel grow along this coast, sir?' asked the chaplain. 'Wild laurel? I had always imagined it to be Greek. I do not know the Mediterranean, however, apart from books; and as far as I recall the ancients do not notice the coast of Languedoc.'*
>
> *'Why, it has been gathered there, sir, I believe,' said Jack. 'And it is said to go uncommon well with fish. A leaf or two gives a haut relievo, but more is deadly poison, I am told.'* —H.M.S. Surprise, *38–9*

Converting to Metric

WHEN THIS IS KNOWN	MULTIPLY IT BY	TO GET
Teaspoons	4.93	Milliliters
Tablespoons	14.79	Milliliters
Fluid ounces	29.57	Milliliters
Cups	236.59	Milliliters
Cups	.236	Liters
Pints	473.18	Milliliters
Pints	.473	Liters
Quarts	946.36	Milliliters
Quarts	.946	Liters
Gallons	3.785	Liters
Ounces	28.35	Grams
Pounds	.454	Kilograms

Fahrenheit and Celsius Equivalents

FAHRENHEIT	CELSIUS
150°	70°
175°	80°
200°	95°
225°	110°
250°	130°
275°	140°
300°	150°
325°	170°
350°	180°
375°	190°
400°	200°
425°	220°
450°	230°

Select Bibliography

Eliza Acton, *The English Bread-book for Domestic Use,* London: Longman, Brown, Green, Longmans, & Roberts, 1857.

——, *Modern Cookery for Private Families,* London: Longman, Brown, Green & Longmans, 1845.

——, *Modern Cookery in All Its Branches,* London: Longmans, 1845.

L'Albert moderne, ou nouveaux secrets éprouvés et licites, recueillis d'après les découvertes les plus récentes . . . , Paris: Veuve Duchesne, 1777.

Ann H. Allen, *The Orphan's friend and housekeeper's assistant, is composed upon temperance principles: with instructions in the art of making plain and fancy cakes . . . also for the cooking of all the various kinds of meats and vegetables . . . by an old housekeeper,* Boston: Dutton & Wentworth, 1845.

John L. Anderson (comp.), *A Fifteenth Century Cookry Boke,* New York: Charles Scribner's Sons, 1962.

L'art de la cuisine recherchée, ou nouveau recueil des mets les plus délicats à la portée de tout le monde et devenu un talent de bonne compagnie, Leipzic: Reinicke et Hinrichs, 1799.

Louis-Eustache Audot, *La Cuisinière de la Campagne et de la Ville,* Paris: Audot, 1818.

——, *French domestic cookery, combining elegance with economy, describing new culinary implements and processes . . . twelve hundred receipts . . . ,* New York: Harper & Bros., 1855.

Elisabeth Ayrton, *The Cookery of England, Being a Collection of Recipes for Traditional Dishes of all Kinds from the 15th Century to the Present Day, with Notes on their Social and Culinary Background,* Bungay, Suffolk: Chaucer Press, 1974.

Henri (Ali-Bab) Babinski, *Gastronomie Pratique,* Paris: Flammarion, 1904.

Isabella Mary Beeton, *The Book of Household Management,* London: S. O. Beeton, 1861.

Mrs. Ann Blencowe, *Receipt Book of Mrs. Ann Blencowe, A.D. 1694,* London: Adelphi, Guy Chapman, 1925.

Frank C. Bowen, *Sea Slang: A Dictionary of the Old-Timers' Expressions and Epithets,* London: Sampson Low, Marston & Co. Ltd., 1929.

Mrs. Martha Bradley, *The British housewife, or the cook, housekeeper's, and gardener's companion . . . ,* London: S. Crowder & H. Woodgate, 1757.

Henderson William Brand, *Simpson's cookery, improved and modernized; The complete modern cook, containing a very extensive and original collection of recipes in cookery, as now used at the best tables of London and Paris, with bills of fare . . . ,* London: Baldwin & Cradock, 1843.

Jennifer Brennan, *Curries and Bugles: A Memoir and a Cookbook of the British Raj,* New York: Harper Collins, 1990.

Richard Briggs, *The English Art of Cookery,* London: G. G. and J. Robinson, 1794.

Charlotte Campbell, Lady Bury, *The Lady's Own Cookery Book, and New Dinner-Table Directory, in which will be found a large collection of original receipts . . . adapted to the use of persons living in the highest style as well as those of moderate fortune,* London: H. Colburn, 1844.

Marie Antonin Carème, *Le cuisinier parisien, ou, l'art de la cuisine française au dix-neuvième siècle: traité élémentaire et pratique des entrées froides, des socles et de l'entremets de sucre; suivi d'observations utiles aux progrès de ces deux parties de la cuisine moderne,* Paris: Firmin Didot, 1828.

———, *Le pâtissier national parisien, ou, Traité élémentaire et pratique de la pâtisserie ancienne et moderne, suivi d'observations utiles au progrès de cet art,* Paris: Garnier Freres, 1815.

Charles Carter, *The Compleat City and Country Cook,* London: A. Bettesworth and C. Hitch, 1732.

———, *The Compleat Practical Cook,* London: W. Meadows, C. Rivington, R. Hett, 1730.

Susannah Carter, *The Frugal Housewife, or Complete Woman Cook,* Boston: Edes and Gill, 1772.

Lady Charlotte Coltman Clark, *The Cookery Book of Lady Clark of Tillypronie,* ed. Catherine Frances Frere, London: Constable, 1909.

H. E. Acraman Coate, *Realities of Sea Life,* London: L. Upcott Gill, 1898.

Mrs. Mary Cole, *The Lady's complete guide, or, Cookery and confectionary in all their branches: containing the most approved receipts, confirmed by observation and practice, in every reputable English book of cookery now extant, besides a great variety of others which have never before been offered to the public . . . to which is added, in order to render it as complete and perfect as possible, The complete brewer, containing familiar instructions for brewing all sorts of beer and ale, including the proper management of the vault or cellar: also, The family physician, consisting of a considerable collection of approved prescriptions . . . ,* London: G. Kearsley, 1789.

Francis Collingwood and John Wollams, *The Universal Cook, and city and country housekeeper, containing all the various branches of cookery . . . ,* London: J. Scatcherd & J. Whitaker, 1792.

Charles Henry Cook, with John Greville Fennell and J. M. Dixon, *The Curiosities of Ale and Beer*, London: Field & Tuer, 1886.

Captain James Cook, *The Journals of Captain James Cook*, ed. J. C. Beaglehole, New York: Cambridge University Press, 1955.

Nicholas Culpeper, *Complete Herbal, to which is now added, upwards of one hundred additional herbs, with a display of their medicinal and occult qualities, physically applied to the cure of all disorders incident to mankind. To which are now first annexed his English Physician Enlarged and Key to Physic*, London, 1814.

———, *Pharmacopoeia Londinensis*, London: George Sawbridge, 1679.

Mrs. Dalgairns, *The Practice of Cookery, adapted to the business of Everyday Life*, Edinburgh: Robert Cadell, 1829.

Elizabeth David, *English Bread and Yeast Cookery*, London: Viking Penguin, 1977.

Ivan Day, "Further Musings on Syllabub, or Why Not 'Jumble It a Pritie While?'," *Petits Propos Culinaires*, Vol. 53 (1996), p. 33.

Kenelme Digby, *The Closet of the Eminently Learned Sir Kenelme Digby, Knight, Opened*, London: H. Brome, 1668.

Mistress Margaret Dods (Christine Isobel Johnstone), *Cook and Housewife's Manual*, Edinburgh: Oliver & Boyd, 1826.

Alexandre Dumas, *Le Grand Dictionnaire de Cuisine*, Paris: A. Lemerre, 1873.

Henri Louis Nicolas Duval, *Manuel du cuisinier et de la cuisinière, a l'usage de la ville et de la campagne . . . Par. P. Cardelli [pseud.]*, Paris: Roret, 1826.

William Ellis, *The Country Housewife's Family Companion*, London, 1750.

Auguste Escoffier, *Le Guide Culinaire*, Paris: E. Colin, 1907.

William Falconer, *A New Universal Dictionary of the Marine*, London: T. Cadell, 1815.

John Farley, *The London Art of Cookery*, London: J. Scatcherd & J. Whitaker, 1783.

Lady Elinor Fettiplace, *Elinor Fettiplace's Receipt Book, 1604*, ed. Hilary Spurling, New York: Viking, 1986.

Mrs. Fisher, *The Prudent Housewife, or, Complete English cook, for town and country: Being the newest collection of the most genteel, and least expensive receipts in every branch of cookery, viz. going to market; For roasting, boiling, frying, hashing, stewing, broiling, baking, and fricasseeing. Also for making puddings, custards, cakes, cheese cakes, pies, tarts, ragouts, soups, jellies, syllabubs, wines, &c. To which are added, selected from the papers of a lady of distinction, lately deceased, new and infallible rules to be observed in pickling, preserving, brewing, &c. And, in order to render it still more valuable than any other publication that hath appeared, a treasure of valuable medicines, for the cure of every disorder crowns the whole of this work; which contains every instruction that relates to the pleasing of the palate, and the preservation of that inestimable blessing, health*, London: printed by T. Sabine, 1750.

292 The Adventures of John Wetherell

C. S. Forester, ed., *The Adventures of John Wetherell,* Garden City, N.Y.: Doubleday, 1953.

Charles Esmé Francatelli, *The Cook's Guide and Housekeeper's Assistant,* London: R. Bentley, 1861.

———, *The Modern Cook,* London: Richard Bently, 1865.

———, *A Plain Cookery Book for the Working Classes,* London: Routledge, Warne, & Routledge, 1852.

William Gelleroy, *The London Cook, or the whole art of cookery made easy and familiar, containing a great number of approved and practical receipts in every branch of cookery,* Dublin: T. & J. Whitehouse, 1762.

Mark Girouard, *A Country House Companion,* London: Century Hutchinson Publishing Group Ltd., 1987.

———, *Life in the English Country House: A Social and Architectural History,* New Haven, Conn.: Yale University Press, 1978.

Hannah Glasse, *The Art of Cookery, Made Plain and Easy, Which far exceeds any Thing of the Kind ever yet published . . . By a Lady,* London: printed for the Author, 1747.

———, *The Complete Confectioner, or, The whole art of confectionary made plain and easy. Shewing the various methods of preserving and candying, both dry and liquid, all kinds of fruit, flowers and herbs . . . Likewise the art of making artificial fruit . . . To which are added some bills of fare for deserts for private families,* London: I. Pottinger & J. Williams, 1762.

Peter Grey, *The Mistress Cook,* New York: Oxford University Press, 1956.

Harold J. Grossman, *Grossman's Guide to Wines, Spirits and Beers,* New York: Charles Scribner's Sons, 1964.

Dorothy Hartley, *Food in England,* London: MacDonald & James, 1954.

Karen Hess, *The Carolina Rice Book,* Columbia: University of South Carolina Press, 1992.

———, *Martha Washington's Booke of Cookery,* New York: Columbia University Press, 1981.

Karen Hess et al., "More Musings on Syllabub," *Petits Propos Culinaires,* Vol. 53 (1996), p. 62.

Edward Hewett and W. F. Axton, *Convivial Dickens: The Drinks of Dickens and His Times,* Athens: Ohio University Press, 1983.

Peggy Hickman, *A Jane Austen Household Book, with Martha Lloyd's Recipes (1806),* Newton Abbot: David & Charles, 1977.

Constance B. Hieatt and Sharon Butler, *Pleyn Delit: Medieval Cookery for Modern Cooks,* Toronto: University of Toronto Press, 1976.

Howard Hillman, *The Cook's Book,* New York: Avon Books, 1981.

Alexander Hunter, *Culina famulatrix medicinae, or, receipts in modern cookery, with a medical commentary,* York, Eng.: J. Murray, 1810.

Joseph Jobé, ed., *The Great Book of Wine,* Lausanne: Chartwell Books, 1982.

Hugh Johnson, *Wine,* New York: Simon & Schuster, 1987.

J. F. Keane, *On Blue Water,* London: Tinsley Brothers, 1883.

Peter Kemp, ed., *The Oxford Companion to Ships and the Sea,* London: Oxford University Press, 1976.

William Kitchiner, *The Cook's Oracle, or, Apicius Redivivus,* London: S. Bagster, 1817.

Brian Lavery, *Nelson's Navy: The Ships, Men, and Organisation,* London: Conway Maritime, 1989.

Eliza Leslie, *Directions for Cookery, in its Various Branches,* Philadelphia: Cary & Hart, 1837.

——, *Domestic French cookery, chiefly translated from Sulpice Barue,* Philadelphia: Carey & Hart, 1832.

——, *75 Recipes for pastry, cakes, and sweetmeats, By a lady of Philadelphia,* Boston: Munroe & Francis, 1828.

Le Manuel de la friandise, ou les talents de ma cuisinière Isabeau mis en lumière . . . , Paris: Janet, l'an V (1796–7).

Manuel du cuisinier amateur, ou l'art de la cuisine mis à la portée de tout le monde . . . , Paris: J. D. Simon, l'an XIII (1805).

Mlle. Marguerite, *Le cordon bleu, Nouvelle cuisinière bourgeoise,* Paris: Baudouin Frères, 1828.

François Marin, *Les dons de Comus, ou l'art de la cuisine, réduit en pratique,* Paris: L. Cellot, 1775.

Gervase Markham, *The English Hous-wife, Contayning, The inward and outward vertues which ought to be in a compleat woman. As, her skill in Physicke, Cookery, Banqueting-stuffe, Distillation, Perfumes, Wooll, Hemp, Flax, Dayries, Brewing, Baking, and all other things belonging to an Houshould. A Worke very profitable and necessarie, gatherred for the generall good of this kingdome,* London: Roger Jackson, 1615.

John Masefield, *Sea Life in Nelson's Time,* London: Methuen & Co., 1905.

Robert May, *The Accomplisht Cook, Or the Art and Mystery of Cookery . . . Expert and ready wayes for the Dressing of all sorts of Flesh, Fowl and Fish; the Raising of Pastes; the best Directions for all manner of Kickshaws, and the most Poinant Sauces; with the Tearms of Carving and Sewing . . . ,* London: Nath. Brooke, 1660.

Harold McGee, *The Curious Cook: More Kitchen Science and Lore,* New York: Macmillan, 1990.

——, *On Food and Cooking: The Science and Lore of the Kitchen,* New York: Macmillan, 1984.

F. Marian McNeill, *The Scots Kitchen,* London: Blackie & Son, 1929.

Stephen Mennell, *All Manners of Food: Eating and Taste in England and France from the Middle Ages to the Present,* Oxford: Blackwell, 1985.

M. Menon, *La cuisinière bourgeoise, suivie de l'office, à l'usage de tous ceux qui se mêlent de dépenses de maisons . . . ,* Paris: Pigoreau, 1807.

Elizabeth Moxon, *English Housewifry, Exemplified In Above Four Hundred and Fifty Receipts . . . ,* Leeds: G. Copperthwaite, 1769.

MM. Moynier, *De la truffe, traité complet de ce tubercule, contenant en description et son histoire naturelle la plus détaillée . . . contenant les meilleurs moyens d'employer les truffes en apprêtes culinaires . . .* , Paris: Barba, 1836.

Naval Chronicles, 1800 to 1812.

Jill Norman, *The Complete Book of Spices: A Practical Guide to Spices and Aromatic Seeds,* London: Dorling Kindersley, 1990.

Patrick O'Brian, *Joseph Banks: A Life,* London: C. Harvill, 1987.

———, *Men of War: Life in Nelson's Navy,* New York: Norton, 1995.

A. des Ormeaux, *Le Trésor des ménages, ou recueil complet de recettes journellement utiles et peu connues, pour faire des confitures, des marmalades, des gelées . . . augmenté de recettes pour faire l'eau de cologne . . .* , Paris: Desbleds ainé, 1838.

Oxford English Dictionary, Oxford: Oxford University Press, 1971.

Annabella Plumptre, *Domestic Management, or, The Healthful Cookery-Book,* London: 1810.

Dudley Pope, *Life in Nelson's Navy,* London: George Allen & Unwin, 1981.

Provence—Le cuisinier, manuel économique, contenant, la cuisine dans toutes ses parties, les soins à donner à la cave et aux vins, le chauffage . . . , Paris: L. Babeuf, 1836.

William Rabisha, *The Whole Body of Cookery Dissected, taught, and fully manifested, methodically, artificially, and according to the best tradition of the English, French, Italian, Dutch &c., or, a sympathie of all varieties in naturall compounds in that mysterie: Wherein is contained certain bills of fare for the seasons of the year, for feasts and common diets. With a book of preserving, conserving and candying, after the most exquisite and sweet manner: delectable for ladies and gentlemen,* London, 1682.

Elizabeth Raffald, *The Experienced English Housekeeper, for the Use and Ease of Ladies, House-Keepers, Cooks &c. Wrote Purely from Practice,* London: Robert Baldwin, 1786.

Mary Randolph, *The Virginia Housewife, or Methodical Cook,* Washington, D.C.: Davis & Force, 1824.

M. de la Reynière, *Dictionnaire Général de la cuisine française ancienne et moderne, ainsi que de l'office et de la pharmacie domestique, enrichi de plusieurs menus, prescriptions culinaires, et autres opuscules inédits de m. de la Reynière,* Paris: H. Plon, 1866.

I. Roberts, *The Young Cook's Guide, with practical observations: a new treatise on French and English cookery, combining economy with elegance, to which is added an appendix containing M. Appert's method of preserving fruit without sugar, the rudiments of ices and many useful performances in the art of confectionery,* London: Laking, 1836.

William Robinson, *Nautical Economy, or, Forecastle recollections of events during the last war dedicated to the brave tars of old England by a sailor, politely called by the officers of the navy, Jack Nasty-face,* London: W. Robinson, 1836.

N. A. M. Rodger, *The Wooden World: An Anatomy of the Georgian Navy*, New York: Norton, 1996.

John G. Rogers, *Origins of Sea Terms*, Mystic, Conn.: Mystic Seaport Museum, 1984.

Mrs. Maria Eliza Rundell, *A New System of Domestic Cookery, Formed Upon Principles of Economy, and Adapted to the Use of Private Families*, Boston: Andrews and Cummings, and L. Blake, 1807.

Calvin Schwabe, *Unmentionable Cuisine*, Charlottesville: University Press of Virginia, 1979.

Frederick J. Simoons, *Eat Not This Flesh*, Milwaukee: University of Wisconsin Press, 1961.

Eliza Smith, *The Compleat Housewife, or, Accomplish'd Gentlewoman's Companion: being a Collection of upwards of Five Hundred of the most approved Receipts in Cookery, Pastry, Confectionary, Preserving, Pickles, Cakes, Creams, Jellies, Made Wines, Cordials . . . fit either for private families, or such publick-spirited gentlewomen as would be beneficent to their poor Neighbors*, London, 1727.

William Henry Smyth, *The Sailor's Word-Book, an alphabetical digest of nautical terms, including some more especially military and scientific . . . as well as archaisms of early voyagers, etc.*, London: Blackie and Son, 1867.

Alexis Soyer, *A Culinary Campaign*, London: George Routledge & Sons, 1857.

———, *The Gastronomic Regenerator*, London: Simpkin, Marshall & Co., 1846.

———, *The Modern housewife or ménagère, Comprising nearly one thousand receipts for the economic and judicious preparation of every meal of the day, with those of the nursery and sick room*, New York: D. Appleton & Co., 1851.

———, *A Shilling Cookery for the People*, George Routledge and Sons: London, 1854.

F. W. H. Symondson, *Two Years Abaft the Mast, or Life as a Sea Apprentice*, Philadelphia: David McKay, 1884.

Louis Eustache Ude, *The French Cook, or, the art of cookery, developed in all its various branches*, London, 1813.

Joseph Dommers Vehling, ed., *Cookery and Dining in Imperial Rome; Apicius de re Coquinaria (c. 4 A.D.)*, New York: Dover, 1977.

Alexandre Viard, *Le cuisinier royal, ou l'art de faire la cuisine, Suivi d'une notice sur les vins par M. Pierhugue*, Paris: Barba, 1817.

Margaret Visser, *The Rituals of Dinner: The Origins, Evolution, Eccentricities, and Meaning of Table Manners*, New York: Grove, 1991.

C. Anne Wilson, *Food and Drink in Britain*, London: Constable, 1973.

Index

297